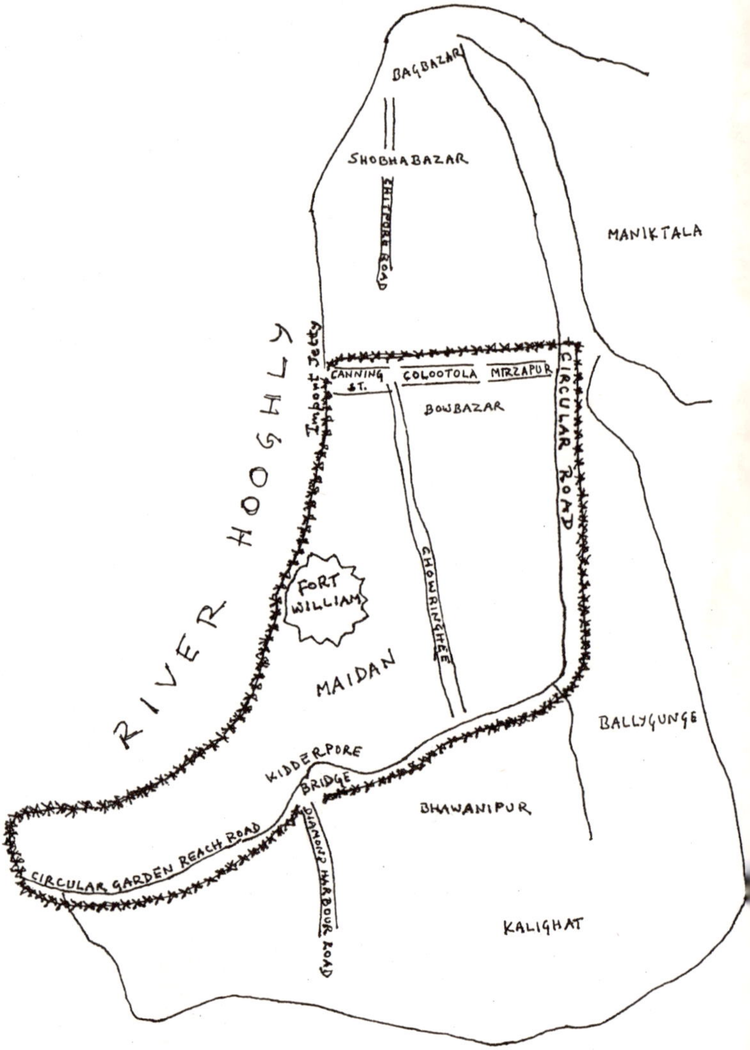

The boot-shaped outline in this map of Calcutta is the 'ring fence' proposed to be set up by the city's Commissioner of Police in 1881 in order to enforce the Contagious Diseases Act within this area to protect the soldiers of Fort William

UNDER THE RAJ
PROSTITUTION IN COLONIAL BENGAL

SUMANTA BANERJEE

Monthly Review Press
New York

Frontispiece
A diagram of the 'ring fence' proposed to be set up in 1881 in order to enforce the Indian Contagious Diseases Act.
Based on Plate 8A in *Atlas of the City of Calcutta and its Environs* (National Atlas and Thematic Mapping Organisation; Ministry of Science and Technology. Government of India. Calcutta. 1990)

Cover image: Chittrovanu Mazumdar
Cover design: Naveen Kishore
Printed in India by Seagull Books
First published as *Dangerous Outcast: The Prostitute in Nineteenth Century Bengal* in 1998 by Seagull Books
26 Circus Avenue, Calcutta 700 001, India.

US ISBN 1-58367-035-1Hbk

Published in the US by:
Monthly Review Press
122 West 27th Street
New York, New York 10001

CONTENTS

Acknowledgements

I am indebted to many friends who have helped me—directly or indirectly—with information and suggestions, during my work on a subject, which, to my knowledge, generally provokes prurient curiosity or shocked silence in 'respectable' society as well as 'academic' circles.

I must, however, express my gratitude particularly to two friends who are working in allied fields, and were gracious enough to share their findings with me—Ms Rimli Bhattacharya, former Fellow, Indian Council of Social Science Research, and Ms Ratnabali Chatterjee of the Department of Islamic History and Culture, Calcutta University. Of the other two friends who deserve special thanks, one is Robi Mukherjee, an aficionado of the old Calcutta pastime of spinning popular jokes and songs, who over several sittings with me, unrolled his own collection of songs and sayings from the red-light areas of the past, which have travelled down to the present through the oral cultural tradition. The other friend is Dr Pradip Sinha of the Rabindra Bharati University of Calcutta, who remained unfailing in his encouragement to me, with helpful suggestions garnered from his rich research on 19th century Calcutta.

I also wish to acknowledge the help and services that I received from the staff of the National Archives of India, New Delhi; the Nehru Memorial Museum and Library, New Delhi; the National Library, Calcutta; the Bangiya Sahitya Parishad Library, Calcutta, and the Uttarpara Library.

Needless to say, the opinions expressed, and the conclusions arrived at, are my own.

Finally, a few words by way of explanation—I have used the word 'prostitute' all through the book, instead of the recently introduced term 'commercial sex worker.' Although the well-meaning inventors of the new term may feel that they are using a less depreciating word, some practitioners of the trade are reported to have resented its use. During a recent educational programme among prostitutes in a Calcutta red-light area, 'in the course of dialogue, they were asked if they liked their new name: sex worker. At least three women said that they didn't because "after all (the word) sex is there."' ('Education for Sex Workers—A Unique Experiment' by Sandip Bandyopadhyay, in *Frontier*, 8 June 1996). In the absence of a better term that would be acceptable to the practitioners themselves, I feel that it is better to stick to the old word 'prostitute', which originates from the more generic, and less pejorative, Latin 'prostituere-utum', meaning 'to set up for sale.'

Sumanta Banerjee
New Delhi

1998

'. . . the cantonment authorities can keep . . . the immediate vicinity of barracks free from the outcasts, who are so dangerous to the men.'

From an official note prepared by the British military department in India, 8 October 1886. (File nos. 34-58. Home Sanitary. June 1887.)

Prologue

Unlike the peasantry and the tribal population, the housewives and the working women, the artisans and the fledgling industrial proletariat of 19th century Bengal—the changed status of all of whom in a colonial society has engaged the attention of some Marxist scholars and the new breed of 'subaltern' historians in the course of their efforts to reconstruct history from below—the prostitutes of that period seem to have escaped such serious attention till now.[1]

Yet, like other pre-colonial socio-economic formations, the profession of prostitution also underwent a dramatic change in Bengal soon after the British take-over. It attracted a wide variety of women from different segments of the population from both within and outside Bengal, and acquired new types of clientele who were products of the colonial order. It was also subjected to attempts at control and surveillance by the colonial administration, as well as reassessment by the newly educated *bhadralok* descendants of the old Bengali households. From the relative obscurity of the periphery of rural society in pre-colonial Bengal, the prostitute suddenly emerged into the full glare of publicity in Calcutta, the capital of colonial Bengal, and its suburbs. There was an explosion of morbid curiosity and prurient voyeurism around her life style—in the Bengali chapbooks and farces that flowed from the cheap printing presses of 19th century Calcutta and other towns. There were also nervous outpourings of fright and consternation about her increasing success in making inroads into vulnerable wings of the colonial establishment (mainly the army—as expressed in contemporary administrative records), as well as into Bengali *bhadralok* society (as voiced in Bengali newspapers and literature). Both the colonial administrative responses and the indigenous socio-cultural reactions to the phenomenon of prostitution in 19th century Bengal could be indicative of a pathological society that was developing during that period in a territory brought under the aegis of a colonial administration, which had just introduced new commercial relations in economy, and tried to bring in simultaneously new ethical norms in social relations. The tensions generated in the process threw up unpredictable and intractable problems. One such quandary—for both the British administrator and the Bengali *bhadralok*—was the proliferation of prostitution in multifarious forms and polymorphic stages of development, all through the 18th–19th century period in Bengal.

The present work is an attempt at exploring some of the cobwebbed corners of the profession of prostitution when it was developing as a trade in 19th century Bengal. It investigates group consciousness over a long period among the practitioners of the trade. The method used here consists first in breaking down the profession as it existed into its different constituent elements, and then reassembling it, by observing the mentalities and behaviour pattern of those who embodied and practised it, as well as of those who observed it from the outside, including the participants (i. e. the clientele).

The crucial areas in the commercial and social relations that marked the profession of prostitution in that period—and which are being examined in the present work—are: (i) the class structure that emerged within the profession in response to the different grades of status and demand, primarily of a new Bengali clientele spawned by colonial, commercial and administrative requirements; (ii) British official efforts to revamp the profession, first to meet the needs of the 'Tommies', and later under various pressures of what constituted the colonial ethos of Victorian society at that time; (iii) the attitude and behaviour of the Bengali *bhadralok* society—a colonized community, shaped partly by the colonizer and partly by pre-colonial traditional social norms—towards prostitution in contemporary Bengali society; (iv) popular perceptions of prostitution as reflected in contemporary folk literature; (v) and finally—the most important and controversial also—the responses of the prostitutes themselves to the changes that were taking place in the socio-cultural milieu of their profession.

The exploration of these areas has unearthed important repositories of confidential official policy decisions, records in contemporary newspapers and journals, and travelogues and reminiscences of both British and Bengali observers—a large and rich body of evidence about prostitution in 19th century Bengal as seen from outside, by the representatives of the elite. They are often counterbalanced—and sometimes corroborated—by another set of evidence (also excavated through the same exploration) provided by the insiders, whether in the realm of iconography or oral tradition. These insiders are the prostitutes themselves and the folk chroniclers of their exploits (the poetasters and the authors of cheap chapbooks)—whose narratives have been given equal space and importance in the present work, in an attempt to arrive at an understanding of the concept of prostitution, and the position of the practitioners of that trade, in the complex and changing reality of 19th century Bengal.

An analysis of these records—both written and oral—suggests the need for reformulating the sociology of prostitution in order to move beyond the simplistic tendency to band together all the prostitutes of that period into a homogenizing category. A single notion of the experiences of prostitutes can never be adequate for understanding the complex, and often contradictory, activities that the profession involved. Was there a collective mentality of prostitutes in 19th century Bengal that was composed of unconscious layers of memories of training in skills, but operative, nevertheless, as in the case of artisans, cultivators, petty traders and other professionals of the period? Or, was there among them a co-existence of different forms of collective representation? Or, an overlapping of different sensibilities, like sloping tiles on a roof, moving from one generation to the succeeding one?

Our findings indicate a variety of mentalities, changing from one period to another, from one class or religious group to another, from the urban to the rural. The analysis presented here, therefore, makes way for a more supple definition of the idea of prostitution in a colonial society. What is being proposed here is a search for a much more fluid, complex and changing reality in an area of research where—let us be modest enough to admit—the techniques of exploration of sources pose a whole series of problems.

First, most of the sources on which we are dependent today for an understanding of the causes of prostitution and the living and working conditions of its practitioners in 19th century Bengal, are external—official records by bureaucrats (whose business it was to supervise and punish); reminiscences by observers from outside (mostly hostile, a few sympathetic); contemporary newspaper reports, as seen by the educated gentry with a cold and ironic stare, and a host of popular farces—usually making fun of the prostitutes. While these sources are no doubt important (both in terms of the rich statistical data and the rare descriptive texts about the life-style of the prostitutes of those days), one, at the same time, has to take into account the distortions and omissions in their views, as they themselves subscribed to a set of self-righteous socio-cultural values that prejudiced their attitude towards prostitution and prostitutes.

Given this lacuna in the secondary sources that are available to us today, the researcher in this area of study will have to search for alternative and unconventional sources by crossing the barricade onto the other side—the dishevelled and embattled world of the prostitutes themselves. Such a search demands from the researcher a different—a 'weighted'—approach to these sources which could provide evidence that is more direct and, therefore, more authentic than what we find in the available records mentioned earlier. The technique of exploring these alternative sources also requires a methodology that is different from that usually adopted in analysing written texts.

Modern continental historians and theoreticians of early modern popular culture are grappling with the problem of searching for alternative sources in oral traditions and coming up with a different methodology to explore them. As one of them puts it: 'Just because the common people, both townsmen and peasants, did not commit their religious views to paper, for very good reasons, does not mean that they are therefore lost in silence. It is necessary to turn to non-written sources to find this expression; to study what was done—belief expressed in actions;

what was seen, through iconography and archaeology; and what was said and recorded in the oral tradition.'[2]

When we turn our attention to the possibility of unearthing alternative sources in the history of prostitution in 19th century Bengal, initially, we quickly discover the extent to which the culture of prostitution is shrouded partly in silence, and partly in distorted versions by contemporary observers. But then, there are ways of cheating the silence, as well as of infiltrating the images of distortion, in order to reconstruct a scene which surely cannot recapture that history in all its authenticity, but can indeed approximate to a large extent to the various nuances in the mentalities of the prostitutes of that period.

First, to cheat the silence—both the silence of the prostitutes and the silence imposed by contemporary society—we have to tune our ears and train our eyes to what had remained unheard and unseen, or in other words, unrecognized in the methodology adopted in conventional academic research. Were they really silent, or were they condemned to a historically silent category because their voices were not recorded on paper? How can one discover these voices of theirs?

The continuity of oral cultural tradition in India—which is being recognized as an important source of historical research—provides us with the opportunity of direct observation of surviving practices and cultural representations among successive generations of prostitutes in Bengal. This helps us to rediscover their voices to a certain extent. Even as late as the 1950s, any visitor to the well-known bordello called 'Nandarani's flat' in the red-light area of Sonagachhi in north Calcutta (which dates back to the early 19th century) could come across old grannies who could be teased into breaking out into songs which they used to sing when they were young in the closing decades of the 19th century. A few of their songs are quoted in chapter V of this book. Such songs and sayings have been handed down from one generation to another—and even today one can hear snatches, although in changed form, with modern contemporary motifs and imageries replacing the old.

There are other ways, also, of assessing the authenticity of these songs. We should remember that most of these songs were sung by Bengali prostitutes who usually came from the rural poorer classes and castes. Among them, uninhibited references to certain parts of the human body and jokes about certain bodily functions (which shocked the obscenity-obsessed Western-educated Bengali middle classes), were a component of their traditional folk culture. Some of the profanities and oaths, the double entendres and bawdy quips that marked the speech and proverbs of the Bengali rural women of the lower orders were related to the body. Terms like *dabka* (a girl with a well-endowed youthful body), *dhoska* (a woman with an aging and withered body), *dhumshi* (a fat woman with ungainly movements), *aantkuri* (a barren woman), *gatar-khaki* (literally meaning a woman who eats up her body—in other words, allows her body to go waste by remaining idle) were common expressions in use among women. Most of these terms are still current in women's speech patterns in rural Bengal.

The women were equally merciless—and perhaps more ribald—in their verbal treatment of the male body. One term used by them for a man whom they considered useless was *phalna-tusku.* A veteran Bengali historian and linguist, Sukumar Sen, pursuing relentlessly the origins of the term, came to a conclusion which suggests a long history of innovative adaptations in popular slang in general and in female dialect in particular, in 19th century Bengal. According to him: 'Women in my childhood days would often refer to their demised husbands as '*phalna*'. It is an Arabic word that was adopted in Persian and therefrom, was transferred to Bengali. It means 'such and such', that is a person unnamed . . . In the parlance of women, the phrase 'phalna-tusku' meant insignificant persons, persons not worthwhile to be mentioned by name. The part 'tusku', also, is of Arabic origin: 'tashakhkhus' (meaning the same as in Arabic: 'penis, pudendum muliebre').'[3]

Worthless husbands were also butts of ridicule, as evident from the following saying:

> *Kapal amar bakto,*
> *Sakto dekhey bhatar nilam,*
> *Hagey sudhu rakto!*[4]
> (Just my luck! I chose a husband who, I thought, would be strong. But now I find that he can only shit blood!)

If we now turn our attention to the songs of the prostitutes (some of which we have examined in the present work), we find that they were marked by the same speech pattern and occasional scatological humour that were common in the parlance of women belonging to the lower strata of the 19th century Bengali countryside.

It is obvious that the prostitutes in the red-light areas of Calcutta and its suburbs, who mainly came from among the rural poor and lower caste communities, carried their traditional reservoir of womanly patois into the environs of their new profession. In the same uninhibited and boisterous style that characterized their earlier folk culture (sayings, proverbs, jokes and songs), they now spun new songs that reflected their daily experiences with a variety of clients, their squabbles with their landladies and similar professional hazards. As in the past, the body remained the focus of attention. But given the nature of their profession, the sexual attributes of the body—both the female and the male—tended to be accentuated in their new cultural representations. Double entendre with erotic suggestion, or more explicit reference to the sexual act—sometimes with a liberal sprinkling of four-letter words—came to characterize the songs of the prostitutes.[5]

The close affinity between the speech pattern and mood of the women of the Bengali rural lower orders on the one hand, and the language and spirit found in the songs of contemporary prostitutes on the other, strongly reaffirms the authenticity of the authorship of these songs.

In a similar effort to assess the authenticity of the available writings of prostitutes who could have belonged to a middle-class and literate background (unlike their counterparts in the oral culture of the lower orders), we have tried to cross-check their style and language against those followed by contemporary Bengali women writers who came from the same socio-cultural background. It is necessary to remember in this context that a large number of women who flocked to the red-light areas from the late 18th to the mid-19th centuries belonged to Brahmin *kulin* families—daughters who could not be married off, and widows who were considered liabilities by their in-laws. As was the custom in many Brahmin households in those days, as children, the girls learnt the three 'R's. It should not come as a surprise, therefore, to find some among the middle-class prostitutes writing letters or attempting autobiographies.

A comparison of the oral culture of the prostitutes of the lower orders and the written literature of those coming from a middle-class background indicates the differences not only in their style of representation but also in their emotional responses to the surrounding situations. The oral culture contained a system of representations that stressed the theme of a world turned upside down, inversion, laughter and derision. These constituted a series of defensive and subversive mechanisms fighting against the mutilating forces of commercial domination. But the middle-class prostitutes negotiated with the given cultural form of literary discourse—the chaste Bengali as structured by the educated society. As the contents of their letters and writings suggest, their style also reflected their urge to re-enter the respectable society from which they had been exiled, or 'fallen.' The term 'fallen', or *patita* (in chaste Bengali), which was used by them quite often to describe themselves, is significant. Unlike the poor prostitutes who had no qualms about using the bazar terminology to describe their role as sex workers (*khanki, beshya, ranrh,* were the common terms), the educated middle-class prostitutes preferred the term *patita,* or the more elegant Sanskrit *barangana*—both of which harked back to a more genteel past.

As we move from these direct sources of oral and written cultural representations of the prostitutes themselves, to the secondary sources provided by the contemporary observers from the outside, we have to infiltrate the curtain of distortion, which requires a profound process of decoding. We face a complicated mesh of fixed likes and dislikes, prejudices and biases, fantasies and assumptions. These records left by British travellers and administrators, Bengali *bhadraloks* and social reformers, contemporary poetasters and writers of farces, reflect a variety of viewpoints of people who observed the prostitutes from different angles. From a selective approach to one class of prostitutes, or one part of their profession, they often tended to draw general conclusions.

When examining the documents of these external observers, therefore, we have to cross-check the information given by one against that provided by some other among them, or by the prostitutes themselves (in their oral or written records), in order to get a clearer picture.

It is also necessary to remember that these documents span a long period—from the mid-18th till the late 19th century. The recorded impressions of prostitutes at the turn of the 18th century need not conform to the modalities of the profession and the mood of its practitioners in the mid-19th century. For instance, the class of prostitutes known as *baijis* underwent a lot of change during the century—although one could still discern a certain continuity in their socio-cultural behaviour.

What emerges from the records of these external sources is a highly variegated and constantly moving panorama of the history of prostitution and prostitutes in 19th century Bengal. For the modern historian, the task of arranging these disjointed and fleeting scenes into a coherent and chronological narrative is both fascinating and challenging. It involves an inter-disciplinary approach which requires serious probings into contemporary subjects of thought—like differences along economic class lines, affinities around religious beliefs and practices, cultural representations of different socio-economic groups, unity and fragmentation in the collective perceptions of the practitioners of a commercial trade, the changing values and demands of the clientele, and the responses of the intelligentsia.

It is only by probing into these different areas of thought and practice in 19th century Bengal that we can understand to some extent the changing and complex reality of prostitution in those days.

The fluidity and complexity in the mentalities of the prostitutes of 19th century Bengali society have to be mapped against questions of religious, class and caste identities. In the perception of later-day historians and sociologists, the differences between responses and religious habits of Hindu and Muslim—as well as a large section of Christian—prostitutes of the period often get blurred, again due to the not infrequent tendency of treating them as a homogeneous professional community. But contemporary records suggest that there was an unwritten law that prohibited Hindu prostitutes from entertaining Muslim clients, and discouraged Hindu clients from visiting Muslim prostitutes—although, in practice, this law was more often honoured in its breach than in its observance, quite predictably because of the predominating commercial interests of both the prostitutes and their clientele, which prevailed over the traditionally ordained religious norms. The song of a Hindu prostitute expressing surprise (in a mock-scandalized tone), at the 'discovery, in her bedroom, that her client is a circumsized Muslim (quoted in chapter V), is an interesting indication of the prevailing norms in the red-light areas of 19th century Calcutta.

The conflict—that nagged the Hindu prostitute's psyche—between the obligation to adhere to religious dictates on pollution (with regard to Muslim clients) on the one hand, and the compulsions of the trade, that operated against any such discrimination, on the other, is vividly described by a Hindu prostitute who entertained Goniur Raja, scion of a 19th century Bengali Muslim zamindar family in Dhaka in east Bengal around 1896. The relevant extracts from Goniur Raja's memoirs are quoted in chapter III.

While life stories of Hindu prostitutes can be reconstructed from the records and anecdotes of 19th century Bengal, it is slightly more difficult in the case of their Muslim fellow-workers who operated in the red-light areas of those days. For one thing, the number of Muslim prostitutes was fewer, due—as suggested by official records—possibly, to the opportunity for Muslim widows to remarry, and to other securities enjoyed by them under Islamic law. From both official and non-official accounts, one could surmise that there were two types of Muslim prostitutes. The first consisted of descendants of courtesans, singers and dancers of the north Indian feudal courts who, during the declining stages of the Moghul empire in the 18th century, began to migrate to Calcutta and other parts of the new British colonial territory in eastern India.[6] The other comprised members of poor, indigenous Muslim rural families of Bengal who were pauperized by famines, displacement, and the loss of traditional means of livelihood in the wake of British commercial forays into the countryside. While these poor Muslim prostitutes shared the same socio-economic background and concerns as those Hindu fellow-workers who came from indigent, depressed and 'untouchable' castes, the slightly better-off and richer prostitutes of north Indian origin—known as *baijis* in popular parlance—

were different in their customs and norms of behaviour from their middle and upper-class counterparts among the Hindu prostitutes. They did not suffer from any religious inhibitions in the choice of their clients. In fact, during the later 19th century period, most of their clientele came from the old Bengali Hindu aristocratic families or the nouveau riche Hindu compradore community—the *banians* and *dewans* who were making fortunes by helping the East India Company to conduct business and administration in its newly acquired territory of Bengal. These tycoons could afford to ignore or bypass traditional Hindu taboos in the choice of their mistresses (invited from among these Muslim *baijis*, who were reputed for their grace and proficiency in classical music and dance). When Kaliprasad Dutta was threatened by a section of his co-religionists with a ban on his performing the last rites at his father's funeral on the ground that he had a Muslim *baiji* as his mistress, he approached another Calcutta tycoon—Ramdular Sarkar. Sarkar advised Kaliprasad to placate the city's Brahmin priests (who were indispensable for any religious occasion in Hindu households) with money and gifts. The advice bore fruit, and Ramdulal summed up the situation with a laconic comment: 'I keep caste in my coffer!'—implying that money could decide whether one violated traditional caste norms or not.[7]

It is obvious, therefore, that the taboos ruling relationships between Hindu prostitutes and Muslim clients, or Muslim prostitutes and Hindu clients, in 19th century Bengal, were confined—and that, too, tentatively—to the middle-class range of the red-light areas. In the upper-class range, both the prostitutes and their clients could afford (through their mutually interlacing superior socio-financial positions) to ignore the prevailing religious injunctions (mainly ordained by the Brahmin clergy for the Hindus) that could obstruct the smooth commercial transactions involved in their trade.

Among the prostitutes, Muslim *baijis* followed norms of behaviour which were different from those displayed by the Hindu *khemtawalis*, who were also singers and dancers, but who came from the humbler background of Bengali rural folk culture—unlike the *baijis*, who tried to adhere to the code of conduct and the discipline of cultivating north Indian classical and semi-classical music and dance forms, as handed down to them by their mothers and grandmothers.

While the upper- and middle-class Hindu prostitutes quite often strove for accomplishment in the arts (like classical music and dancing),[8] among those Bengali prostitutes occupying the lower rungs of the socio-economic hierarchy of the red-light areas, the common form of cultural representation was usually the *khemta.* This was a strongly rhythmical dance form set to lively music accompanying equally ebullient love songs. Practitioners of this dance form (known as *khemtawalis,* one of whom Goniur Raja met in Dhaka), harked back to the vivacious folk dances and songs that had been traditionally popular in the countryside of western Bengal, like *jhumur.*[9]

There was a significant difference between the importance attached (by the clientele) to the cultural representations of the prostitutes belonging to the *baiji* group and those known as *khemtawalis*—although, quite often, both lived cheek by jowl in the red-light areas of 19th century Calcutta, Dhaka and other cities.[10]

The *baijis* were the darlings of the late 18th–early 19th century Bengali grandees, who used to organize their famous 'nautches' (described by contemporary European travellers in their memoirs) for British patrons and friends. More than their dances, they were known for their vocal rendering of the semi-classical north Indian love lyric. The most famous among them was Nikki, who seemed to have had ruled the scene for more than two decades, and was compared by the European listeners to contemporary singers in Europe—Angelica Catalani (1780–1849) and Elizabeth Billington (1768–1818), the two sopranos, the former Italian, and the latter German, who were fascinating connoisseurs of music in Europe in those days. We hear about her from 'Maria, Lady Nugent'—wife of Sir George Nugent, Commander-in-Chief in India in 1812–1814—who, describing Calcutta in 1812, narrates her encounter with Nikki at a party hosted by the 'Nawaub of Chitpore'. At the party, 'the woman who sung so well is the Catalani of Calcutta—the gentlemen call her Nicky (sic.)' and then Lady Nugent adds, in a suspicious vein: 'But I suppose that is not her real name.'[11]

Two years later, an English visitor to Calcutta invited by Raja

Rajkrishna Dev (of the old aristocratic family of Shobhabazar in north Calcutta) to one of the usual 'nautch' performances in the Raja's palace, seemed to be completely bowled over by Nikki. He found 'her black eyes, full and piercing, reflected the pleasurable sensations of her heart; her mouth, around which a smile was ever playing, enclosed teeth, regular, perfect, and white as ivory; her voice was feeble; but inexpressibly sweet . . .', and he then added the information that 'the twelve hundred rupees (one hundred and fifty pounds), and two pair of shawls of the same value, the price of Neekhee's (sic.) attendance for three nights, was only commensurate with her singular accomplishments.'[12]

Nikki's name pops up in the journals of Fanny Parks (who visited Calcutta in 1822) and Mrs Heber (in 1823–24), and again in 1835, when, during a visit to Calcutta, Emma Roberts informs us that Nikki was being paid Rs 1000 every night wherever she was engaged.[13] In the course of her two-decade-long reign, she was, for sometime (in 1819), employed exclusively to serve on a regular monthly salary, by 'some fortunate gentleman who was fascinated by listening to her songs and watching her dances', according to a contemporary Bengali newspaper.[14]

Nikki—as well as other well-known contemporary *baiji* singers and dancers like Ushoorun, Begum Jan, Hingool, Nanni-jan, Supan-jan, who used to grace the 'nautch' parties in early 19th century Calcutta and its suburbs—appeared to inhabit the twilight zone of an independent career (as professional singers and dancers), quite often restrained by compulsions of concubinage.[15]

A similar twilight zone emerged among the women of the lower orders in the second half of the 19th century, when prostitution often became a means of seasonal employment or regular moonlighting for poorly-paid female workers in factories and domestic maid-servants in Bengal.

Another group—the traditional female folk singers and dancers (with their distinctive styles of popular cultural representation) like the *jhumur* dancers and *khemtawalis*, occupied the same ambiguous social status among the lower orders as the *baijis* did among the upper classes. Some were known for their professional skills in their art forms, while many appeared to interweave their profession as pure *khemtawalis* with that of prostitution—as is evident from contemporary Bengali reports and farces which tend to equate *khemtawalis* with prostitutes.

But although both the *baijis* and the *khemtawalis* shared the same reputation as 'disreputable women' in the contemporay Bengali *bhadralok* discourse, the *bhadralok* as well as their English mentors and friends were highly class-conscious in making a distinction between the two groups of women. There was a somewhat sneaking attraction for the *baijis*—who evoked the ambience and charm of the feudal aristocracy of the Moghul era—among the newly arrived British settlers in Bengal who were enamoured of the exotic Orient, the members of the old Bengali aristocracy who inherited the pre-British cultural norms and love for north Indian classical music and dance, and the new class of parvenu *banians* and *dewans* who wanted to impress their British patrons by flaunting their patronage of the *baijis*. Some of this upper-class ethos rubbed off on the middle-class educated *bhadralok* who were prepared to tolerate the *baijis*, even to invite them to sing at their homes on occasions like weddings or birthday parties—but never to allow their children to study at the same school with their own children, as is evident from the uproar created over the admission of Heera Bulbul's son to the Hindu College in 1853! (see chapter IV).

The *khemtawalis* were a different kettle of fish altogether, in the perception of the *bhadralok*. Since they came from the poorer classes and lower castes (often regarded as 'untouchable'), the *bhadralok* considered them as belonging to an inferior species and their cultural performances as catering to the needs of the vulgar plebs!

This discriminatory attitude comes out clearly in the writings of the contemporary Bengali *bhadralok*. The Bengali journal *Banga-darshan*, edited by the well-known novelist Bankim Chandra Chattopadhyaya, denounced the *khemta* dance as originating from barbarian Bengali *tantrik* practices, and marked by 'abominable contortions of the middle part of the body', while praising the dancing of *baijis* as inspired by the (north Indian) Hindu religious scriptures, and discovering in them a 'seriousness that is similar to that of the (Hindu) *puranas*.'[16]

Another contemporary Bengali journal, while demanding the

'expulsion of the filthy khemta dance that provokes the basest instincts' from Bengali society, added that there was no harm if the dances of the *baijis* were allowed to continue.[17]

Unlike the love lyrics sung by the *baijis* (both in Urdu and Bengali), which usually dealt with traditional romantic themes as structured by the male poets—unrequited love, pangs of separation from the lover, and longing for a meeting with the beloved—the songs and sayings of the *khemtawalis* of the lower orders were an unabashed expression of earthy needs and desires that quite often reflected living and working conditions in the cheap brothels. The risque jokes and cynical guffaws at the expense of their male customers that marked their cultural representations were not likely to endear them to the respectable *bhadralok*!

These different nuances in the mentalities of prostitutes of 19th century Bengal, mapped against their religious, class, caste and socio-cultural backgrounds, prompt the modern historian to examine another dimension which was germane to their profession. This was the question of identity—as a woman, as an individual, as distinct from the other fragments of their collective identity which they could have inherited at different levels from their respective religious, class or caste origins. Did the prostitutes carve out an autonomous niche—each in her own way—which allowed them to discover themselves as individuals? Did their trade, with all its exploitative constraints, unwittingly encourage them to explore alternative avenues for self-assertion?

When we listen to the cultural representations of the prostitutes of the lower orders, and read the descriptions of their behaviour by contemporary observers, we are struck by certain common traits—aggressiveness, boorish remarks, and swagger. They defied the middle-class male construct of the female stereotype as a demure and submissive woman. Part of their aggressiveness was inherited from their rural socio-cultural tradition, which, as we have discussed earlier, allowed them a certain space to express their attitude towards men in particular in an uninhibited manner. This aggressive streak was accentuated in the commercial world of the red-light areas, where they had to constantly contend with male aggression. At times, their responses to male propositions almost took on the attributes of male bellicosity—in the form of furious abuses and insulting acts. Contemporary Bengali accounts, which have been extensively used in the present work, suggest that these prostitutes sought to express their grievances through such gestures in the public sphere of their profession. This enabled them to create an alternative version of autonomy.

We discover a different world when we turn our attention to the upper- and middle-class Bengali prostitutes. How did they carve out their autonomous space? Contemporary records about them suggest that there was a tussle between their being reconciled to prostitution, and the prospect of a respectable married life (which a few among them experimented with when their lovers offered). The latter prospect, however, entailed the claustrophobic domesticity that was prevalent in middle-class households in those days. The former status of a prostitute, on the other hand, notwithstanding the exploitation and oppression, allowed the practitioners access to the outer world, apart from an independent income.

Among those who had the chance of negotiating with these opposing constructions of feminity—domesticity (in marriage) and independence (in prostitution)—the trade-off was perhaps not always conducive to their emotional health. Golap, one of the most talented actresses from the red-light area of Calcutta in the 1870s, created a sensation by getting married to a Bengali *bhadralok* actor, Goshthabihari Dutta, in February 1875. Her name was changed to Sukumari Dutta. But this did not make her acceptable to *bhadralok* society or Goshthabihari's relatives, who disowned the young couple. Living in extreme poverty, and unable to maintain the new household that they had set up, Goshthabihari left for England as a sailor on a ship, and died there soon after, while working as a waiter in a hotel. Left alone in Calcutta, Sukumari had to maintain the household and look after her newborn daughter. In order to help her tide over the crisis, her colleagues and admirers held a charity show in Calcutta on 23 August, 1875, where they staged a play written by her—*Apurba Sati.* Sukumari spent her last years in penury.[18]

The other well-known actress of that period, Binodini, did not marry, but withdrew from the stage at the early age of twenty-four after having found a lover and guardian in a scion of an old aristocratic family of north Calcutta. Desire for a home made her abandon not only her old profession, but also her prospects of a successful career as an artiste.[19]

To come back to the issue raised at the beginning of this chapter—the problems of research in an area as contested and confused as that of prostitution in the colonial setting of 19th century Bengal! The infinite variety of individual mentalities and the great complexities of group mentalities in the profession suggest strongly the need for a more refined methodology that could be specifically suited to the exploration and examination of sources in this particular area. While the oral sources may be more down-to-earth, and, therefore, recognized as more authentic, the modern researcher has also to take into account the possible dilutions that might have taken place over the years in the handing down of the oral tradition. The fast-disappearing residues of that cultural tradition in today's red-light areas of Calcutta have to be checked and cross-checked against the written records of the songs and sayings of prostitutes of 19th century Bengal as found in contemporary literature.

Similarly, while trying to analyse the printed records, the researcher will have to distil the characteristics of a different system of behaviour and beliefs as practised by the prostitutes, from what were basically negative and veiled impressions left by British bureaucrats and *bhadralok* commentators.

Any comprehensive definition of the problematique through an examination of these issues, therefore, requires an ambitious inter-disciplinary exercise and a resolutely dynamic approach to a fluid and changing reality. The present work proposes to identify only some of the landmarks and crossroads that the author had come across during his investigations into the twisting back-lanes of the history of what was known as the red-light areas of 19th century Bengal.

I
Introducing Phulmoni and Her Sisters

> *'Phulmoni, Joymoni, Andi, Lakhhi, Padmamonistatha, Pancha beshya smarennityam mahapatakanashanam.'*
> (Phulmoni, Joymoni, Andi, Lakhi, and Padmamoni: honour these five prostitutes by taking their names every moment, and even the worst of your sins will be wiped out.)
>
> —a satirical Sanskrit couplet.[1]

In the purely clinical terms of market economy, prostitution can be stripped of its emotive sexual overtones and reduced to the status of yet another profession where a person hires out his/her body or physical labour and sells skills in the market like a wage worker in piece work. But in the case of the prostitute, she hires out the most tender and innermost parts of the female body—the reproductive system and its physical components— which remain a major, if not basic, constituent of the man-woman relationship, emotional and otherwise. With the societal attribution of moral value to the reproduction system, woman's fertility has come to be regarded as 'sacred', which, in a patriarchal society, means the monopoly of the husband. But unlike the wife, who in this society sells her body to the husband 'into slavery once for all'[2] and is turned into a breeding machine for producing sons (e.g. the much-quoted Hindu religious precept—*putrartha kriyate bharjya*), the prostitute hires out her body without the obligation to reproduce.

What the prostitute produces in the course of her labour of replicating every night (and day) the same act of simulated love-making, is a purchasable commodity for her male client in which she can never claim any share. The traditional artisan, or the industrial worker, sells his skills—and distorts his product in the process—to meet the commercial needs of the market, and stands 'related to the product of his labour as to an alien object'.[3] The prostitute's alienation, both from her work and the end product, is more pervasive. Forced to distort what could have been her spontaneous sexual responses into commercial 'skills' to feed the market, she cannot even perceive her labour's product, which remains elusive and intangible to her.

The modern prostitute—or the 'commercial sex worker' in a capitalist society—belongs to a class which stands apart from her predecessors. Although exploited by the same patriarchal system, she occupies a position which is in many major respects different from that of the ancient Greek *hetaera*, or of the courtesan in Buddhist India, or the old Hindu temple dancer, or the concubine in Moghul and Hindu royal households. Courtesans and temple dancers of the past were quite often members of a state enterprise—required to serve the public, and enjoying in return certain privileges and protections from the state. Unlike these professionals—usually described as 'public women'—the concubines were captives within feudal households, without the freedom to hire themselves out in the open market. In all these various manifestations, the institution was essentially tuned to feed the sexual needs of the men. Even in the state of comparative freedom enjoyed by the courtesan or the *hetaera*, she had to cultivate skills mainly for the entertainment of the male. But significantly enough, the cultivation did not remain confined to skills of sexual entertainment alone. It embraced the fine arts—music, dancing, painting. It was this space provided to the courtesan, temple dancer and even concubine, which marks out the ancient practitioner of the profession from the modern prostitute in a capitalist society. Whether they performed for immediate financial gain for members of the public, or for long-term security for themselves in the private role of concubine or mistress attached to, and dependent upon, the male patron, their sexual functional role was, interestingly enough, bound up with the wider cultural world and social festivals.

In contrast, in a capitalist society, like other wage workers in a system that thrives on the intensification of the division of labour and specialization of skills, the prostitute, also, is pushed into a strictly defined narrow space. She is condemned to the exclusive role of a specialist in sexual entertainment. Stripped of all emotional and intellectual attributes, she becomes the female body—an input required at one level in the long line of the production process in a capitalist society. Reduced to a source of purely utilitarian needs, her body is expected to produce the regular nocturnal fantasy of pleasure that deceptively fills up the vacuity of the soul of the alienated worker who comes to her as a client. She represents the ultimate in alienation in a capitalist society. The alienation of one section of the exploited feeds upon the alienation of another.

I

When we look back at the pre-capitalist social formations in ancient India, we find that as early as the 4th century B.C., Kautilya, the chief adviser of the Maurya emperor Chandragupta, in his treatise on governance, *Arthashastra*, not only laid down rules as to how the prostitutes should deal with their customers, but also provided for punitive measures like fines to be imposed on customers who cheated the prostitutes, or harmed them in any way. The tax paid by the prostitutes (two days' earnings) was an important source of revenue for the state. Prostitution was neither a crime nor a sin, but was treated like any other trade. Its practitioners—as in other professions—were expected to abide by the regulations formulated by the administration which also protected them from acts of misdemeanour.[4]

Significantly, the prostitute continued to enjoy a similar privilege and social status in medieval Bengal, also. Contemporary poets and their lyrics offer interesting glimpses of the life-style of prostitutes, who were painted in flattering colours, indicating the prevalent social attitude towards them. The following lines in Sanskrit by an anonymous poet in a 13th century anthology compiled in Bengal are quite illuminating:

Basah sookshmam bapushi bhujayoh kanchanee changadesreer
Malagarvah surabhimasrinairgandha tailaih shikhandah.
Karnottangse nabashashikalanirmalam talapatram,
Beshah kesham na harati mono, Banga-baranganam.[5]
(A fine cloth over the body, both arms beautified with gold

> ornaments, flower garlands inside the smooth tresses rendered fragrant by perfumed oil, ear-ornaments clear like a new digit of the moon—whose mind would not be stolen by such a dress worn by the courtesans of Bengal?)

Even 400 years later—in the 17th century—prostitutes continued to be major partners in social and cultural festivities and royal expeditions in Bengal, as is evident from the following description, in a Bengali poem, of the entourage accompanying a prince embarking on a journey:

> *Alim, pandit aar jyotish, ganak,*
> *Nana jantra, Raj-beshya, Gahon, Nartak*[6]
> (Learned Muslims, Sanskrit pandits, astrologers and astronomers; musical instruments, courtesans, singers and dancers).

In an early 18th century Bengali poetical narrative—composed on the eve of the establishment of the full-fledged colonial administrative norms—we catch echoes from the earlier-quoted 13th-century verses of the favourite topic of descriptions of a prostitute's toilet:

> *Haste Kori nilo beshya subarner chiruni*
> *Mastaker kesh chiri ganthilo bianee.*
> *Gandha pushpa taila beshya porilo mathatey*
> *Subarner jaad beshya porilo khompatey.*[7]
> (The prostitute took up the golden comb, brushed through her hair and plaited her tresses. The prostitute applied perfumed oil made from flowers on her head. The prostitute then bound her hair into a coiffure with a golden lace.)

Such laudatory references to prostitutes and eulogistic descriptions about their life-style—which continued in Bengali literature from the medieval period to the early 18th century—indicate a continuity of certain societal values as well as state patronage which allowed the prostitutes to enjoy a privileged space in society. Reputed for their proficiency in singing and dancing (which was required due to their traditional and professional obligation to please their clients—and in the medieval period, the clientele were a feudal gentry fond of classical songs and dances), they apparently commanded a certain respect in society, and were treated on an equal footing with other professionals who were experts in their respective occupations. This was in continuation of the tradition set by Vatsyayana in his famous *Kamasutra*: 'A courtesan of a pleasant disposition, beautiful, and otherwise attractive, who has mastered the arts . . . has the right to a seat of honour among men. She will be honoured by the king and praised by the learned, and all will seek her favours and treat her with consideration.'[8]

From all these accounts, one should not rush away with the impression that prostitutes of medieval Bengal were a highly independent and powerful community of women (as understood in today's terms of women's emancipation and empowerment). They were operating within the parameters of a patriarchal society and state which defined and determined their role—as in the case of other trades and occupations. Like other professionals such as artisans, craftsmen, priests, traders, and shopkeepers who catered to the various needs of society and state, prostitutes were also allotted a slot and officially recognized as an important professional community serving particular interests. But, although gratification of male sexual needs was the main function that they were required to carry out at the purely physical level, contemporary society and the ruling powers also assigned them tasks like the cultivation of the arts, and provided them with avenues for participation in social and cultural activities that made them very much a part of the wider society. In fact, if we go by Kautilya's accounts, the Maurya administration even elevated prostitutes to the position of undercover agents to spy on enemies![9]

With the arrival of British colonialism and the introduction of the capitalist economy in India, all this changed and the status of prostitution underwent a radical transformation. The colonial system not only gave birth to a new breed of prostitutes, treating them exclusively as what we today describe as 'commercial sex workers', but also set up moral and legal boundaries which excluded them (as well as their colleagues from the pre-colonial past—the dancing girls and courtesans) from the rest of society. They were driven away from society as outcasts, and branded by the state as criminals.

There was a distinct shift of stress in state policies towards prostitutes under the colonial regime. The restrictive and punitive attitude adopted by the British administration was in sharp contrast to the permissive and accommodating policies pursued by generations of rulers in pre-colonial India, although the latter subscribed to the same patriarchal values that compelled the British to accept prostitution for their soldiers as essential. The British administration, however, introduced a moral dimension by attaching a stigma to prostitutes, and banishing them from society.

The moral attitude towards prostitutes as betrayed by the colonial administration was underpinned in a large measure by the Judaic–Christian religious tradition, and reinforced by contemporary Victorian ethical norms. A comparison of this religious tradition with those prevalent in pre-colonial India, with respect to the position of prostitutes, reveals striking differences. In the Old Testament, while the prostitute is tolerated, she always suffers from a degree of opprobrium.[10] Even when praised for noble character or action, the stigma, somehow, continues to stick to her.[11] In the New Testament, her position seems to have fallen further—representing the lowest class in moral terms.[12]

In the ancient puranas and mythology of India (from which Hindus derive their religious inspiration), the prostitute is allotted a well-defined position bereft of any moral reproach. In the Padma-purana, for instance, we are told that in the war between the *devas* (gods) and *asuras* (demons), women who were ravished by their enemies were asked to follow the life of prostitutes at the royal palaces or at temples, or in Brahmin households![13] It is, thus, obvious that during wars, women victims of rape who were not taken back by their families became prostitutes—as concubines in royal households, or as temple dancers, or as mistresses of the Brahmins. The purana, thus, merely legitimized the age-old practice. It also set apart the prostitutes from other women by insisting that they should not love any man, whether handsome or ugly, but should work only for money:

> *Surupa wa birupa wa,*
> *Drabyameba prayojanam.*[14]

According to some of the puranas, the presence of a prostitute was essential on certain sacred occasions. During the

Deepavali (lighting of lamps) festival, a prostitute used to go from house to house uttering auspicious words, heralding the advent of the Goddess Laxmi.[15] Again, a prostitute had to be present at the ritual of tying the sacred protective cord (*raksha-bandhan*) in the case of a king, whose waist also used to be purified with clay from the threshold of a prostitute's house.[16]

In fact, in Bengal, even today, according to religious rules, the making of the image of the Goddess Durga cannot be perfect unless it is made of clay collected from the earthen floor of a prostitute's threshold (*beshyadwara-mrittika*). The popular logic behind this age-old custom was the belief that the earth on the threshold leading to a prostitute's house was the purest since it contained all the accumulated virtues which were shed by the men who lost them once they entered a prostitute's room! By turning her into an appendage to religious rites, the ingenious Bengali society made a religious virtue of a social necessity.

In Bengal, in particular, the prostitute often occupied an important position in the religious rituals of the *tantrik* practitioners. In their practices, the male devotee needed a female partner, who embodied *shakti* (the primeval power without which no worship could be complete). Among the various types of *shaktis* (the term used for the female partners) mentioned in the *tantrik* texts, there is one who, when watching the implements used for prayers, feels the desire for 'making love'. She is described by the term *beshya* (prostitute).[17] It is quite possible that *tantrik* practitioners in Bengal—who were known for their liberal outlook, and accepted devotees irrespective of caste, class, religious or sex differences—threw open their doors to prostitutes, also.[18]

The acceptance of the prostitute in her own right was not confined to those who followed Hindu customs and rituals in pre-colonial India, but was also shared to a great extent by Buddhist preachers and patrons. The story of Ambapali, the famous courtesan of Vaisali, is well-known. Buddha, on his last journey to the hills, as he passed through Vaisali, preferred dining at her place to attending a civic reception proposed by the city fathers.[19]

The journey of the prostitute through religious customs and practices in India was, however, not a smooth one. Opposition came from orthodox Hindu lawmakers like Manu, who put the prostitute in the same category as the thief and the blackmailer, and imposed punishments on Brahmins who consorted with them. But, as A. L. Basham, writing on prostitution in medieval India, observed: ' . . . the secular attitude differed very greatly from the religious ideal, and here (i.e. in the case of prostitution) it was the secular view which prevailed.' One of the reasons for the ascendancy of the secular over the religious in the treatment of prostitution, according to Basham, was: 'By the Middle Ages the brahmans who propounded the Sacred Law might themselves be attached to temples with hundreds of prostitutes on their staffs.'[20]

Thus, the sheer social and economic compulsions of the situation not only defeated the sanctimonious objectives of the religious lawmakers, but also devoured these lawmakers themselves and turned them into patrons of prostitution.

Ironically enough, centuries later, in a Bengal ruled by a different set of lawmakers—the British administration—similar attempts were made to blacklist prostitutes and punish them. Ironically again, as in the past, the 19th century British counterparts of the ancient Manu suffered the same fate. All their professed pious objectives to cleanse the 'native' society of the ills of prostitution were overtaken by other more important and immediate compulsions that forced the colonial administration to retreat to the unenviable role of an official patron and superviser of an institution that it had earlier condemned as 'un-Christian'. The stubborn resilience of the 'oldest profession' had always stolen a march on the misanthropic plans of the clerics of all religious hues, and the vindictive arm of the law of all states.

II

In the period just preceding the colonization of Bengal by the British, prostitution in the modern sense of wage labour was in a nebulous state. The traditional domination of the male over the female body (outside the institution of marriage) took various forms. The woman's surrender of her body to the male for a remuneration took place in the twilight area of changing social norms brought about by the collapse of the Moghul empire and the prevailing anarchy in the early years of 18th century Bengal. Faint silhouettes of the courtesans of yore were to be found among the free women living on the fringes of 'respectable' society—the singers and dancers from the lower castes; the Hindu widows who joined Vaishnavite 'akhras' or clubs and were free to choose their male partners; and the so-called 'fallen women' (those deserted by their husbands, or seduced by lovers to be abandoned later) forced to eke out a living after having been discarded by their families. Segregated colonies of such women had become a part of urban and village society, tolerated with some indulgence. Not all of them could be strictly called professional prostitutes, since they followed other occupations (e.g. flower-sellers, milk-maids, barbers, etc.). But self-employment allowed them a certain freedom of action and movement which quite often made their company easily accessible to the village male looking for extra-marital or pre-marital sex. In keeping with the norms of their life-style—a grey area—they could, however, exert their own right in choosing or rejecting their clients, on whom, in any case, they did not have to depend solely for their living. An excellent representative of this type of free woman can be found in the portrayal of Hira Malini in the Bengali verse-narrative *Vidya-Sundar* composed by Bharatchandra in the first half of the 18th century. She lost her husband as a child-wife, and grew up to be a flower-pedlar, moving from house to house selling her flowers. As a young, unattached woman, she obviously had lovers, and even later, she apparently retained her charms, as described by Bharatchandra:

> *'Achhilo bistar thhaat prothom boyoshe.*
> *Ebey bura, tobu kichhu gunra achhey sheshey . . .*
> *. . . Chengra bhulaye khaye, kato janey thhuli.'*[21]
> (She was quite a coquette when she was young. Even now, when she's old, some crumbs of that past are still there . . . She lives by seducing youngsters, she knows a lot of tricks to hoodwink them.)

All these women, inhabiting the twilight zone of early 18th century Bengali society, continued to occupy the traditional space—in the participatory roles allotted to them in the various social, cultural (and even religious) functions that dominated rural society in those days (a feature of the Bengali life-style that was expressed in the popular saying: *Baro mashey teroe paban*, which freely translated would suggest: 'A festival every month all through the year'). Thus, there was always a readily available socio-cultural avenue for the display of their talents. The women *jhumur* dancers and *khemtawalis* (some among whom might have been sexually entertaining their male admirers and customers for financial remuneration, or domestic security), were invited to perform at functions during religious festivals like the Durga Puja, or wedding ceremonies in 'respectable *bhadralok*' households.[22]

Similarly, Vaishnavite women *kirtan* singers (many among whom were reputed to have left their homes and struck up temporary alliances with male partners through the still-acknowledged Vaishnavite practice of *kanthi-badal*—marriage by just exchanging the string of beads—a practice that allows both the male and female partners to dissolve their association, if any one chooses a new partner and decides on another *kanthi-badal*) were a must in musical soirees organized during religious festivals like 'Rasa-leela' (celebrating Krishna's dance with the milk-maids). In fact, the female *kirtan* singers of Bengal—despite their personal life-style, considered as non-conformist by middle-class standards—continued to enjoy popularity among both the Bengali rural masses and the urban educated gentry even into the colonial period. They were invited to sing at funeral ceremonies or other occasions at the homes of rich Bengali citizens.[23]

To go back to pre-colonial Bengal, we also come across a class of female go-betweens—known as *kutni*—who used to arrange liaisons between daughters or wives of rich households and their paramours. They were not professional procuresses (or counterparts of the male pimps, who were to dominate the transactional part of the flesh-trade in 19th century Bengal), but self-employed women like flower-sellers or hair-dressers who had free access to these households. The previously mentioned Hira Malini played the role of a go-between in the liaison between the heroine Vidya and her paramour Sundar. Such mediation did not often lead to the happy ending that marked the 'Vidya-Sundar' romance. More often, lured from their homes by *kutnis*, young women from these homes were abandoned by their lovers and left to fend for themselves, and invariably ended up as prostitutes.[24]

III

In sharp contrast with these free women inhabiting the peripheral areas of Bengali rural society, there was another class of women who could be described as the later variant of concubines. Although, in the 18th century, the Muslim *nawabs* of Bengal still maintained large 'harems', among the common run of the rich people, concubinage seemed to have shrunk from its old form of multiplicity to the status of the single mistress 'kept' by a male patron. The newly arrived European settlers—traders, freebooters and servants of the East India Company—gravitated towards the local ways of living and acting. Along with the adoption of local customs like smoking the hubble-bubble and wearing Indian clothes, they also picked up Indian women as mistresses. Some among these women were fortunate enough to live upon the jointures left to them by their English 'husbands' who returned to England with large fortunes—rarely or never honestly acquired. But others, most often, faced a bleak future. English missionaries from the beginning of the 19th century were found to be increasingly voicing concern over the rapid rise in the number of children 'born to Europeans by native women', since 'to provide employment for them has already become a matter of serious consideration . . .'[25] Another class of concubines or mistresses came from among the displaced Muslim musicians and dancers of northern India. The decline of the Moghul empire and the loss of patronage of the old aristocrats led to their emigration from places like Delhi, Lucknow, Agra, Benaras. By the end of the 18th century, many among these women artistes had arrived in the rising metropolis, Calcutta, seeking patronage among the new breed of Bengali landlords, *banians* and *dewans* who had made money through their transactions with the British traders and administrators. It was these women who were the star attractions in the famous 'nautch' performances that were organized by the Bengali parvenu for the city's European residents. In contemporary journals and publications we frequently come across the name of one such performer, Nikki. In 1819, we learn from a newspaper report, Nikki was being maintained by a rich Bengali on a monthly allowance of Rs 1000.[26]

The worst form of concubinage was the system of keeping *bandis* or slave-girls by rich Muslim households. In fact, the boom in slave traffic, carried out mainly by the Portuguese pirates from Arab settlements in Africa and South-west Asia, all through the 17th and 18th centuries, led to the importation of a large number of black women slaves (known variously as *habshis* or *kafris* in local Bengali) to serve in Muslim aristocratic households in cities like Dhaka, Murshidabad, and later, in Calcutta. Sometimes these women managed to escape—only to be pursued by their masters and apprehended. We learn, for instance, about the plight of two such female slaves in August 1831 in Calcutta: '. . . two grown up girls, the natives of a country which they called Habaish, and who appeared to be what are generally called Coffrees, absconded from the house of Syed Husein, an opulent Mogul, and he, to have them apprehended, made an application at the Thannah of the Division in which he lives, and stated that the women had robbed him of some silver ornaments and clothes which belonged to him. They were immediately taken into custody . . . they stated that they were slaves, and that from having been obliged to do more work than they liked they formed the plan of running away, and had only taken with them some of the articles given to them during the time they were in Sahib Husein's house . . .'[27]

Female slavery was not confined to aristocratic Muslim households. Rich Hindu families in medieval Bengal maintained *dasis* or female slaves, who were primarily objects of sexual exploitation by the males of these families, as evident from contemporary Hindu rules and regulations formulated by the 12th century Bengali lawmaker, Jeemutabahana, who laid down meticulous rules in his *Dayabhaga* as to the distribution of these *dasis*, along with immovable property, among the male heirs of the family. According to Maheshwara, a later commentator on, and interpreter of, *Dayabhaga*, the female slaves were used for male lust only![28]

This tradition of female slavery in pre-colonial Bengal quite often gradually slid into the new commercial enterprise of prostitution that emerged in the colonial state in 19th century Bengal. The female slaves, apart from being used by their owners for personal work, were often hired out for prostitution. We hear of a case that came up before the Government of Bengal in 1859, in which one woman called Ameerun was accused of buying girls and making them serve as prostitutes. She 'had in her possession two young girls, who had been sold or leased to her by their respective fathers for periods of 90 and 91 years, in consideration of which she had undertaken to supply them with food, and other necessaries, and had paid to the parents the sums of Rupees 12.0.0 and 8.0.0 respectively, the services of the children, and the right to employ or dispose of them as she thought fit being . . . secured to her by documents which had been executed and attested before the Cazee, or Mahomedan Notary Public of Monghyr.' On investigation, the local magistrate found out that the 'girls were employed by . . . Ameerun for purposes of prostitution', and he commenced a prosecution against her. But when her case went up to the Sudder Court, it broke down since the majority of the judges decided that there was no 'formal complaint as required by law . . .'![29]

As for the rural Bengali women, their position became insecure in the mid-18th century with the depradations of the Marhatta raiders (known as *bargis*), which created widespread anarchy in the countryside with the abduction and raping of women.[30] In accordance with the conservative norms of Hindu society, families seldom took back these unfortunate victims, since they were considered 'polluted.'

Again in 1770, a disastrous famine wiped out a third of the population of Bengal and forced the survivors to sell their children. One could see boats filled with children coming down the river for open sale at Calcutta. 'Most of them were stolen from their parents, or bought perhaps for a measure of rice in time of scarcity.'[31]

It was these rootless and displaced women—girls sold away by their famine-stricken parents, singers and dancers fallen on evil days, widows and daughters from *kulin* Brahmin families rejected as liabilities by their families, female slaves seeking escape from captivity, victims of seduction and abduction—who formed the first generation of prostitutes in the colonial world of market economy in 19th century Bengal.

It is, thus, obvious that violence was crucial to the growth and development of prostitution in this period. Direct physical violence againt women, ranging from rape and abduction to slavery and abortion (particularly in the case of young widows and unmarried women who, as a result, were excommunicated by society), played a major role in driving a large number of women to prostitution. It is interesting to note that violence against women, in general, continued in the countryside throughout the 19th century. Official records indicate a steady increase in cases of rape, abduction, enticement and exploitation of minor children and women for prostitution in certain eastern districts of Bengal (Mymensingh, Nadia, Dhaka, Patna, Rajshahi, Faridpur) between 1866 and 1904.[32]

Beginning with forcible recruitment to prostitution, violence continued to pursue these women even after they had joined the profession, as evident from the numerous cases of murders, attempts at murder, deadly assaults, burglaries and other criminal acts that the prostitutes had to suffer in those days.

Indirect violence against prostitutes took various forms—ranging from sophisticated official measures like the repressive Act XIV of 1868, to aggressive campaigns by the Bengali *bhadralok* against their participation in socio-cultural activities (which, as we have noticed earlier in this chapter, were important avenues for their self-expression in pre-colonial days). These were accompanied by a systematic psychological assault through verbal violence—abuses that were aimed at reinforcing their inferior and degrading position in society. Over the years, these abuses and sayings became a part of popular culture in Bengal—building up the stereotype of a blood-sucking vampire, out to fleece 'unwary' and 'innocent' men who walked into her den!

The first settlements of this new breed of 'commercial sex workers' in colonial Bengal sprang up in the small mofussil towns that had developed as centres of trade and commerce and business transactions in the economic network created by the East India Company. The Company's Bengali *banians* (brokers to the British traders), in order to collect the exportable merchandise from the rural producers, appointed *gomastahs* who set up their offices or 'cutcheries' in these towns with their subordinates—the peons, the *paiks* (armed servants), messengers, etc. etc. In the daily transactions of these people, along with cotton, raw silk, salt petre and other goods, female flesh also became a purchasable commodity—sometimes for direct consumption, sometimes for better exchange value through their transport to the brothels of Calcutta—the metropolitan centre created by the British to organize the linkages necessary for extracting from the vast hinterland of the Indian subcontinent the resources required for developing the economy of England.

Along with the expansion of trade and commerce, the colonial administration also extended its network of offices and courts in these mofussil towns. A contemporary Bengali observer has given an interesting account of how all these contributed to the development of brothels in a part of a typical mofussil town in the early years of the 19th century: 'In Goari (a locality in Krishnanagar town), at one time there were a few settlements of *gope* (milkmen), *malo* (fishermen and boatmen) and other lower-caste people. Later, when the British government found that it was a spacious spot and situated on the banks of the river, it chose to set up courts and other establishments there. The British began to build houses for themselves in the western part of Goari, while their (Bengali) subordinate officers, lawyers and others built their houses in the eastern part.' The observer then adds that these Bengali employees mostly came from outside the town—villages where they left their families behind. As a result, 'almost all the subordinate officers, lawyers and others needed concubines. Consequently, brothels sprung up in the neighbourhoods adjoining their houses. As in ancient Greece, where even scholars gathered at brothels for intellectual discourse, here, also, the same custom became the vogue. Even those who were not given to sensual pleasures came to these brothels for the fun of it, or to meet friends. The brothels were full of people from evening till late night. During festivals, in particular, one could hardly find any space to stand in these places. Just as during the [Durga] puja festivities people used to spend the nights moving from one spot to another to watch the images of the goddess, on the night of *vijaya* (the last day of the festivities when the images were immersed in the rivers) they moved around to look at the prostitutes.[33]

Prostitutes began to acquire a new utilitarian value among their new clientele in these towns. Another 19th century writer, recalling social customs in Jessore in the early part of that century, tells us: '. . . the (Bengali) officers and lawyers of the courts, when introducing themselves and their colleagues to some newly arrived *bhadralok* used to describe them in these terms: "This gentleman has built a *pucca* house for his mistress." Building a *pucca* house for a mistress was considered a sign of honour and prestige.'[34]

In the spatially hierarchical society of early colonial Bengal, prostitution in its new commercial form percolated down from these mofussil towns (which were the district headquarters of the colonial administration) to the rural hinterland of these towns. The administrative network created a new breed of middlemen and minions in the villages who occupied a privileged position in rural society by virtue of the official sanction that they enjoyed in collecting rents, organizing inter-district trade and commerce, extorting money from gullible villagers and playing a crucial role in mediating in litigations over land disputes—which became a perennial feature of Bengali rural society. It was this section of the rural parvenu, along with the hangers-on and employees of the old (fast declining) local zamindar families, who constituted the clientele in the proliferating commerce of prostitution in the 19th century Bengali countryside.

A mid-19th century Bengali author recalls a story (which might be apocryphal, but unerringly captures the spirit of the times), according to which, some time in *Sravana*, 1242 (July–August 1835), a Brahmin went from his village to a market in another village some two miles to the north of his own, in order to buy a prostitute! But no such 'commodity' was available in the open market. There were a few fisherwomen around, a couple of whom were persuaded to accompany him back to his village where they were installed as prostitutes, and thus their breed increased and spread out in all the villages of Bengal![35]

The same author gives us a graphic account of the habits and customs of these rural prostitutes and their clients (as distinct from the more popular and better publicized accounts of the life-style of the urban prostitutes of 19th century Calcutta). As evident from the abovementioned story, they were recruited from among the poorer, lower caste communities (e.g. fisherwomen). Their dress and cosmetics were, therefore, knocked together from whatever resources were available in the rural environment. '. . . they stick to their coiffure circular, gilded flowers which look like mushrooms; to their 'anchals' [ends of their saris] they tie a ring of a dozen of keys; on their foreheads they scrawl round dots in chalk which resemble Vishnu's 'chakra' (disk); . . . they paint their teeth with antimony, and eyes with lamp black . . .' As for their regular customers, there is a long list: '. . . swanky carters, tailors, sweetmakers, school-teachers, cooks and gatekeepers employed by zamindars, rent-collectors, bench-clerks, milkmen, peons, lawyers' clerks, and head-constables (and sometimes the officers also) of police stations. . .'[36]

But it was Calcutta, the metropolitan centre of colonial trade, and headquarters of colonial administration, which emerged as the main flesh-pot for the new patrons of prostitution during the 18th–19th century period. During the early years of the 18th century, Calcutta was still to emerge as a metropolis from the conglomeration of the three villages—Sutanati, Dihi Kolikata and Gobindapur—over which the East India Company had acquired a licence (*firman*) from the Moghul Court in Delhi in 1698 to collect revenue from the farmers. The Company's officers were in a hurry to clear these villages of their inhabitants to build their warehouses amd a fort (the latter for defence against their Dutch, Portuguese and French rivals). Along with the cultivators and artisans who lived in these villages, the prostitutes, who apparently carried on their trade according to the old rural societal norms, also had to make way for the colonial establishments which represented a new order that introduced a different system of commercial norms for prostitution (among other occupations) in Calcutta. We hear of two such prostitutes whose properties were confiscated by the Company, in the latter's account of expenditure in Tank Square, which was its business centre, situated in the centre of the rural conglomeration that was emerging as Calcutta, as early as 1753. A notice issued by the Company on 1 February that year announced 'For sale at public outcry of sundry effects belonging to Isury and Bovee, prostitutes . . . confiscated to the Company . . .' The expenditure (as compensation to the two prostitutes for the confiscation of their 'sundry effects', or otherwise?) claimed by the Company officials stood at: 'Rs 539.4.3'.[37] If we make allowances for the notoriety of the English clerks' misspelling of Bengali names, it is not difficult for us to discover behind the two un-Bengali sounding names—Isury and Bovee, in the colonial records—two living characters respectively known as Ishwari and Bhobi, which were common names for women in Bengal in those days.

Curiously enough, prostitution thrived in Calcutta not so much due to the direct needs of the British settlers there, but because of the indirect impact of the British colonial order on the life-style of the Bengali citizens there. It was from among them that a new generation of clientele emerged.

In an ironical twist to the pre-colonial tradition of a living link between prostitutes and religious rituals (whether through temple dancers or *tantrik* practices, as suggested earlier), a 19th century Bengali satirist composed a couplet lampooning the habits of these Bengali citizens, in the same religious terms of reference to which they were used. Manmohan Basu (1831–1912), noting the popularity of prostitutes among this new breed of urban Bengalis (who usually came from 'respectable' and devout Hindu upper caste families), came up with a spoof on a well-known invocatory Sanskrit couplet. In his parody, he daringly brought together an evocation of heroines of mythology with a celebration of the virtues of contemporary prostitutes of Calcutta. He, thus, compared the Calcutta 'babu's' devotion to the city's famous five prostitutes with his equally ardent adoration of the famous five *satis* (the five heroines of mythology known for their chastity, who were worshipped by the Hindus), Ahalya, Draupadi, Kunti, Tara and Mandodari. The original Sanskrit couplet ran as follows:

> '*Ahalya, Draupadi, Kunti, Tara, Mandodaristatha,*
> *Pancha kanyah smarennityam mahapatakanashanam.*'
> (Ahalya, Draupadi, Kunti, Tara, Mandodari—honour these five women by taking their names at all times, and even the worst of your sins will be wiped out.)

In his parody, Manmohan Basu replaces the five *satis* with five contemporary prostitutes, and, thus, welcomes the arrival of the new heroines in the pantheon of Calcutta's commercial world:

> *'Phulmoni, Joymoni, Andi, Lakhhi, Padmamonistatha.*
> *Pancha beshyam smarennityam mahapatakanashanam.'*[38]
> (Phulmoni, Joymoni, Andi, Lakhi, and Padmamoni—honour these five prostitutes by taking their name at all times, and even the worst of your sins will be wiped out.)

But behind this hyperbolic sneer about the prostitutes by a Bengali *bhadralok* satirist, there was a hidden story of their long struggle of what can be described in today's terms as 'career management' in an occupation that was increasingly becoming hazardous and illegal in 19th century Bengal. The occupation drew a pool of women who were driven into a disadvantaged position in society and had fewer legitimate professional opportunities available to them than men. Although a variety of social, economic and personal factors might have influenced their entry into the profession, once they became full-time prostitutes, interaction with their clientele, as well as members of their own profession, brought about subjective changes regarding self-image, perception of prostitution as a profession governed by its own rules, assessment of threatening situations (like encounters with the police, or jealous and homicidal lovers, and affliction with venereal disease), and evaluation of options that often came their way in the shape of reformist offers of rehabilitation, or promises of marriage by lovers.

II
British 'Sahibs' and 'Native Women'

'These are the Syrens of the East, bedeckt
With anklet-bells and nose-rings—such are they
Valued in tender youth, but cold neglect
Scorn, or contempt, marks their declining day . . .'

—James Atkinson
'The City of Palaces, A Fragment.'[1]

The attitudes and policies of the British administration towards prostitution in India need to be located in the wider context of the changing construction of relations between European male settlers and indigenous women all through the 18th and 19th centuries, as well as of the changing notions of sexual behaviour in British society during this period.

Right from the end of the 17th century—when London was getting increasingly involved in the administration of Bengal—the 'native' woman was also acquiring a new importance in colonial discourse. In the European male imagination, her image was being fashioned by the impressions about Oriental women provided by travellers from the West.[2] These travelogues conjured up fantasies of 'seraglios' of languid and compliant dark-skinned beauties adept in offering pleasures of an exotic nature! They also evoked sentiments of chivalry among many a crusading European male heart, by their narration of the woes of these women, shut up inside 'harems', or of the Hindu females as victims of *sati*.[3] As a result, one discerns in contemporary British attitudes towards Indian women a curious mix of erotic fascination and a missionary zeal to rescue them from their societal prisons (whether a Muslim 'harem' or an orthodox Brahmin household). Byron, in a moment of facetiousness, summed up the mood of his contemporaries who sought pleasures in the Orient:

> 'What men call gallantry, and gods adultery,
> Is much more common where the climate's sultry.'[4]

Although Byron was describing the Mediterranean environs in his poem *Don Juan*, the 'sultry climate' in Bengal in those days apparently stimulated the same impulses of 'gallantry' and 'adultery' among the British traders, administrators, lawyers, teachers and adventurers of various types, who started to settle down in Bengal from the early years of colonization.

I

One of the earliest examples of this ambiguous liaison between a British trader and an Indian woman, is the life-story of Job Charnock, the man who is known as the founder of Calcutta. Although much of the story has been found to be apocryphal by modern researchers,[5] it bears repetition, since the common thread that runs through all the various accounts of Charnock's romance as narrated in contemporary British records indicates the mix of impulses that characterized the male colonialist's attitude towards the Indian woman. Some accounts portray Charnock (who was the East India Company representative in Bengal from the middle till the end of the 17th century) as rescuing an Indian widow from the funeral pyre of her husband as she was about to commit *sati*. According to one contemporary: '. . . he was so smitten with the Widow's Beauty, that he sent his guards to take her by force from her executioners, and conducted her to his own lodgings. They lived lovingly for many years, and had several children; . . . but instead of converting her to Christianity, she made him a Proselyte to Paganism, and the only part of Christianity that was remarkable in him, was burying her decently . . .'[6] Yet, another contemporary looks at Charnock's relationship with this woman in a different light—and with a different story, also. William Hedges, Agent and Governor of Bengal during Charnock's tenure there, noted in his Diary: '. . . a

Gentoo . . . made complaint to me that Mr Charnock did shamefully, to ye great scandall of our Nation, keep a Gentoo woman of his kindred, which he has had these 19 years . . .'[7] Echoing similar sentiments of official embarrassment at the life-style led by Charnock, one of his colleagues even complained to his bosses in the East India Company in the following terms: 'As in the case of Mr Job Charnock and the Women hee kept tho' of a meane Cast, and great poverty, which occasioned Great trouble . . .'[8]

Through all this maze of laudatory accounts of Charnock's 'gallantry' in rescuing a Hindu woman from death and emerging as her lover and protector on the one hand, and the abusive accounts of his 'adultery' in living with a 'Gentoo's Wife (her husband being still living, or but lately dead) . . .'[9] on the other, there is, however, a common thread that runs all through and which confirms the historical fact of Charnock's relationship with an Indian woman. Her name is forgotten, but the names of the children borne by her through her liaison with Job Charnock, were meticulously recorded in the baptismal register of St. Mary's Church of Madras in 1689, where Charnock's three daughters—Mary, Elizabeth and Katherine—were baptised.[10] As one modern researcher points out: 'Mrs Charnock's name was deliberately omitted from the baptismal register as he (Charnock) was not married to her in the legal sense and he had not converted her to Christianity.'[11]

While the story of Charnock's liaison with an Indian woman has to be unravelled from a tangle of versions found in the early records of the East India Company in the 17th century, we can have more direct access to an account of a similar liaison from an autobiography left by an English barrister, who lived in Calcutta during the last decades of the 18th century. William Hickey (not related to his more famous contemporary, the newspaper-editor James Hickey, who, at around the same time, was bringing out the first English journal in Calcutta, the *Bengal Gazette*) lived in Calcutta from 1777 to 1808, and his memoirs covering that period, apart from giving us a glimpse of the politics and the life-style of the British settlers in the city, also tell us about his own peccadilloes. His memoirs are in the tradition of the genre established in English literature by the diaries of his predecessor in 17th century England—Samuel Pepys and John Evelyn. Hickey's frank disclosures about his relationships with Indian women in his memoirs hark back to that genre. The reminiscences of British settlers who followed Hickey in 19th century Calcutta were often controlled by the newly emerging British notions about sexual behaviour and the code of conduct in colonies, that were to be crystallized into what was known as 'Victorian Morality'; as a result, these later accounts were written in a style that was less uninhibited than that of Hickey.

Hickey tells us of one of his earliest encounters with a Bengali woman, soon after the death of his English wife in Calcutta, sometime in 1785. A friend of his, who was the British Resident in Murshidabad, sent him a handsome-looking 'native' woman for his 'private use' while he was living in Calcutta. Her name was Kironbala, and after living with Hickey for a year, she gave birth to a son. Hickey, although fond of the son, could not help feeling puzzled by his dark colour. The secret was out when one day he returned home early and found her sleeping with his Indian *khidmadgar* (waiter). Needless to say, Hickey drove out both of them. But, when he heard later that Kironbala was living in distress, he arranged for a monthly allowance for her. Hickey's next experience with an Indian woman was to be a more lasting and pleasing one. A north Indian woman known as 'Jamadarni', she joined Hickey after having served an English friend of Hickey's who left her following his transfer from Calcutta. Hickey's account of his life with her is a picture of romantic bliss—with Hickey putting her up in a garden house in Garden Reach (one of the riverside outskirts of Calcutta in those days) with a retinue of maid-servants to look after her, in real 'seraglio' style! But, unlike the Indian owners of 'seraglios', Hickey introduced his mistress to his friends, and Jamadarni seemed to be quite a draw among them—judging by Hickey's adulation of her smart demeanour in such company. Hickey seemed to be totally devoted to Jamadarni and committed to her needs and requirements. On a boat-trip along the Hooghly river, Jamadarni took a fancy to the environs of Chinsurah (a small town a few kilometres away from Calcutta), and in order to please her, Hickey bought a house there and set up a home with Jamadarni. In 1796, she gave birth to a son, but died soon after delivery. A sad and shocked Hickey, unable (or unwilling?) to bring up the newborn son, handed him over to an English couple, acquaintances of his in Calcutta. But the boy died soon after.[12]

The practice of maintaining Indian mistresses among male European settlers in Calcutta (as described by Hickey in the 18th century) apparently continued without attracting any social opprobrium (from the substantially large European community living in the city) even into the early decades of the 19th century. An English writer—who chose to be anonymous—in his memoirs about Bengal during 1811–14 tells us: 'Concubinage is so generally practised in India by the Europeans, and at the same time so tacitly sanctioned by married families, who scruple not to visit at the house of a bachelor that retains a native mistress (though were she an European they would avoid it as polluted), that when, setting aside the married men, I calculate three parts of those who remain as retaining concubines, I fancy I shall be only confining myself within the strictest bounds of truth and moderation.' Explaining the reasons, the writer harks back to Byron and says: 'The climate is undoubtedly one of the chief causes of this great propensity to sexual intercourse the results of which prove generally so unfortunate to my countrymen.' He then describes the other cause: 'The Hindoostanee women (under this denomination I class both Hindoos and Moslems) are in general exquisitely formed, after the truest models of symmetry and beauty. Their countenances, more pleasing than handsome, are very expressive; their large black eyes in particular, full of the softest fire, convey volumes, and almost supercede the necessity of speech. They take much pride in their hair, which is usually very long and glossy, and tied simply in a knot at the back of the head. The delicacy and nice proportions of their limbs, must be seen to be admired; their finely-shaped necks, small and tapering waists, well turned ancles and infantine feet, form a cluster of delights, to the temptation of which it is not surprising if we see men, in other respects prudent, fall the victims.'[13]

Here is, in short, the summation of the Englishman's fantasy of the sensual promise of the exotic Orient. The concept of the Oriental woman as the odalisque, ready to offer 'a cluster of delights' (like a cluster of succulent fruits!), was an extension in gendered terms of the colonial ideology of treating the colony as passive and virgin soil for exploitation, from where the colonialist could pluck at his will whatever resources he needed. Even when Hickey writes about his life with Jamadarni—to whom he was obviously devoted—one cannot escape the feeling, when reading him, that his concern for her was structured by the same assumption of white superiority and civilization that shaped imperial policies towards India. Among many other qualities of hers, Hickey was particularly impressed by her ability to join his European friends at dinner parties and please them with her intelligence. This was in keeping with his patronizing attitude towards Indians. While describing, for instance, a dinner party at the palace of the Nawab of Murshidabad, he remarks condescendingly that it was 'quite in the English taste'!

II

But while Hickey—and most of his European upper-class contemporaries in 18th century Calcutta—were quite uninhibited in publicly owning to keeping Indian mistresses (or even marrying 'native' women), later British settlers who succeeded them (particularly in the last half of the 19th century) followed a more discreet life-style, which was also marked by a decreasing trend in contracting unions with 'native' women. There were several reasons. First, the onset of Victorian morality in Britain compelled the British civilians and professionals to lead a more circumscribed and circumspect sex-life in India to avoid censure by colonial authorities back in London. Secondly, while in the 17th–18th century period, Hickey and his European peer-group were seldom able to find any but Indian mistresses in Calcutta, by the middle of the 19th century, there were flocks of women from England arriving at Calcutta (and other Indian cities) in search of husbands among the British civilians there. They drifted to cities like Calcutta in a matrimonial odyssey that was termed 'damsel-errantry' in those days. Thirdly, apart from the new moral codes of Victorian life-style and the availability of British wives for the British settlers in India in the mid-19th century, there was also a distinct change in the administrative role of the East India Company in Bengal during this period which shaped

British attitudes to, and relationships with, 'natives'—and particularly their women. The British, by now, had emerged from the role of traders into that of well-entrenched colonial rulers. This required a new breed of Englishmen and the relinquishing of old habits like smoking the hubble-bubble, attending 'nautch' performances or keeping an Indian mistress (customs that were adopted by the first generation of European settlers in Bengal). There was an insistence on rigid norms of behaviour which led to a sort of self-segregation of the British ruling elite in Calcutta from the local Bengali society (in marked contrast with the social bonhomie of the previous century) and became a means of establishing the image of exclusiveness of the colonial rulers.

One notes with some amusement how later British residents of Bengal, in the last half of the 19th century, reared up on the strict regimen of Victorian norms, sought to find excuses and explanations for the habits of their predecessors in 18th century Calcutta. One such writer, admitting that the 'beginning of the eighteenth century was the nadir of our morality', still tried to bear with the fact that 'many of the (English) exiles in that distant land (of Bengal) formed unions, sometimes lawful, sometimes unlawful, with . . . Indian women', by consoling himself and his readers with the words: 'We do not expect the wall to stand firm when its buttresses have been removed, and Calcutta was then so far away from London that all the common moral restraints and supports were to a great extent inoperative.'[14]

But facts are stubborn! As far as contemporary British morals were concerned, 18th century London was not very far away from Calcutta of those days. Gambling, duelling, drinking, adultery, concubinage, were fashionable among the British gentry, as immortalized by Hogarth (1697–1764) in a series of paintings like 'The Rake's Progress' and 'Marriage a la Mode'. Those were the days when Henry Fielding (1707–1754) was writing *Tom Jones* and Laurence Sterne (1713–1768) *Tristram Shandy*—which give us a glimpse of the life-style of English men and women of that period.

Those Englishmen who arrived in Bengal in the 18th century naturally carried with them the baggage of values and habits with which they grew up in England. The following excerpts from a satirical catechism published in 1780 in James Hickey's *Bengal Gazette* sum up the prevailing English morals in Calcutta:

> 'Q.— What is commerce?
> A.— Gambling . . .
> Q. — What is punctuality?
> A.— An observation of the appointments of duelling and intriguing . . .'[15]

Given this state of affairs in 18th century Calcutta English society, there was a general acceptance—if not approval—of happenings like the seduction of the wife of George Grand by the senior East India Company official Phillip Francis on the day of their wedding[16] or of the common practice of keeping Indian mistresses by affluent English traders and merchants and well-to-do professionals. But when some among English settlers in Bengal chose to continue the same practice in the mid-19th century, they incurred opprobrium from fellow English residents. Even a Shakespearean scholar of repute like Captain D. L. Richardson (who taught in the Hindu College, and later became the Principal of Krishnanagar College in 1846) could not escape reproach for having maintained a Bengali mistress in a secluded house set up for her alone. John Drinkwater Bethune, then Chairman of the Education Council (who founded the women's school in Calcutta known as Bethune College today) publicly denounced him as 'a hoary-headed libertine.'[17]

Such liaisons, however, were contracted on an inter-personal level between the 'sahib' and the 'native' female, and remained confined within the framework of concubinage. A more promiscuous opportunity was offered by Calcutta to the newly arrived British 'writer' (clerk) of the East India Company, or the soldier, in the shape of commercially institutionalized prostitution. From the middle of the 18th century, the trade in flesh was carried out in the gorgeous garb of 'dancing girls'—the ethnic chic that was calculated to allure the 'sahibs'—through an elaborate network of sales-agents.

We get an interesting account of a typical transaction on these lines from the viewpoint of a British representative of the colonial order. Captain Thomas Williamson published in 1810 the *East Indian Guide and Vade Mecum*, where he offered information and warnings to his countrymen who were about to land in

Calcutta. Presumably based on his personal experiences, he described the fate of the newly-arrived Englishmen: 'Totally ignorant of the language, and without any guide, it is by no means surprising that so many impositions are practised on our countrymen as soon as they arrived in India. A debash of the lowest order, and of the most crafty disposition, perfectly experienced in all the ordinary requirements of Europeans, and prompt to gratify their desires so long as profit attends the speculation, is ever at the elbow of the novice, serving as banker, purveyor, pimp and interpreter.' He then proceeded to describe the next stage of the 'gratification of desires' of his countrymen: 'Add the allurements held out by the sable beauties, who will contrive means to retail their charms so long as they think money is to be had, and no trifling expense will be incurred. Some fellow who can speak English, and thoroughly understand whatever relates to the interest of the concern, which, among other things, includes thieving, lying, cheating, pimping etc. is imployed to delude the unwary stranger. The first essay is ordinarily made by describing the elegance of the native women, and their great perfection as singers and dancers; and rarely fails, especially with youths under such circumstances, to excite something more than curiosity. The dancing-girls are introduced, and so many fatal consequences follow, that nothing can be more dangerous than this irregular indulgence; it never failing first to drain the purse, and, in a few days or weeks, the constitution also.'[18]

It, of course, did not occur to Williamson that similar methods of 'thieving, lying, cheating, pimping' were being employed by his own countrymen in Bengal, with consequences that were far more fatal for this land's economy and its people than those suffered by a few young Englishmen who encountered the 'dancing-girls'—and those among them who might have ruined themselves in the process. But that is another story!

The young English 'writers'—the term used for clerks and junior officers employed in the new colonial administrative set-up in Bengal—seemed to have acquired the rakish habits of their senior predecessors in India, by the mid-18th century. Around this time, we come across official records of the East India Company which betray its increasing concern about the life-style followed by these young employees in Bengal. Letters to the Court of Directors complained about 'the younger servants being incapable themselves to (*sic*) discharge the functions of their several offices, were forced to have recourse to the industry of their Banians and black writers', who advanced 'large sums of money to their Masters, which served no other purpose than to support their extravagance and render them dependent on their servants instead of being obedient to the Governor and Council.'[19]

One of the 'extravagances' indulged in by some of these junior English officers of the Company was the maintenance of garden houses on the outskirts of Calcutta, where they installed their 'Hindoostanee female friends.'[20] Many among them were sons of impoverished middle-class families, who, on their arrival in Calcutta, were opened up to privileges and facilities that were unimaginable to them at home. It was quite likely that they would make use of these advantages to replicate, in their life-style in India, the libertine habits of their aristocratic contemporaries in 18th century England—habits which they had watched with envy from a distance, and aspired to follow as marks of a status symbol. Denied the choice of a similar permissive life-style in their own home-towns, these young English 'writers' who chose to come to India naturally found an avenue for their aspirations in a colony where they could acquire rank and fortune that enabled them to assert their authority, to maintain a 'seraglio', or keep a mistress in a 'garden house'—symbols of aristocracy.

They must have also been inspired by the lavish dinners and dance performances that were held by the Bengali zamindars and millionnaires in the palatial garden houses, where the superiors of these junior servants of the Company thronged, whenever invited for wedding ceremonies or religious festivals.

Possession of garden houses on the outskirts of Calcutta and suburbs on the banks of the Hooghly river thus became a status symbol with most of these young writers in the 18th century. It reached such an extent that the East India Company's Committee of Inspection felt constrained in the 1760s to recommend that 'an order be issued that no writer shall be allowed to keep a house without the express permission of the governor, or be permitted either of himself or jointly with others to keep a garden house.'[21]

III

While the monogamic alliances of the Company's senior officials and traders (or of Englishmen in the upper echelons of professions) with Indian mistresses in 18th century Calcutta might have been somewhat grudgingly accepted with the cynical tolerance that marked contemporary social life in London, it was the vulnerability of the young English clerks to the promiscuous temptations of the 'sable beauties' that seemed to worry the Company's directors in London. After all, it was these young people who had to be depended upon for running the daily administration in Bengal. They could not be allowed to dissipate their energies on 'dancing girls' and orgies in garden houses!

Two major steps taken at the beginning of the 19th century were aimed at contributing to the control of—among other proclivities—sexual involvements of English clerks with Indian women. The first was the establishment of the Fort William College in Calcutta in 1800. Explaining the reasons why the College had to be established in Calcutta, Marquis Wellesley, then Governor-General of India, said: 'The age at which writers usually arrive in India is from sixteen to eighteen . . . Once landed in India their studies, morals, manners, expenses and conduct are no longer subject to any regulation, restraint, or guidance. Hence, they often acquire habits destructive of their health and fortunes . . .'[22]

While the Fort William College was expected to take care of the morals of those young writers who had already arrived in Calcutta, another college was set up in England itself (Haileybury College in Hertfordshire) to prepare the new recruits before they set sail for India for moral resistance to the temptations that they might face in that country! One of the civilians trained there, who later rose to the position of the Secretary to the Government of Bengal (in the 1860s), was to recall how at that college he 'first became cognizant of the fact that we were members of the Civil Service, a body whose mission it was to rule and to civilize that empire which had been won for us by the sword . . . (and) as members of such a body, there were certain traditions to be kept up . . . and a code of public and private honour to be rigidly maintained . . .'[23]

The 'traditions to be kept up' and the 'code of public and private honour' that were being taught at Haileybury College (which was set up five years after the establishment of the Calcutta Fort William College) were a far cry from the 'traditions' and 'codes' that ruled English social life in the 18th century and permitted the young 'sahibs' in India to strike up relationships with 'native' women. The cultural mission of the colonial power to 'civilize' the 'natives', which began to be firmly entrenched in official policies from the beginning of the 19th century, led to the development of a new set of values among the young English civilians who arrived here that kept them away from intimate relationships with 'native' society—leave alone 'native' women.[24]

Apart from these official steps to control the social behaviour of the Company's officers in Calcutta and other towns in India, another development around the beginning of the 19th century also contributed to the change in the sexual life-style of the new generation of young British civilians. By the beginning of the 19th century, Bengal was to acquire the reputation of an attractive colony which began to draw shiploads of women from England who were in search of husbands among the European residents in Calcutta and other parts of the colony. The return of the first generation of British 'nabobs' (the English traders and Company officials who amassed fortunes in the 17th–18th century period in Bengal) to their homeland with all their riches, created the impression among English families that India was an El Dorado, and prompted what came to be known as 'damsel-errantry' from the shores of England. According to a French visitor to Calcutta in the 1820s: 'Girls with no money who have not succeeded in getting married in England arrive here in cargoes for the purpose of selling themselves—in the most honourable sense of the word, of course—to young officers and civilians who receive, in addition to their appointment and the assurance of a fortune sufficient for two, orders to go and be rich all by themselves in some village two hundred leagues from Calcutta and govern an area equal to that of several French departments.'[25] Thus, marriages with women from their own community, which replaced inter-racial unions, were expected to hold in leash the sexual impulses of the young civilians, as well as provide them with domestic bliss. An Englishwoman visiting Calcutta in 1835 was to observe, while noting the very young age at which they were getting married: '. . . such unions are not considered imprudent, for they are often the means of preventing extravagance, dissipation, and all their concomitant evils.' She then added that the majority of these English civilians were 'exceedingly anxious to obtain for themselves a security against the tedium and ennui of a solitary jungle—a being interested in their welfare, and not only attached to them by the tenderest and most sacred of all ties, but who supplies the place of relatives whom they may never hope to see again.'[26]

Still later, the opening of the Suez Canal (in November 1869) made the journey to India comparatively easy, and a different category of English women began to arrive in Calcutta. They were employed to serve behind hotel bars in Calcutta and other cities. They usually came from lower-middle-class English homes and were employed by Spiers and Pond, then the leading restauranteurs in England. But while some among these women succeeded in acquiring bridegrooms and settled down to marital bliss, others who failed drifted into prostitution. Contemporary records suggest the existence of a large number of English women among European prostitutes who plied their trade from lodgings in Kerr's Lane (now Collin Lane) and Dacres Lane in Central Calcutta, and later in Kareya in south Calcutta. The barmaids in the taverns of Khidirpur (the dock area) catered to the needs of the European sailors. A song of apocryphal origins, invented later, celebrated their charms in the following lines:

> 'Gone away are the Kidderpore girls,
> With their powdered faces and tricked up curls;
> Gone away are those sirens dark,
> Fertile of kisses, but barren of heart . . .'[27]

By the mid-19th century, therefore, inter-racial relationships in Bengal had undergone a sea change. Within the new framework of colonial administration, where the type of bonhomie with 'natives' that marked British social life in 18th century Calcutta had no place, the new generation of upper- and middle-class 'sahibs'—the civilians and commercial agents, the barristers and solicitors, the doctors and teachers—could have no dealings with 'native' women. The free-wheeling days of the era of Job Charnock and William Hickey were over. The new 'sahibs' had to be protected from contamination by 'native' women, and 'damsel-errantry' from their homeland took care of this problem by bringing the wayward 'boys' into the fold of marriage.[28]

III
White Mars and Black Venus

'It is probably true to say that Venus has been
in constant attendance upon Mars wherever the
British soldier has served in our far-flung
Empire, both in an official and unofficial capacity.'

—Dr Fernando Henriques
Stews and Strumpets.[1]

While 'damsel-errantry' served to meet the physical and emotional needs of the middle- and upper-class 'sahibs' (the civil servants, army officers and other professionals in Bengal), the vaster number of English soldiers and sailors—who had to be imported every year into the province to bolster the colonial administration's defence against external and internal offensives—had to be satisfied, too.

In fact, from the earliest days of their involvement with Indian affairs, the East India Company authorities in London expressed their concern about providing women for soldiers sent to this country. We come across a quaintly worded order from the Company, dated sometime in 1692, saying: 'Encourage by all means that you can invent that our Soldiers do marry with the Native women, because it is impossible to get ordinary young women, as we have before directed, to pay their own passages, although Gentle-women sufficient do offer themselves.'[2] Quite obviously, as we have noted in the previous chapter, this was in keeping with the prevailing social attitudes in 17th century London, which permitted—or winked at—marriages or liaisons by British traders, freebooters, officials and professionals in India contracted with local women.

But this permissive attitude towards its soldiers in the early days of the Company's rule in Bengal created problems of an insurmountable nature that forced the colonial rulers to formulate a different strategy altogether to satisfy the sexual needs of their soldiers. It brought into existence a special category of Indian prostitutes. The history of their emergence and development—under the strict supervision of the British military authorities—constitutes an important and interesting chapter in the annals of the colonial administration of the Army in India.

Unlike the 'sahibs' of the 18th–19th century period, the white soldiers and sailors who arrived in India at that time were mostly drawn from lower-middle- and working-class homes. These people were looked down upon by their superior officers as a sub-human species who were thought to lack the intellectual and moral resources required for continence. To quote such a soldier who served in India in the 1840s ' . . . the British soldier is a neglected man. He is looked on in every country as a being of inferior species; as the paria of the body politic; and thought to be almost incapable of moral or social improvement. His own officers despise him, and the public at large despise him. Surely then, when he finds himself treated with universal contempt, it cannot be a matter of surprise that he loses all self-respect, and becomes the reckless and degraded being that he is . . .'[3]

The British soldiers and sailors were, indeed, notorious for their drunken brawls in Calcutta in the 18th and 19th centuries. Complaints about their misbehaviour in the streets were quite common. They thronged the Lalbazar area (where the Calcutta police headquarters are situated today) which was known as 'Flag Street' because of the string of flags across the street leading to eating houses, grog shops and brothels. Soldiers and sailors drank and fought to their hearts' content in 'Flag Street'. As early as 1745, the Company authorities had to investigate into allegations of outrages in the area by English troops.[4]

Faced with the disorderly behaviour of its soldiers, British officialdom explored various options to control them. In the proceedings of the Select Committee on 26 May, 1761, we find an interesting reference, made approvingly, to the French East India

Company's policy of controlling their soldiers who were posted in Mauritius ('to be sent to India on extraordinary occasions'). The French colonial authorities, while responding to the 'frequent complaints of the disorders which the (French) soldiers commit when scattered at their liberty', and apprehending 'all the inconveniences attending licentious soldiers', proposed the setting up of barracks in Mauritius. The justification of the French East India Company's proposal is significant as it harks back to the same attitude, shared by its English counterpart, of regarding the ranks as an inferior species that needed to be held in leash: 'A good prison or guard house is not less necessary to hold the blacks, than the barracks for the soldiers, in keeping the Company's slaves, under good management shutting them up by night . . .'[5]

By establishing barracks, the colonial administration was thus institutionalizing the hierarchical system within its core of white armed personnel—the lowest in rank among whom had to be 'shut up by night.' In fact, as early as 1758, the East India Company in Calcutta was complaining about the absence of barracks in the city, as a result of which the soldiers were dispersed, and, therefore, the 'impossibility of preventing their committing great disorders and destroying themselves with spirituous liquors when so dispersed, and the necessity of keeping them together for their discipline.'[6]

The 'great disorders' and the tendency to 'destroy themselves with spirituous liquors', of which they were accused in the above-mentioned official report, could have reflected the mental disorder that these soldiers must have suffered from, having been displaced from their homes and environment. It was these ranks who had to face the brunt of the armed resistance put up by the Indian peasantry in a series of rebellions that swept the countryside in the early years of British colonial expansion in the 18th–19th century period. They were also used by their generals to carry out reprisals against the peasantry after the suppression of these rebellions. The brutalization of their behavioural instincts, encouraged by their superior officers during such tasks of suppression and reprisal, revealed itself during peacetime in cities like Calcutta in the form of criminal outrages. The East India Company authorities felt alarmed by these tendencies, not out of any concern for the woes of the common citizens (who were victims of these outrages by the British soldiers), but because of the physical dissipation by 'spirituous liquors' that would cripple their armed minions, and the growing lack of discipline among these ranks which, in future, could pose a threat to the Company itself.

The construction of Fort William in Calcutta in 1758 (after the old Fort was abandoned following the sacking of Calcutta by Nawab Siraj-ud-Dowla in 1756) helped the military authorities to 'shut up by night' their soldiers in the barracks that were set up on the Fort premises. But even this did not stop drunkenness among the troops. Visiting the Fort in 1829, the French scientist Victor Jacquemont found: 'At the present moment there are hardly more than fifteen thousand [European troops]. The mortality among them is very high. Drunkenness, which in England stupefies men, kills them here.'[7]

Drunkenness and death from alcoholism continued unabated among British troops in India. As one British soldier posted in India in the 1840s observed: 'It is absolutely astonishing to see the eagerness with which the mass of European soldiers in India endeavour to procure liquor, no matter of what description, so that it produces insensibility, the sole result sought for. . .'[8] According to the same source, out of the 1800 odd European soldiers dying annually in India, at least 800 were killed by liquor. Five-sevenths of the court-martials in India were assembled to try 'delinquents for habitual drunkenness, drunkenness on duty, or crimes committed while under the influence of liquor.'[9]

I

If the British soldiers had to depend on liquor to produce the 'insensitivity' essential for them to adapt themselves to the brutalization that was demanded of them, they also had to look for female company to meet both their physical and emotional needs. While similar needs of their British bosses—the army top brass, the officials of the East India Company, and even the junior 'writers' posted in India—were taken care of by their expensive Indian mistresses in the 18th century, and 'damsel-errantry' in the 19th, the ordinary British soldier all through these years had to fend for himself in India. Their poor income, and even worse barrack-life, could never inspire a 'damsel-errantry' from their own classes in England.

The colonial authorities also recognized the impossibility of importing prostitutes from home to feed the increasing number of soldiers who were being despatched to India. The women who plied their trade in the streets of West End, Burlington Arcade and Haymarket in those days could not be shipped en masse to India.

As a result, members of the *gora paltan* (platoon of white soldiers), as they were known in Bengal at that time, had to take recourse to the only outlet available to them—the public brothels that had sprouted in the cities and towns. But such indulgences by the soldiers created problems of a serious nature for the Army authorities. Venereal diseases spread at an alarming rate among the British soldiers posted in India.

In fact, as early as 1766, the colonial administration was compelled to take note of the spread of the deadly disease among its soldiers. In an order dated 22 September that year, it was stated that 'a distinction should be made on account of common and natural disorders and venereal cases.' Stressing the need to take measures against soldiers picking up venereal diseases, the order 'as a further discouragement and punishment to the latter' recommended that '5 instead of 3 rupees should be deducted from their pay . . .'[10]

Curiously enough, the historical sources of venereal diseases still appear to remain shrouded in mystery. In Bengal, their origins have been attributed to the arrival of Portuguese sailors to India after the discovery of the Cape route to this country. They were supposed to have carried the germs of syphilis, which was an epidemic in 15th century Europe. According to one Bengali observer: 'The disease [of syphilis] is first mentioned in the 'Bhabaprakasa', under the name of Feringhi Roga, and mercurial preparations are recommended for its treatment.'[11] 'Feringhi Roga', if translated literally, means a disease (*roga*) caused by the *Feringhi* (the term used in Bengal in the 17th–18th century period, for the Portuguese sailors and colonizers—but which was later extended to embrace the descendants of Indo-European parentage in colonial Bengal).

Whatever might have been the origins of venereal diseases, the British administrators in Bengal were getting worried by their spread among their soldiers. An analysis made over a five-year period in the 1830s showed a rate of 32–45 per cent incidence of venereal diseases among British soldiers compared to 2–3 per cent among their Indian counterparts. Among the troops in Bengal, the rate rose from 29 per cent in 1827 to 31 per cent in 1829.[12]

Physical disability due to disease among the troops was a far more serious cause of concern than its prevalence among their superior officers. It was these troops—the Tommies from the British lower classes—who were required to take the field to suppress the rebellions of the Indian masses. The administration could not afford the loss of man-hours among its troops due to disability caused by venereal diseases—apart from the cost involved in treating them. According to an official estimate made in the 1860s, at least 'one-third of the British Army passed through the hospitals in the course of a year, suffering from these [venereal] diseases. . . at many stations the proportion amount to 50, 60 or 70 percent of the total force . . . a part of the invaliding which occurred every year owed its origin to these diseases, which also indirectly aggravated the mortality from other causes. . .'[13]

Some years later, a British official noted: '. . . the number of days spent last year [1867] in the Calcutta General Hospital alone, by Europeans and a few Eurasians, on account of venereal disease, was 9,808. The cost of this to the hospital principally was rupees sixteen thousand one hundred and sixty-four, this is exclusive of the suffering and cost entailed by numbers of other men, whose other diseases were owing to or aggravated by, this same cause.'[14] No wonder a later British commission of inquiry, while observing this development, was to comment: '. . . the imported British soldier is enormously costly'![15]

Special provisions, therefore, were called for to meet the demands of these cannon-fodders, as also to protect their health to keep them fit to face any eventuality that the administration might face. The colonial authorities, one must admit, displayed a remarkable sense of planning in organizing such provisions. In their policies regarding their upper- and middle-class employees, they took care to keep them chaste—and away from pollution by 'native' women. In formulating measures for the lower class 'other ranks' of their Army, they saw to it that there was an ample supply of 'native' prostitutes to satisfy their physical needs—but adequately sanitized!

In this respect, the colonial authorities betrayed a typical class attitude towards the Tommies. The strong upper-class prejudice against them which made the Company's Directors treat them as an inferior species to be shut inside barracks in the 18th century, persisted in the later period, also, when the British government set them apart as a special category of people who were supposedly on heat all the time! The following observation made by no less a person than the Surgeon-General of Her Majesty's Forces in the 1880s brings out the attitude: 'Although much has been effected, during recent years, to improve the condition and social surroundings of soldiers and sailors, and so to promote morality among these classes, it cannot be expected, by those acquainted with physiology, that, in any large body of men, particularly if situated as soldiers and sailors are circumstanced, the sexual passions will be kept in such perfect control that there shall be no incontinence . . . Such physiological instincts must be satisfied in some way or other; or they must be repressed by force of will aided by severe physical exertion, abstemious habits, and the high moral capacity arising from culture. That the classes (soldiers and sailors) . . . will not repress their animal instincts by the means above mentioned, is patent to all aware of the characteristics of such classes.'[16]

Given this characterization of the 'other ranks' in Her Majesty's Forces, the colonial authorities who succeeded the East India Company in India made every effort to see to it that the 'sexual passions' of their armed minions were kept 'satisfied in some way or other.' In 1692, as we mentioned at the beginning of this chapter, the Company encouraged all means so that 'our Soldiers do marry with the Native women.' Less than two hundred years later, instead of marriage with 'Native women', the British officials were to propose provision of 'native' prostitutes for their soldiers. A typical illustration of this policy is available from the contents of a letter written in 1873 by a junior English official posted in the Andaman and Nicobar Islands, requesting his senior officer in the Army to allow him to provide prostitutes for the English soldiers under his command there! The entire letter is a sort of treatise on the morals of armed personnel posted in India, particularly in the island of Andamans, where they were required to guard the detained rebels of the Wahabi movement, and the 1857 War of Independence. (In fact, a year before the letter was written, on 8 February 1872, Lord Mayo, the Viceroy of India, while on a visit to the Andamans penal settlement in Port Blair, was assassinated by a Wahabi rebel who was serving life sentence there. More guards were posted on the island after this, for reasons of security). The official, in his letter, referred to the 'necessity, which appears . . . to exist for the provision of some outlet for the passions of men [i.e. personnel of the Port Blair Free Police] hitherto wholly unused to the exercise of any curb upon whom religion or morality exercise no check, principle or restrain (*sic*), and which, in the absence of their accustomed tributaries, will, there is every cause to fear, find vent in other channels far more perilous.'[17]

Having whipped up this bogey of unrestrained passions of the English soldiers (who were posted in the Andamans as members of the Free Police), the official then proceeded to explain how these men possessed enough purchasing power—thanks to the generous pay scale that they enjoyed—and were, therefore, ready to buy the commodities that the official was proposing to supply them in the shape of 'public women.' He pointed out that his corps consisted of 'young, strong and physically able-bodied men, whose circumstances will be those of comparative ease, and even, it may be said, of affluence, as experience proves that considerable savings may be effected from the liberal scale of pay sanctioned by the government, more particularly where the opportunities for disbursements are too limited.' He then appealed to his superior officer to recognize the fact that prostitution was 'an unavoidable and inevitable part and sequence of every considerable aggregation of human beings', and drew his attention to the 'special expediency' and 'further considerations which the peculiar local circumstances of the place [i.e. Andamans and Nicobar] cannot fail to suggest.'[18]

Thus, even whore-mongering among the ranks had to be organized in accordance with the code of British Army discipline! Like military drill, or maintenance of knife-edge creases on their uniform, or honouring of ranks in order of precedence, fornication, also, had to conform strictly to a new set of rules from the mid-19th century. While the administration took pains to train the Tommies in India in these newly formulated rules, it simultaneously began to groom a special class of Indian prostitutes who would feed the needs of the British soldiers according to the new norms.

II

The government promulgated in 1864 Act XXII—popularly known as the Cantonment Act—clauses 7 and 25 of Section 19 of which provided that rules might be made for cantonments by the local governments with the object of securing the 'inspection and control of houses of ill-fame, and of preventing the spread of venereal disease.'

A committee appointed under the Act divided prostitutes into two classes: (i) those frequented by European soldiers, and (ii) those outside that category. Only the first class was subjected to the regulations provided by the Act, the sole object being the protection of the British troops. Army authorities set up brothels in the regimental bazars and other appointed places within the cantonments. They were known as *chaklas* (or 'rags' in the parlance of the British Tommy).

According to an official report (by an Inquiry Commission set up by the government some years later), 'the officer commanding a regiment, used . . . to arrange for the provision of women for the use of his men. A hereditary pimp or a prostitute (more commonly the latter) would offer to bring the women required. If the offer was approved, she collected women from among her acquaintances, and became responsible for their management and good conduct. From them, she received fees, generally in the form of a levy on their earnings; while in some cases, but apparently rarely, she also received an allowance from regimental funds. She lived with her women in the regimental *chakla*; and her duties were to attend generally to the comfort and welfare of the women, to fill up vacancies in their ranks, to take them to the periodical examinations by a doctor, and personally make periodical examinations, to settle disputes . . .'[19]

These women managers of the *chaklas* were known as *mahaldarnis*. An official document defines a *mahaldarni* as a 'forewoman of prostitutes' who performed for them the duties which a foreman performed for workmen. She was a 'paid Government servant,' according to this document.[20] It appears that the authorities were officially legitimizing the role of the traditional 'madams' (usually retired prostitutes, who ran brothels—also known as *mashis* or aunties, in Bengali red-light areas), and the *kutnis* (the go-betweens-cum-procuresses, who operated in pre-colonial Bengali society).

A late 19th century account divides the *chaklas* into three categories: *gora chakla*, reserved for the white army officers; *lal kurti chakla*, for the white infantry ranks who wore red coats; and *kala chakla* for the Indian soldiers. The latter were not allowed to enter the *chaklas* reserved for the whites. If they attempted to do so, the military police threw them out.[21] Explaining—and justifying—the discrimination, another contemporary official report observed: 'If English soldiers and natives were to openly consort with the same set of women, jealousies would certainly arise, and quarrels, which are specially to be deprecated as inter-racial, would frequently occur. . .'[22]

The Army authorities were not only extremely considerate about the sexual needs of their ranks, but also careful about improving the professional efficiency of those women who were required to serve the Tommies. A memorandum issued from the Army Headquarters at Simla, in the name of the Commander-in-Chief (a certain Sir Frederick Roberts) dated 17 June 1886, makes interesting reading: 'In the regimental bazars [shops, bazars occupied by traders and others who have been allowed to settle within regimental limits for the convenience of the troops], it is necessary to have a sufficient number of women, to take care that they are sufficiently attractive, to provide them with proper houses . . .' He then added: 'Attention is called to the following points . . . the desirability when constructing free quarters for registered women of providing houses that will meet the wishes of the women. Unless their comfort and convenience of those who consort with them is considered, the results will not be satisfactory.'[23]

These women who were reserved for the white soldiers used to be registered by the Cantonment Magistrate, and were issued tickets. Official attempts were made to train the British soldiers to 'consort' with these certified and sanitized Indian prostitutes, instead of the unregistered outsiders. The Army Headquarters memorandum, quoted above, stated: 'If young soldiers are carefully advised in regard to the advantage of ablution, and recognize that convenient arrangements exist in the regimental bazar, they may be expected to avoid the risks involved in association with women who are not recognized by the regimental authorities.'[24]

A typical *chakla* was an extension of the familiar caravanserai that used to dot the ancient highways in India. It consisted of a high wall enclosing a larger or smaller area, to which a strong gate gave access. The middle of the interior was occupied by an open space, while round all four sides were ranged numbers of small rooms or quarters where the prostitutes lived and entertained their customers. A late 19th century account provides us with the rates charged by the prostitutes—one rupee from a sergeant, eight annas from a corporal, and four annas from a private soldier. The *mahaldarni* took between one-fourth and one-eighth of the girls' receipts.[25]

Besides adopting—and adapting—old institutions (like the brothel landlady as the *mahaldarni* and the caravanserai as the model for the *chakla*), the authorities also introduced a new institution to monitor the state of health of both the prostitutes and the soldiers. This was the 'lock hospital' to treat venereal diseases. The beginnings of this institution could be traced to four hospitals set up before the end of the 18th century at Berhampore, Kanpur, Dinapur and Fategarh for the 'reception of diseased women.'[26] This was followed by the establishment of regular lock hospitals by the mid-19th century in major towns and cantonment areas, where registration and inspection of prostitutes suffering from venereal diseases were made obligatory. The Government of India in 1869 sanctioned a proposal to set up a number of lock hospitals in Calcutta and its suburbs at a cost of Rs 3,300 per month, expecting to accommodate 900 prostitutes. It was also proposed to levy a registration fee of rupees six per annum from each prostitute.[27]

The records of the lock hospitals of Bengal in the 19th

century reveal interesting dimensions, like fluctuations in the number of prostitutes taking admission, racist overtones in the treatment of Indian and European prostitutes, resistance of the prostitutes themselves to the medical treatment, persecution of the prostitutes by the military authorities, and, last but not the least—the failure of the lock hospitals to stem the spread of the diseases. We shall have occasion to dwell on these various aspects in subsequent chapters.

To go back to the Cantonment Act of 1864, the meticulously devised plans by the colonial administration to dovetail the 'animal instincts' of its soldiers with the vivacity of the 'sufficiently attractive', but medically certified, Indian prostitutes, did not quite take off, and the incidence of venereal diseases among the British soldiers continued unabated. A later-day official document was to complain: 'The enthusiasm inspired by novelty [of the Cantonment Act], however, soon began to flag, and with increasing ratios [of venereal diseases] as a result, the fault began to be laid to imperfections of the system. . .'[28]

The 'flagging of the enthusiasm' and its disappointing consequences were caused by a number of imponderables. One of the main features of the British military establishment in India was the frequent transfer of troops from one part of the country to another—to quell revolts, to annex territories in wars of expansion, etc. This came in the way of fastening down the British soldiers to their reserved partners among the regimental prostitutes in the *chaklas* of their local cantonments. As another late 19th century official correspondence, while commenting on the functioning of the 1864 Cantonment Act, was to observe: 'The movement of troops about the country. . . also afforded opportunities to the men of consorting with women of a class not met within a cantonment . . .'[29] A contemporary report prepared by the Surgeon-General pointed out in unambiguous terms: 'There can be little doubt that troops on the march in our own (Indian) territories act as accumulators of venereal disease. When they have crossed the frontier, the subsequent prevalence will depend much upon the nature of the country occupied, and upon the amount of hostility displayed by its inhabitants.' He, then, added the interesting information that in Afghanistan, the British troops (belonging to the Bengal Presidency which occupied that country during the wars) 'could not become affected to any large extent with venereal disease' (obviously because of the Afghan 'hostility' that did not allow their women to consort with the British soldiers).[30]

III

Before we move on to the next stage of administrative measures regarding prostitution in 19th century India in general and Bengal in particular, it may be useful to examine an interesting facet of the British colonial attitude towards the problem of venereal diseases that emerges from the official correspondences and documents quoted earlier. Although the prevalence of venereal diseases among British soldiers in India was discovered as early as 1766 (when, as mentioned previously, the East India Company authorities proposed imposition of fines on their soldiers who were found infected with the diseases), it was only later, in the mid-19th century, that we find an increasing tendency on the part of 'Her Majesty's' administrators (who took over from the Company the reins of governance in India) to blame the outbreak of venereal diseases among their soldiers on Indian prostitutes, and to penalize them.

Yet, long before the British colonization of India—as far back as the early 15th century—we come across historical evidence of the prevalence of syphilis in England. A police regulation of 1430, during the reign of Henry VI, ordered the exclusion of patients suffering from the disease from London hospitals and required them to be strictly guarded at night. Later, in the 16th century, during the times of Henry VIII, six 'lazar-houses' (medical homes) were set up in London for the reception of victims of venereal diseases.[31] In 18th century England, we come across a revealing diary left by the eminent James Boswell, which, among many other daringly candid confessions about his sexual peccadilloes, narrated how he caught the disease soon after picking up a prostitute (obviously a native English one, since Indians had not yet arrived there!) from a London street, and sleeping with her.[32]

It is quite evident that venereal diseases were prevalent in England before her soldiers arrived in India. But there appears to be a definite attempt by the 19th century British administrators in India to trace the roots of venereal diseases to Indian prostitutes, and stress the danger of these diseases being imported into England by British troops who got afflicted by them while posted in India. The authorities in London, also, were disposed to consider venereal diseases as a newly imported malady—conveniently forgetting that they had existed in their country for centuries! The colonial and racist overtones of a discourse considered 'disagreeable' in the polite circles of Victorian society, was, therefore, never subjected to a rigorous analysis, and led to the perpetuation of the myth that British soldiers and sailors were 'importing' venereal diseases from India, and infecting not only their families, but also the British prostitutes in port and garrison towns like Plymouth and Southampton.

It was this that prompted the British government to enact a number of legislations known as the Contagious Diseases Acts in the 1860s in England that authorized the detainment and forcible medical examination of women designated by local authorities to be 'common prostitutes.'

IV

Meanwhile in India, the 1864 Cantonment Act, as we have noted earlier, was failing in its aims, since soldiers tended to move out of their cantonments (either due to paucity of prostitutes in the regimental *chaklas*, or because of troop movements) and consort with 'common prostitutes' outside, and get afflicted with venereal diseases as a result. The authorities, therefore, planned to extend their operations beyond the cantonments and impose control over those prostitutes plying their trade outside. In the past, there were a few occasions when the administration did come up with proposed measures to discipline prostitutes who operated among the civilian population in cities and towns. In 1857, Sir John Peter Grant, Member of the Governor-General's Council (who, two years later, was to become the Lieutenant-Governor of Bengal) was reported to have proposed that if three or more local residents complained about disturbances in a neighbouring brothel to the police magistrate, the latter would take measures to control them, and if such disturbances persisted, the residents of the brothels would be fined Rs 20 every day.[33]

A more comprehensive legislation to bring prostitution (outside the cantonments) under state control came in 1868, when, taking the cue from the Contagious Diseases Acts in operation in England, the colonial authorities in India enacted the Indian Contagious Diseases Act (Act XIV—or *Choudda Ain*—the dreaded term by which it came to be known among the prostitutes of Bengal at that time). The main objective of the legislation was to protect British soldiers and sailors from venereal diseases that they might contract from the 'common prostitutes' outside the regimental bazars. Dr C. Fabre-Tonnerre, Health Officer in Calcutta, who was to frame the first draft (of what later became the Indian Contagious Diseases Act) of an Act to prevent venereal diseases and control prostitution in Calcutta, in a despatch dated 16 September 1867 (a year before the enactment of the Act) pointed out: '. . . syphilitic diseases exist amongst the public prostitutes of the town [Calcutta] in the following ratio: Hindoo women of high caste 15 percent; Hindoo women of inferior caste 30 percent; Mussulman and low caste Hindoo women 50 percent; low Christians and other non-descript prostitutes 70 percent. The last two classes of women are frequented mostly by soldiers and sailors, and reside in Jaun Bazar, Bow Bazar and Champatolla.'[34]

This official perception that the Tommies and sailors picked up the diseases from prostitutes of the lower orders was widely shared by British civilians, army officers and medical superintendents all over India during this period. Relevant extracts from some of the contemporary official correspondences are worth quoting in this context. An officiating commander of an army division in a north Indian town in 1870 described his dilemma in the following words: ' . . . every poor woman of certain working classes seems to be available in the neighbourhood of cantonments. These are not professionals; no one knows or cares what their practices or means of livelihood are. It would be quite impossible to register all the coolie women, who labour by hundreds or by thousands near our cantonments; but if we have learnt nothing else, we have learnt beyond a doubt that these are the women to whom the soldier resorts, and from whom he contracts disease.'[35] Another army commander, heading the Meerut Division, reporting on measures for the prevention of venereal diseases among his soldiers, in a letter in the same year (1870) asserted: 'One cannot deny the assertion that disease amongst the European soldiers is not taken from the avowed [i.e. the professional prostitute recognized by society, or the regimental prostitute certified by the army authorities] prostitute, but from the hypocritically honest labouring women . . .'[36]

These 'labouring women'—denounced as 'hypocritically honest' by the colonial army top brass—continued to be objects of suspicion, and often victims of the repressive provisions of the Indian Contagious Diseases Act of 1868, all through the last decades of the 19th century. A senior British medical official posted in Calcutta in the 1870s, while attributing the rise in venereal diseases among the soldiers in Fort William there to the 'existence of a prostitute class in the Fort not under the law', went on in his official despatch to identify this 'prostitute class'—not only in Calcutta's Fort William, but in other cantonments in India also—in the following way: 'There is perhaps not a military station in India in which prostitutes, under the guise of day-labourers employed by the Department Public Works, or others, do not infest European barracks and give disease to the soldiers.' He then added ominously: 'These women are the terror of military men who have been long in India.'[37] This suspicious and hostile attitude towards female labourers continued among the British bureaucrats in the 1880s also, as is evident from the annual report of medical transaction of the lock hospital in Darjeeling in Bengal, which, while explaining the persistence of venereal diseases among the British soldiers, added among other causes, the following: 'There was also a large number of cooly women belonging to the hill tribes notoriously dirty in their habits and persons, employed in and about cantonments; some of whom undoubtedly added to their gains by prostitution.'[38]

V

The Contagious Diseases Act that was enacted in India was more stringent in its operation against the prostitutes than its model in England. Under the Act, the prostitutes were required to (i) compulsorily register themselves; (ii) subject themselves to periodical medical examination; and (iii) compulsory treatment; and were (iv) forbidden to live in specified areas. C. Fabre-Tonnerre, the brain behind the Act, insisted that every woman registered under the Act must be provided with 'a ticket bearing her name, caste and residence,' and must be 'compelled to exhibit such tickets on being required to do so by a Superintendent of the police.' Violation of the provisions of the Act by the offender invited for her imprisonment 'with or without hard labour for any term exceeding three months.' Fabre-Tonnerre spread quite a wide net by his catch-all provision: 'Public prostitution or women of ill-fame or reputed as such shall be liable to those rules and regulations.'[39]

While the primary objective of both the 1864 Cantonment Act and the 1868 Contagious Diseases Act was to protect the British troops from venereal diseases, their implications varied from one strata of prostitutes to another. The Cantonment Act was geared to groom a breed of Indian prostitutes who were to be trained exclusively for the British Tommies, and kept captive in the *chaklas* in the cantonments. The Contagious Diseases Act was meant to control the movements and operations of the 'common prostitutes' who dominated the wider spectrum of the profession, so that the Tommies did not have access to them, and to put them under medical surveillance so that if some errant Tommy did visit them, he would be protected against the diseases.

The training of the regimental prostitutes was similar to the exercise outlined by Thomas Babington Macaulay in his famous 'Minutes' of 1835, where he wanted to mould a certain type of professionals for administrative purposes into a 'class of persons, Indian in blood and colour, but English in taste, in opinions, in morals and in intellect.' His British colleagues in the Army, in a similar manner, attempted to create a class of prostitutes 'Indian in blood and colour, but English in professional skills and hygiene.' The regimental prostitutes were the 'labour aristocracy' among the Indian prostitutes. They were certainly earning more than their sisters outside, and other labourers. Their houses were quite well furnished, and they enjoyed better food and standards of living. Yet, in the eyes of their compatriots, they were worse than the cheapest whore. *Gora-kamana* (to earn one's living from the British soldier) was a term of reproach used against them.

But, being captive and subjected to forcible medical examination, all regimental prostitutes were apparently not happy. Two American women social workers who travelled through India in 1891–92, visiting different military stations to study the plight of prostitutes there, came across residents of *chaklas* who appealed to the two to rescue them from the cantonments. One, in the Lucknow cantonment, was all prepared to leave with the American women, but at the last moment panicked when the local magistrate warned her that she could get molested by the soldiers![40]

Medical examination was one of the main causes of discontent among the regimental prostitutes. The cantonment authorities induced the soldiers suffering from venereal diseases to identify the women from whom they had caught them. These women were then forcibly dragged away and detained in lock hospitals.[41]

The Cantonment Act reflected the 19th century capitalist concern about how to keep the body (of the labourer) fit for its optimal functioning and productivity. English Victorian society was obsessed with hygiene, longevity and physical exercises. In this framework of thinking, the body (of the mercenary soldier) could not be allowed to be dissipated in promiscuous whoring and reckless drinking—which used to be the norms among soldiers and officers in 18th century India. Such practices had to be replaced by an ordered structure of sexual behaviour, out of the sheer necessity of keeping fit the main pillar of the colonial administration—the Army. Similarly, the body of the prostitute—which was an 'unavoidable and inevitable' cog in the wheels that kept the Army moving smoothly—had to be kept fit to enable it to lock itself into the needs of the British privates.

The imposition of strict norms of sexual behaviour among both the British soliders and the Indian prostitutes recruited to serve them was also reinforced by the contemporary Victorian concepts of gender domination current in the metropolitan centre. Male control over sexual relations was being codified in pseudo-scientific terms of male superiority versus female inferiority. Such theories governed the treatment of the problem of prostitution in Britain at that time. The following extract from a late 19th century official report is quite revealing: '. . . we may at once dispose of any recommendation founded on the principle of putting both parties to the sin of fornication on the same footing by the obvious but not less conclusive reply that there is no comparison to be made between prostitutes and the men who consort with them. With the one sex the offence is committed as a matter of gain; with the other it is an irregular indulgence of a natural impulse.'[42]

It is interesting to observe how this official attempt at codification of the client-prostitute relationship in Britain in 1871 is grounded in the gut-level reaction of a British soldier in India in 1810. The words hark back to the sentiments expressed by Captain Thomas Williamson in his *East Indian Guide and Vade Mecum* published that year (excerpts from which have been quoted earlier) where he made the same distinction between what he perceived as the commercial interests of the Indian 'dancing girls' and his countrymen's 'irregular indulgence' (the exact euphemism that was to be repeated 70 years later by a Royal Commission to describe—and condone—whore-mongering among males in contemporary British society).[43]

It was thus the pragmatic considerations and immediate compulsions of the colonial administration in India, buttressed by the new ideological attempts at codification of sexual relations and practices in Victorian England, that led to the enactment of the Cantonment Act of 1864.[44]

The prostitutes covered by the Cantonment Act—captives under direct administrative supervision and control—could be described as belonging to what we today term as the 'organized sector'. Beyond this sector, which was confined to the regimental bazars and the cantonments, there existed the vast majority of women who practised the trade in Calcutta and other major cities in the 19th century. They had always remained outside any centrally-run organization. The Contagious Diseases Act of 1868 was an administrative intervention in the practice of their occupation. While allowing them to pursue their occupation and retain their unorganized structure, the Act sought to curb their free movement by imposing regulations like compulsory registration at police stations, medical examination at certified clinics, segregation and confinement to specified areas of the cities and towns, and heavy penalties for violation of these regulations.

The Contagious Diseases Act, therefore, went beyond the confines of the cantonments (which were taken care of by the Cantonment Act) and spread its dragnet to the red-light areas outside. The fear that the British soldiers could get infected by the 'common prostitutes' (as distinct from the captive regimental prostitutes) led the administration to build up an elaborate machinery of surveillance under the CDA (Contagious Diseases Act) that not only affected the business of these prostitutes (by driving away their regular customers, the local indigenous clients who were put off by the sudden police raids), but also subjected them to the most horrible medical examination. When reports of their humiliating experiences in the clinics and the lock hospitals, collected by contemporary Western feminist social activists in the late 19th century, reached England, womens' organizations like the Ladies' National Association, and women leaders like Josephine Butler, mounted a campaign against the CDA, demanding its repeal and denouncing it as a violation of the personal liberty of a woman.[45] Within Bengal, also, the *bhadralok* gentry—sections of which had earlier welcomed the CDA as a measure to control the spread of prostitution—began to protest at the end of the 19th century because of the indiscriminate powers enjoyed by the police to harass and persecute any woman under the catch-all provisions of the Act. The ostensible plea of controlling the spread of venereal diseases became a cover for police atrocities not only on the 'common prostitutes' and women from the poorer classes (like female labourers working near the cantonments), but also on members of the upper strata of the prostitute community, like the *baijis* or the dancing girls and singers (mainly from North India, settled down in Calcutta) and mistresses maintained by the rich Bengali citizens in houses situated in the traditional red-light area of Sonagachhi in north Calcutta, which came under surveillance under the CDA.

Protests against the functioning of the CDA in India, both within India and in England—as also the realization among the colonial administrative and military authorities in India that the Act had failed to serve its purpose (the prevention of the spread of venereal diseases among the British soldiers)—finally led to the repeal of the CDA in 1888. The official explanation for the repeal was: 'It certainly has not had the anticipating result of extirpating disease . . . The Government of India recommended the repeal of the Act on the grounds that it did not . . . effect appreciable good . . . and was liable to abuse' (24 June 1888). The government, however, retained the regulations which enforced compulsory medical examination under the Cantonment Act, thus keeping the regimental prostitutes (who served the British soldiers) under firm control.[46]

As mentioned earlier, the majority of prostitutes in 19th century Bengal plied their trade outside the cantonments and catered to the demands of a variety of clients. It is necessary, therefore, to take a look at their professional norms and social life-style, as well as their clientele who, distinct from the British Tommies, came from different levels of indigenous society.

IV
The 'Beshya' and the 'Babu'

> 'You should practice love in such a way that you do not get swayed by any lover; but try to bring the 'babu' under your thumb. . .'
>
> —Advice by an old prostitute to a young practitioner of the trade in 19th century Calcutta.[1]

With the growth of Calcutta and other mofussil towns and cities in Bengal, and in response to the demands of the new clientele spawned by the colonial system, brothels began to spring up haphazardly in these places from the early years of the 19th century. According to one later-day survey of 44 centrally located streets of the most important parts of Calcutta of 1806, out of a total of 7,633 residential premises, 655 were owned by prostitutes (who were—and still are—known as *beshyas* in colloquial Bengali).[2]

The survey reveals interesting facts and figures. For instance, in Moonshy Suderuddy's Lane at Machooa Bazar in north Calcutta, there was a prostitute called Moynah Tackooraney who owned '14 straw huts, one upper roomed house and a mosque.' The old records showed up a 'brothel in 235 and 236 Bow Bazar Street, owned by a member of Dwarkanath Tagore's family. It had 43 rooms for prostitutes. . .'[3] The profession appears to have been commercially profitable enough—and without the moral stigma in those early years of the 19th century—to allow a member of a Bengali aristocratic family to rent out his premises to its practitioners.

It seems that by the early 19th century, some distinct patterns had emerged in the profession of prostitution as practised in Calcutta and its suburbs. Among some practitioners, it was vertically stratified—corresponding to the different classes of the clientele. Some, again, were divided at a horizontal level on linguistic and religious lines.

Evidently, the demands of the market shaped the pattern of prostitution in 19th century Bengal. It is essential, therefore, to examine first the clientele who patronized the prostitutes. In the parlance of the red-light areas, these customers were known by a variety of terms—babu, *khodder, nagar,* etc. The word 'babu', popular in 19th century Bengali discourse, was a catch-all term that embraced respectable dignitaries (like the novelist Bankim Chattopadhyay, or the zamindar Digambar Mitra—to whose names the prefix 'Babu' was always attached) from one end of the contemporary Bengali social hierarchy to the members of that society's parvenu and their spoilt sons who occupied the other end, dissipating their wealth on drinking, whoring and other amusements.[4]

It was this latter section of the 'babus' (from the early 19th century) in Calcutta on whose patronage prostitution began to thrive in the city. Their sexual behavioural norms and demands and their cultural tastes shaped to a great extent the life-style of the prostitutes in the red-light areas of the city's northern part—known as 'Sonagaji' in those days (after the name of a Muslim religious preacher, whose tomb still graces the entry to the lanes).[5]

This class of Bengali parvenu sprang up in Calcutta from the first decade of the 19th century. They made money through diverse transactions with the British traders and administrators in a hierarchically defined system—ranging from operations of the *banians* and *dewans* (who acted as direct agents of the colonial commercial and administrative systems respectively) at the top, to those of their subordinates, hangers-on, flunkeys and parasites (known as *mosahebs*) at the bottom. These upstart fortune-seekers, along with the 'absentee zamindars' (the new rentiers created by the Permanent Settlement) formed a distinct urban group of pleasure-hunters with new social habits, who were in search of entertainment to fill up their leisure time. It was these people who constituted the first generation of patrons of the prostitutes of early 19th century Calcutta.[6]

Contemporary Bengali farces and belles-lettres abound in the portrayal of these people, as well as of the prostitutes with whom they consorted. They sometimes appear as touts and toadies, sometimes as fops and dandies—but always revolving around the ubiquitous Bengali 'babu' of the 19th century. This archetypal period-piece was usually the pampered son of a rich *dewan* or *banian*, or a zamindar who, having inherited his father's wealth, dissipated it on drinking, whoring and other amusements in the company of sycophants (the *mosahebs*), including lecherous Brahmin priests.

A brief analysis of this literature which flowed from the newly established printing presses of north Calcutta all through the 19th century, will indicate the socio-economic changes taking place at the source of the 'babu' phenomenon, in the 'babu's' habits and tastes, in his choice of extra-marital adventures—and, in response to his demands, corresponding changes in the institutionalized system of prostitution through different stages in 19th century Bengal.

I

One of the earliest literary documentations of the life and manners of the first generation of Calcutta's 'babus' is available from a series of highly entertaining satirical pieces composed by a versatile journalist and poet of that period—Bhabanicharan Bandyopadhyay (1787–1848). His *Naba-babu-bilash* (1825), *Dooti-bilash* (1825) and *Naba-bibi-bilash* (1822?) offer invaluable glimpses into the system prevalent at that time to recruit prostitutes and train them in the art of entertaining customers.

As for the customers, according to the prevailing norms of sexual adventures, they were apparently required to graduate from adultery to whore-mongering. In *Naba-babu-bilash*, the 'babu's' toady—who claims to be a veteran in debauchery—advises the 'babu' in the following words: 'He who achieves success in the four 'p's will be a half-babu. The 'p's are—*pasha* (game of dice), *paira* (pigeon-fights—a sport popular among Calcutta's rich gentry in those days), *para-dar* (liaison with another man's wife), and *poshak* (dress). He who achieves success in both the four 'p's and the four 'kh's will become a complete babu. The four 'kh's are *khushi* (pleasure), *khanki* (whore), *khana* (lavish meals), and *khairat* (charity—the euphemism used to persuade the 'babu' to spend all his wealth on his hangers-on!).'[7]

Bhabanicharan's *Naba-bibi-bilash* turns to the prostitute. It describes in details the various stages in the life of a typical prostitute of early 19th-century Bengal, from which we get an excellent idea of how prostitutes were recruited, and trained, how they moved up the social ladder and how their fortunes declined with advancing age, how they gradually sank to the position of maid-servants, and were finally reduced to begging. The heroine, when we first meet her, is introduced as the neglected wife of a hemp-addict living in a village. A *napitini* (woman hair-dresser) pretends to take pity on her, tempts her with stories of the good life in the city, lures her away from her home, and introduces her to a foppish 'babu'. The latter deserts her after some time, and she drifts into the house of an old prostitute in the city, where she is trained to sing and dance by a variety of *ustads*. Once she completes her training, the old madam advises her on how to attract male customers and retain herself in the favours of the rich among them. She is required to cultivate the 'chh's—*chhalana* (tricks and artifices), *chhenali* (coquetry), *chhelemi* (pretending to be younger than her actual age), *chhapan* (hiding the other customers from the main patron—the 'babu' who keeps her as a mistress), *chhemo* (deceiving the 'babu' with false stories when/if he comes to know about her entertaining other customers), and *chhenchrami* (collecting money from the sundry customers—other than the patron 'babu'—before entertaining them).[8]

If one reads between the overtly erotic lines of *Naba-bibi-bilash*, one discovers an extraordinary treatise on how to transform a woman's emotions and passions, her mind and body into commodities in a commercial transaction that is sought to be made profitable to both the seller and the buyer. It is a contemporary version of the *Kamasutra*, in which the old *nayika* (heroine) is transformed from a feudal courtesan into the 19th century Calcutta prostitute who is required to cultivate a new set of skills to attract her purchaser—the 'babu'. The cultivation of the skills is very explicitly attuned to the acquisitive objective of acquiring assets—in the shape of cash, jewellery and a house. The repeated stress on this objective has to be understood in the contemporary context, where the 'babus' who patronized these prostitutes were themselves an uncertain and unreliable component in the commercial transaction. Their lavish indulgences were quite often a nine-day wonder. Contemporary accounts record the rise and fall of the parvenu within the span of a few years. The prostitutes who were favoured by them, had to make the most of their indulgences as long as the 'babus' were capable of spending, so that they could ensure their future security.

In a very revealing passage in *Naba-bibi-bilash*, the old madam warns the heroine against accepting the conventional concept of love in her profession, and comes up with a different concept which should be more suitable for her requirements. She quotes a contemporary Hindi couplet—

> '*Kasbi kiski joru?*
> *Ar bherua keska sala?*'

which she translates as—'How can a whore become the wife of anyone? How can her brother become an in-law?' She, then, proceeds to advise her: 'Therefore, my daughter, our love is only with those from whom we can get more money. Even that should not be pure love; it must be false. You should practise love in such a way that you do not get swayed by any lover; but try to bring the 'babu' under your thumb. . .'[9]

This warning against getting involved in any emotional entanglement—and, particularly, in the institution of marriage—suggests the prevalence of a variety of desires and attitudes among the prostitutes: the hope among some to tie up with a 'babu' patron in a permanent attachment, preferably in the shape of marriage, or as a mistress (the latter was a more common phenomenon in 19th century Bengal), which could provide them with security—financial, and sometimes, emotional. This was probably countered by the desire, among others, to carve out an autonomous space for themselves in the form of assets earned from their customers in the course of their professional career—money, jewellery and a house—without depending on any lasting attachment to a particular patron. The madam in *Naba-bibi-bilash*—being a veteran in experiencing the changing fortunes and tastes of the 'babu' patrons—evidently opted for the latter course.

Although written by a male, *Naba-bibi-bilash* reflects accurately the moods and manners of the contemporary Bengali prostitutes, as will be evident from our later analysis of their songs and sayings current in the red-light areas of 19th century Calcutta.

II

When we move beyond Bhabanicharan's period and reach the mid-19th century in Bengal, we find that prostitution had expanded—both numerically and spatially—in cities like Calcutta. In 1853, Calcutta, with a population of about 400,000 people was supporting 12,419 prostitutes. More than a decade later, in 1867, their number went up to more than 30,000 (with the total population of the city remaining more or less the same).[10]

In 1862, the famous Bengali satirist, Kaliprasanna Sinha (1840–70), while describing the life-style and manners of the Calcutta idle rich of his generation, wrote: 'Because of these great men, the city of Calcutta has become the city of whores. There is not a single locality where you won't find at least ten houses of whores. Every year, instead of coming down, the number of whores in this city is going up.'[11] A few years later, a Bengali newspaper from Dhaka complained: 'The number of prostitutes in Dhaka is increasing steadily. It will not be an exaggeration to say that there has been a four-fold increase from what it was ten years ago. Almost all the well-built houses on both sides of the main roads have been taken over by the prostitutes. . .'[12]

The rise in the number of prostitutes in Calcutta and other places was also accompanied by a change in their composition. The first generation of prostitutes in the late 18th–early 19th century period, as we pointed out earlier, came from among a variety of displaced women like widows and daughters of *kulin* Brahmin families and neglected wives from middle-class homes, who were often seduced and abandoned by their lovers, and were then left to drift into some 'red-light' area. These women continued to end up in brothels in the 1850–60 period. An interesting interview, carried out by a contemporary Bengali newspaper, *Sangbad Bhaskar*, with twenty-seven prostitutes, throws light on their caste and class composition, age-group and reasons for their joining the profession. Of the women, sixteen were 'comparatively elderly', eight were 'in the middle of their youth', two were 'young women', and one was a 'twelve-year-old child widow.' Of the first sixteen 'comparatively elderly' women, seven were Brahmin *kulin* daughters who had never been married—and had no chances of getting married—since their parents insisted on waiting for the right match to correspond with their respective caste, sub-caste and clan ties. These parents abused the daughters, 'but failed to provide them with appropriate food and lodging, as a result of which they left their homes.' Five were 'Kaistha widows' who were compelled to leave their homes because of their inability to suffer the religious obligation of fasting without drinking a drop of water during *ekadashi* (the eleventh day of a lunar fortnight, when Bengali Hindu widows were required to observe the ritual of fasting). Two from among this first category of 'elderly' prostitutes belonged to the weavers' caste, who left their homes to escape daily beatings by their husbands. Two others from this age-group were widows belonging to the 'Sadgope' caste (a cultivating caste), who 'left their homes at the instigation of their paramours.'[13]

As for the eight women 'in the middle of their youth', five were 'Shudras' and three Brahmins. All of them were widows, and joined the profession 'unable any longer to bear the agony of widowhood, and over and above that, the persecution by their families.'[14]

The next age-group of the interviewees consisted of two 'young women', both of whom stated that although married, they were deprived of the company of their husbands. 'They served their husbands according to the rules, by cooking and carrying out other domestic chores. Despite that, their husbands went out, and indulged in carousals with other women. As a result, unable to suffer this apathy and contempt, they left their homes.'[15]

The remaining interviewee was the '12-year-old child widow'. Her history was different. She lost her husband within a few days of her marriage. What followed in her life was recorded by *Sangbad Bhaskar* in its report, based on what she narrated to the person who was asked by the newspaper to interview the prostitutes. The report about her stated: 'There was no surviving member from this girl's paternal family. Her father-in-law and mother-in-law were old. The father-in-law earned his living by carrying out Brahminical priestly duties [during rituals]. . . The child widow used to cook food and feed these in-laws of hers. In spite of that the father-in-law and the mother-in-law accused her of stealing food and eating on the sly.' Angry at this 'false accusation', the child approached one of her neighbours—a Bagdi woman (belonging to a lower caste)—requesting her to take her to her maternal uncle's home and promising her in exchange a piece of cloth. The Bagdi woman, however, deceived her and sold her to a brothel for just five rupees![16]

For our present purpose, certain significant dimensions that emerge from contemporary records of the changing pattern of prostitution in 19th century Bengal need to be analysed. The *Sangbad Bhaskar* report, while highlighting the reasons for women's taking to prostitution, stresses a number of factors: *kulin* norms that operated against unmarried girls from those families; rigours of leading the austere life-style that was required of Hindu widows; ill-treatment by husbands and/or in-laws; seduction by paramours. Official records as well as observations by contemporary Bengali social reformers and newspaper editors repeatedly echoed these reasons to explain why middle-class and upper caste Bengali women left their homes to become prostitutes in 19th century Bengal.[17]

But these factors had been in existence for several hundreds of years in pre-colonial Bengal. *Kulin* polygamy, along with the strict insistence on following the hypergamous codes in matters like matrimonial alliances among upper caste Hindus, must have been in vogue since the 12th century, when the then king of Bengal, Ballal Sen, was reported to have formulated the *kulin* codes. So, also, were the unsparing rituals that a Hindu widow had to follow in order to live up to the traditional role assigned to her by the Brahminical scriptures—that of a faithful wife who was required to deny herself everything that smacked of her personal choice (especially in food), after her husband's death.

As for the other factors—cited by 19th century colonial administrators, as well as contemporary Bengali educated *bhadralok* observers—which related mainly to individual choices stemming from personal experiences, they had also been prevalent in pre-colonial Bengali society. Ill-treatment of wives by husbands and in-laws and stories of their occasional adulterous love affairs quite often formed the staple of folk ballads (like the popular narrative from Mymensingh in north Bengal, called *Andha-Bondhu*, about a blind flute-player with whom the wife of a prince fell in love[18]) and, of course, the ageless songs about Radha and Krishna.

But these women were not known to have trooped out of their homes en masse to enter brothels to escape the oppressive conditions. What could have made the next generation—these *kulin* wives and daughters and upper caste Hindu widows—react to the same conditions in a different way in a colonial setting? Could it have been because of a certain commercialization of social relations in Bengal in the 18th–19th century period?

In the past, social ties like marriages, in the traditional feudal Bengali society, were also dictated and controlled by the utilitarian interests of the dominating upper caste and upper-class men. The system of dowry (money and assets demanded by the bridegroom), the privileges enjoyed by the *kulin* Brahmins through their right to polygamy (sanctioned by so-called religious precepts), the custom among the Srotriya Brahmins to virtually sell off their daughters to the highest bidders among the bridegrooms (since the parents among this community were obliged to pay bride price for the marriage of their sons)[19]—all these reflected the norms of a feudal society where the woman was treated as so much property to be exchanged between one male and another. Such an exchange, however, had to be justified by the guardians of medieval Hindu Bengali society by invoking the precepts of Manu, who ordained that a woman should always be under the surveillance of a man—as a daughter under her father's, as a wife under her husband's, and as a mother under her son's.

The arrival of the British bourgeoisie in Bengal meant the introduction of new commercial and administrative relations, accompanied by the prevalent values of the 19th century capitalist system (the most clinical—and cynical—analysis of which, so far, had been provided by Karl Marx). In this newly introduced system of values, the woman was no longer the private property of a single man, but a commodity who was free to sell herself in the market to all men. The development of prostitution as an industry in 19th century Bengal offered avenues of escape for daughters and wives of *kulin* Brahmin families—who, for almost 700 years, had suffered deprivation and humiliation locked up within the cell of *kulin* obligations. The collapse of traditional social norms under the impact of colonial economic changes also led to the loosening of the tight hold of *kulinism*. It is not surprising, therefore, that government official records, contemporary newspaper reports and literature repeatedly mention the tendency of wives and daughters from *kulin* families (along with young Hindu widows—the other deprived section of Bengali women) to gravitate towards prostitution in 19th century Bengal. A mid-19th century official report estimates that of the 12,000-odd prostitutes in Calcutta, more than 10,000 were Hindu widows and daughters of *kulin* Brahmins.[20]

III

But the upper caste Hindu female domination of the trade of prostitution was not to last for long. By the beginning of the second half of the 19th century, the composition of the prostitute community was changing. First, a new generation of prostitutes emerged during this period from among the daughters of those who had started to ply the trade from the earlier period. In British administrative terms, they were described as 'hereditary prostitutes'[21] and in the Bengali slang of the underworld as *dobol khanki* (the first word derived from the English 'double', and the second meaning a prostitute—suggesting that the latter is repeating her mother's profession). These daughters of the first generation of debutantes in the profession grew up with a different set of values and tastes.

Secondly, a large number of poor women coming from the depressed castes, who were uprooted from their villages by famine and loss of their traditional occupations, sought work in Calcutta and other mofussil towns (often as maid-servants in Bengali middle-class homes, or as manual labourers in the newly established factories). They supplemented their meagre earnings by working as prostitutes in the evenings.

An official report of the late 1860s divided Calcutta's prostitutes into seven categories. The first category—small in number—consisted of 'Hindoo women of high caste who live a retired life, and who are kept or supported by rich Natives,' residing between Chitpore Road, Cornwallis Street, Baghbazar North and Manicktollah Street. The second category comprised 'Hindoo women of good caste, who, being possessed of small means, live by themselves, receiving a limited number of visitors of their own, or of a superior caste.' The third group was formed by 'Hindoo women living under a *bareewallah* (house-owner), either male or female, who make advances to them for board and lodging. These women receive Hindoo visitors only without distinction of caste.' These latter two groups had no special locality, and lived 'everywhere in the Native town.' The fourth category consisted of 'dancing women, Hindoo or Mussulman, living singly or forming a kind of chummery . . . receiving visitors without distinction of creed or caste,' living mainly on Chitpore Road and adjacent streets and by-lanes. The fifth, sixth and seventh classes comprised respectively 'Mussulman public prostitutes; low caste Hindoos and low Christian prostitutes; and European prostitutes.' That they were numerous in number, and, therefore, difficult to control, is evident from the indignation and irritation reserved for them by the official while writing the report: 'They are the moral plague of our principle thoroughfares, where they exhibit their persons wth a barefacedness unsurpassed in any other part of the world . . . They are also swarming in the neighbourhood of the European and Native grog-shops, more especially in the latter . . .'[22]

That the number of poor women from the depressed castes—'the low caste Hindoos and low Christian prostitutes'—was increasing is evident from another official report of the early 1870s, which, describing the composition of the class of prostitutes in the Presidency Division (Calcutta and the neighbouring districts), states that they were 'chiefly of low castes—the women of the *tantee* (weaver), *mallee* (gardener), *jogee* (weaving caste from East Bengal), *kumar* (potter), *kaman* (blacksmith), *chamar* (tanner), *sonar baniya* (dealer in gold), *tellee* (oil presser), *jalia* (fishing folk), *koyburtto* (cultivator), *moyra* (sweetmeat maker), *badiah* (gypsy), *goalah* (milkman), *napit* (hairdresser), &c . . .' [23]

Following the introduction of the system of registration of prostitutes under the CDA (Contagious Diseases Act), from 1868 onwards, a more systematic record of religion and a nationality-wise list of prostitutes came to be available every year. Although such lists were notoriously deceptive in quantitative terms (since the much larger number of unregistered women who plied the trade avoided registration—and the consequent harassment—by every means at their disposal), they, nevertheless, give us in qualitative terms, and in an encapsulated form, a representative picture of the religious and racial composition of the prostitutes of Calcutta in the last quarter of the 19th century. They also indicate the increasing international dimension that the trade was acquiring in the city. For instance, in 1872, out of the 6,871 registered prostitutes, the number of Hindus was 5,804, that of Muslims 930, and the rest consisted of English, Irish, Russians, Austrians, Poles, Hungarians, Italians, French and Spaniards.[24]

The composition remained more or less the same nearly a decade later, when out of the 7000-odd registered prostitutes in the city, 5834 were Hindus, 1049 Muslims, and 117 Europeans and others.[25]

Along with the growing stratification in the profession—on lines of class, religion, race and language—there developed a parallel spatial distribution of red-light areas in Calcutta. By the end of the 19th century, clusters of brothels had sprung up in well-demarcated localities of the city—the practitioners having chosen the spots according to their respective class and community interests and proximity to their particular clientele.

A graphic account of the spatial distribution of the various classes of prostitutes in Calcutta, their clients and their different modes of operation, is available from a delightful late 19th century travelogue by a Bengali author, Durgacharan Ray. It is a guided tour for the benefit of the gods of the Hindu pantheon who, the author dreams, have suddenly landed in India to watch how the mortals are faring in the 19th century! Towards evening, the gods are taken along the main road of Chitpore, where the creators and rulers of the universe are shocked to find 'on both sides of the road, on the balconies of two-storeyed and three-storeyed mansions, prostitutes sitting and chewing *pans* and smoking the hubble-bubble. . .' These women were probably the privileged lot, the 'Hindoo women of high caste . . . kept or supported by rich Natives,' as described by the British official in the late 1860s. Durgacharan Ray describes their attitude towards the poor clerks who, at the end of their office hours, had to walk down the main Chitpore road on their way home. When one of these clerks dared to protest after a prostitute from the balcony spat *pan* juice on him, the woman along with her colleagues came up with the devastating retort: 'Look at the cheek of the bloke! He is a mere clerk, and yet affords to indulge in anger! . . . We may be prostitutes, but we can keep lots of clerks like you. Here are you—after having spent the whole day as a pen-pusher, what are you bringing home? We earn from eight to ten rupees every hour sitting in our homes. We can earn in one generation what you and your descendants can never hope to gain in three generations.'[26]

The author then takes us to the spots inhabited by the less privileged lot—the lanes and by-lanes twisting out from the main roads. Harkata Lane was—and still remains—one such spot, behind the main Bowbazar Road. Durgacharan describes the habits of the denizens of these areas: 'The whores . . . get up in the evening, dress up in whatever little attire they have, and run along the road creating a stir. At that hour, they try to pull at the sleeves of anyone crossing their way—whether a gentleman or a vulgar fellow.'[27]

But, in 19th century Calcutta, there were other spots inhabited by prostitutes who occupied an even lower rung in the ladder. Durgacharan takes us to the dark alleys behind the by-lanes in Sinduriapatti, 'a mere branch of Chitpore Road', but where 'dirt-cheap prostitutes live who charge two or four paise'. In the evening, they 'collect in groups on the streets, and whenever any male crosses the road, they shout: Come, man! Come, man!'[28] May be these were the women who threatened the morals of the British official who described them as 'the moral plague of our principle thoroughfares.'

While Durgacharan Ray describes the exterior professional habits of these 'dirt-cheap prostitutes', an idea of their domestic living conditions is available from the report of a 19th century

British official, who records his impressions about visits to two brothels in the alleys of Calcutta: 'The first was a lower-roomed house which I inspected some months ago . . . In that house there were no less than 44 women huddled together. The second instance was that of a narrow blind lane, 240 long and 10 feet broad, which I had occasion to visit . . . containing 33 houses and five huts. There are at present not less than 250 prostitutes residing in that lane.'[29]

Durgacharan's account indicates that while the old brothels of the traditional Sonagachhi area (in Chitpore and its by-lanes like Sinduriapatti) continued to thrive, new red-light areas were developing in other parts of the city (like Harkata Lane in central Calcutta) towards the end of the 19th century. Official reports tell us that in 1874, prostitutes were entertaining soldiers and sailors in Bowbazar in central Calcutta and Fenwick Bazar in the south. Further south, in Watgunge, near the Port, another cluster of brothels was reported to be catering to the needs of the sailors.[30]

By 1881, prostitutes had spread out beyond these areas, and settled down in Colootollah and Taltollah in central Calcutta, and Bhowanipore in the south.[31]

The other major spot where they operated and found a special class of clientele (the British soldiers) was Fort William and its neighbourhood. The women who visited the Fort were not only Indians, as is evident from the following complaint made by a British official: '. . . Fort William and its immediate surroundings are visited by European and Eurasian women for purposes of prostitution, who, by the locality in which they ply their calling, are exempt from police interference.'[31] The Fort premises being under military administrative control, fell out of the purview of the authority of the Calcutta Police. The local British military authorities apparently turned a blind eye to the proclivities of their soldiers, whose satisfaction of sexual needs through commercial transactions with prostitutes had been traditionally recognized in the military strategy of the colonial rulers. But this, often, became a bone of contention between the British Army top brass posted in India, and their counterparts in the British civilian administration in the country, as well as in London.

This tussle between the colonial military and civil authorities—over the issue of prostitution—constitutes a major episode in the history of colonial policy on prostitution in 19th century Bengal, which will be examined in chapter VII.

To go back to the expansion of prostitution in the last quarter of the 19th century, brothels were also coming up around the newly established factories 'with astonishing rapidity on both banks of the Hooghly', according to one contemporary official report. Inmates of these brothels obviously served the neighbouring factory workers and the 'babu' clerks employed there.[32]

There was also another class of women who did not reside in Calcutta, but commuted daily to the city from Howrah which lay across the River Hooghly. The same official report, quoted above, describes: '. . . scores of women were seen daily crossing the river in boats who plied their trade in town [i.e. Calcutta] and betook themselves to Howrah in the day time, where the police could not reach them . . .'[33]

From these various contemporary accounts—both official and unofficial—it seems that there developed a class of prostitutes who did not operate from brothels (as residential-cum-working places, as in Sonagachhi and other red-light areas of Calcutta), but were itinerant practitioners who visited the Fort to solicit soldiers (and were smuggled surreptitiously into their quarters inside the Fort), or took a daily trip to Calcutta from neighbouring districts (like Howrah) to pick up customers who were required to provide the temporary space (either in their own homes, or the 'hotels' that were coming up in Calcutta from the end of the 19th century in the northern and central parts of the city) necessary for carrying out the sexual-commercial transaction.

By not being a part of the residential complex (of Sonagachhi and other red-light areas), these itinerant prostitutes were the precursors of today's 'call-girls'.

A contemporary British official described them in these terms: 'There is another class of prostitutes in Calcutta, the existence of which is scarcely known by a great number of persons, and who, morally speaking, are more dangerous and more pernicious than public prostitutes. I mean those women, who, under the most respectable appearances, visit the private residences of gentlemen, or who secretly resort to "empty houses". This class of women generally escape the action of the general laws regulating prostitution on account of the secret protection thrown over them by the persons acquainted with them.'[34] This category of non-residential prostitutes (those not living and entertaining their customers in brothels) embraced women from different classes—ranging from what the above report described as 'married women, widows, or young persons who are led astray by the love of dress', to those poor day-labourers in military stations in India who sold their bodies to the soldiers for a pittance and were described in official parlance as 'clandestine prostitutes.'[35]

The history of the growth, rise, and various ramifications of prostitution in colonial Bengal can be captured in a large measure from the developments that were taking place in the red-light areas—as well as other spots, like Fort William and its environs—in 19th century Calcutta. The metropolis was developing into a flesh-pot, attracting the nouveau riche as well as the rural poor (who came to Calcutta seeking employment in the newly established factories), from all parts of Bengal, and outside, too. Calcutta offered entertainments for these people at all levels. The sex trade in Calcutta developed in response to the needs and demands of the customers who came from these various strata of contemporary Bengali society.

It was in response to these varieties of social-sexual requirements that prostitution in 19th century Calcutta acquired a variegated character. Operating in a strictly structured city (divided by the colonial administration into a 'Black Town' and a 'White Town', into the Army Headquarters at Fort William and the rest of the British population of the city), the prostitutes were compelled to distribute themselves into a variety of categories, each catering to the demands of a particular class of clients—ranging from the Bengali 'babus' to the British Tommies.

This compulsion of creating ghettoes for themselves to entertain their respective clientele led to the geographical stratification of the city into several red-light areas. The one called Sonagachhi in the north spanned a wide belt from Chitpore Road in the west to Sobha Bazar in the east, housing brothels that served the Bengali upper- and middle-class men, as well as 'the most dilapidated and miserable hut of the filthiest bustee' for the poorer customers.

Two- or three-storeyed houses in the division of the town between Chitpore Road from the west running through Cornwallis Street and moving further east towards north Bowbazar and south Manicktollah, belonged to the richer class of Bengali prostitutes, some among whom were kept as mistresses by well-to-do clients, or who were selective in their choice of customers.

Further down, in central Calcutta, Bowbazar and Fenwick Bazar were inhabited by prostitutes who served sailors and soldiers. South of Fenwick Bazar (in Kerr's Lane and the neighbourhood) lived the European prostitutes—whose numbers, as we noted earlier, had been swelling with immigrants from various parts of the continent. Further south, in the dock area, were brothels resorted to by sailors.[36]

IV

British official records reveal one interesting dimension which seems to have been ignored by most of the 19th century Bengali observers of prostitution. Findings from British administrative records point out the preponderance of Hindus over Muslims among the prostitutes of Bengal—although the number of Muslims varied from almost half to more than half, at times, of the total population of the province during the 19th century.

Explaining the reasons, a British official cites the following factors: '. . . widow marriage is common among Mahomedans, but almost unknown among Hindus; destitute Mahomedan girls can frequently obtain a livelihood as unpaid maid servants in the houses of wealthy Mahomedan gentlemen, where they doubtless lead a life of concubinage.'[37] The British Commissioner of Dhaka in East Bengal echoed the same views when he stated in his report: 'The prostitutes [in his zone] are generally Hindus, owing to the prejudice against re-marriage, strictness of Hindu social law, *kulinism*, etc.'[38]

Among the Muslim prostitutes, there seemed to be a tendency to hide their religious identity. An official report from Chittagong states: 'Many Mahomedan prostitutes assume the name of Hindus for two reasons: first to enable them to get Hindu girls (for recruitment), and to induce Hindus (males) to frequent them, which would not be the case if they professed to be Mahomedans, while it does not destroy the chance of *nika* marriage with one of her own race; second, Hindus are more popular, and are credited with having more attractive manners. This accounts for the preponderance of Hindu prostitutes even in Mahomedan districts.'[39]

A slightly different picture of Muslim prostitutes is available from an official report from Coochbehar in north Bengal: 'The Mahomedan (prostitute) is generally a convert from the Kooch tribe, calling herself a Hindu or Raj Bungshee, and who has adopted Hindu manners. The poor of these classes frequently sell their children to prostitutes, who rear and live by them.' It, then, reiterates the same argument explaining the numerically small component of Muslim prostitutes in the zone: 'The number of Mahomedan women is small, as re-marriage is easy among the sect.'[40]

This leads us to another interesting query. How was the Muslim client treated by the Hindu prostitute in the red-light areas of 19th century Bengal? We are lucky in laying our hands on a fascinating autobiography by a scion of a 19th century Bengali Muslim 'zamindar' family, which gives us intimate glimpses of the conflict that nagged the Hindu prostitute's psyche—between the obligation to adhere to her religious dictates on pollution (with regard to Muslim clients) on the one hand, and the compulsions of her trade that operated against any such discrimination on the other. The author, Goniur Raja, describes in his autobiography his visit to a Hindu prostitute (who also happened to be a dancer, proficient in the then popular *khemta* form of dancing—known as *khemtawali*) in Dhaka in East Bengal around 1896. While entertaining him, the *khemtawali*, called Sarala, said to him: '. . . Although you were introduced to me [by your friend] as a Hindu, right from the start I could make out that you were a Muslim.' She then added: 'We Hindu women do not entertain Muslim men. We get abused in our society [if we do it].' Goniur Raja asked her sneeringly: 'Do women of your type also have a 'society' [meaning societal norms and code of behaviour]? . . .' Sarala retorted: 'Of course!

Although I've registered my name as a prostitute, all our Hinduani [practices and customs of Hindus] is still maintained by us.' To give an illustration of the Hinduani, then, she pointed out: 'In this quarter of ours where you are now, you won't find any woman who isn't a Hindu. In other [red-light] areas you'll find women who are Muslim, or belong to other religious communities. But in this quarter, as well as in the neighbourhood of the Kotwali [the local police station] and in 'Sankharipatti' [the colony of the shell workers], there are no women from any other religious community but Hindus. They and us follow the same societal norms.'[41]

We also come across official records about Muslim prostitutes in certain areas of Bengal adopting Hindu names to be able to pursue their business with Hindu customers. This raises certain important questions. Although, during the 19th century in Bengal, the number of Muslims equalled, and sometimes even outnumbered, the total Hindu population, why did the Bengali Hindu clientele appear to be in a more dominating position in the red-light areas than their Muslim counterparts—to the extent of not only ensuring the observance of traditional religious and socially discriminatory norms among the Hindu prostitutes whom they patronized, but also in indirectly compelling the Muslim prostitutes to adopt Hindu names to pretend to be Hindus? Is it because the Hindu clientele came from among the new parvenu that cropped up in Bengal during the 18th–19th century period, who made money and occupied lucrative positions in the commercial and administrative hierarchies—thanks to the patronage of the British colonial rulers? As one perceptive historian of Bengali culture, explaining the absence of Muslims among the Bengali 'nouveaux riches' of 18th century Calcutta, observes: 'The majority of the Muslims were agriculturists; there were few who were in service. Muslims did not want to leave the economic security of land for the city where life was full of financial uncertainties. Those who were engaged in services and administrative work [during the previous Moghul regime] turned to agriculture after the loss of [Moghul] ruling power . . . while the Hindus advanced towards their improvement through seeking opportunities in services by collaborating with the British government and receiving English education, the Muslims lost similar opportunities by turning away from the British government and English education and suffered decline . . .'[42] The Hindu clientele, therefore, appeared to wield more influence on the prostitutes, who tended to please them by adhering to their socio-religious norms of behaviour.

By insisting on—or pretending to—the observance of the codes of Hinduani, the Hindu prostitutes could have also sought, in their own way, to recapture the cultural ambience in which they were born and brought up (many among them were widows and daughters from orthodox Brahmin and upper caste families), before they were uprooted and compelled to enter the red-light areas in a totally alien and hostile environment. The observance of traditional Hindu rituals, therefore, often became a major mode of reasserting and restoring their solidarity with the Hindu society which had cast them off. The worshipping of two deities of the Hindu pantheon in particular—Saraswati, the goddess of learning, and Kartika, the commander of the army of the gods—were important events in the red-light areas of 19th century Calcutta. Newcomers were formally initiated into the profession, and given new names on the occasion of the Saraswati puja (worshipping ceremony).[43]

But although the prostitutes sought to demonstrate their adherence to Hindu religious rituals, the 'respectable' society of the educated Bengali *bhadralok* looked down upon such display. Observing the popularity of the two deities among the Hindu prostitutes, a contemporary Bengali journal ticked them off in the following words: 'People worship Kartika to obtain sons, and Saraswati to become learned. For prostitutes, any entertainment of either of these two objectives is totally unauthorized. Yet, they celebrate the Saraswati and Kartika pujas with a lot of pomp!'[44]

Yet, their decision to propitiate these two deities (associated with learning) could have been dictated by their own logic—a method of reasoning leading them to believe that such a propitiation could fulfil their desire to have children (both sons and daughters) who would get education and escape from the sordid red-light areas—and, if possible, rescue their mothers from their oppressive living conditions.

Education—or learning in general—was an issue which was taken up by some prostitutes in 19th century Bengal in the teeth of fierce social opposition. The most sensational case was that of Heera Bulbul (variously described as a prostitute and a *baiji*) who was determined to educate her son in the prestigious Hindu College of Calcutta. His admission to the College in 1853 triggered off an uproar among the Bengali *bhadralok* families whose sons were studying at the College. They decided to withdraw their wards from the College, protesting against the admission of a *beshya-nandan* (son of a prostitute) into a College that was established from funds contributed by 'Hindu gentlemen'. These disgruntled elements of the city's Bengali *bhadralok* society soon started a new college called the Hindu Metropolitan College. Apparently perturbed by the defection of their students, the Hindu College authorities knuckled down under pressure from the *bhadralok* guardians and expelled Heera Bulbul's son.[45]

Some two decades later, when the British government came out with a directive stating that the 'children of the professional prostitute class are to be admitted to public girls' schools under the control of the State up to the age of puberty on equal terms with all others',[46] it evoked tremendous opposition from the Indian educated gentry—which was, curiously enough, shared by the British bureaucrats posted in India. Following reports of 'Native repulsion against the mixture of prostitutes' children with respectable children,' a British official observed: 'They [daughters of prostitutes] begin at a very early age those bodily exercises which are designed to fit them for their lewd profession. Their earliest home lessons are unclean songs. All that they hear and see around them is unalloyed immorality.' He then added: 'Their earliest training unfits them to be school associates of innocent children from virtuous homes.'[47] A year later, his seniors in the Government of India were to concur with him in opposing the entry of girls of prostitutes into 'native schools', stating: 'It is already difficult enough to get Natives to patronize girls' schools at all without throwing open such schools to a class of children that might contaminate innocent little children,' and objecting to 'the introduction of infant harlots at the bottom of the schools. . .'[48]

We should, however, add in this connection that small girls growing up in brothels were not always daughters of prostitutes. Quite often, they were bought by brothel owners from poor parents. The sale of little girls who later ended up in brothels (as mentioned in the 1872 report of the Calcutta Deputy Commissioner of Police) was quite common. It was caused primarily because of the increase in the number and intensity of famines in the second half of the 19th century. There were six famines between 1851 and 1875 and twenty-four between 1876 and 1900 (as against seven in the first half of the century).[49] During such times, poor parents sold off their girls to procuresses or prostitutes, with all the semblance of a legal transaction. A deed was drawn up, generally on stamped paper, and this was kept hanging as a threat over the child by her purchaser, who frightened her with dire punishment in the event of her leaving.[50] According to a contemporary district official: '. . . every female child who is unmarried or abandoned finds a ready home with the bazar women [i.e. prostitutes]. Once in their power, a girls finds it very difficult to escape; if she runs away, a criminal charge of stealing ornaments is brought against her at the thannah . . .'[51]

What happened to boys during periods of distress like famines? From a contemporary official report, again, we hear of a strange deal—'an exchange being made of a cultivator's girl for a prostitute's boy, on the ground that neither was of any use to its natural parents.'[52] For the poor cultivator, the boy was obviously of more value—far more important than any sentimental ties to his daughter—since the boy could help him in his agricultural work, and look after him in his old age. For the prostitute, the cultivator's girl was naturally considered a more valuable asset than her son, since she could join her profession and take care of her when she became old and infirm.[53]

V

Meanwhile, the composition of the clientele of the brothels in Calcutta, Dhaka and other towns in Bengal was also changing during the latter half of the 19th century. As among the prostitutes, so, also, among their customers, a new generation emerged whose life-style, manners and demands were different from those of their predecessors. The changing values and tastes of these people determined to a large extent the behaviour and expectations of the prostitutes. The nature of the demand in the market shaped the character of the supply.

A comparison of two literary compositions will indicate the change suggested above. Three decades after Bhabanicharan Bandyopadhyay, another Bengali satirist painted the habits of contemporary 'babu' community. Pyarichand Mitra (under the pseudonym Tekchand Thakur), wrote *Alaler Gharer Dulal* (The Spoilt Child of a Rich Home) in 1858.[54]

His hero, Motilal, has the same habits as the hero of Bhabanicharan's *Naba-babu-bilash.* But Pyarichand adds new characters to his entourage, who had emerged in Calcutta during the intervening period—teachers of English, lawyers and the different categories of touts involved in legal proceedings, and the Anglicized sycophants. While the 'babu' in Bhabanicharan's works reminds the readers of the decadent Bengali feudal dandies who still retained some interest in north Indian classical music and pastimes redolent of the preceding Moghul culture, in Pyarichand's farce, the 'babu' and his companions are a new breed who are primarily interested in immediate profits through a fast transaction—whether in commerce, administration, or in their relations with prostitutes. They have no time for cultural trappings like elaborate 'nautch' sessions for transacting deals with singers like Nikki. The carefully prepared training course for the prostitutes—as well as of their patrons—described in Bhabanicharan's *Naba-babu-bilash* and *Naba-bibi-bilash,* was no longer considered essential in the late 19th century terms of trade in flesh in Bengal.

The Bengali farces written during the last half of the 19th century—which proliferated thanks to the expansion of the printing press—provide a fascinating insight into the changing attitudes and habits of both the prostitutes and their patrons of that period.

We are choosing one typical farce which recaptures the generation gap between the two periods and illuminates the changes in the behaviour pattern of the prostitutes. Entitled *Aponar Mukh Apuni Dekho* (Look At Your Own Face), it was written by Bholanath Mukhopadhyay in 1863. Among the various characters, the one who stands out is the elderly prostitute, Rammoni—a woman from the Baiti community (a lower caste people engaged in the manufacture of lime from shells). In the words of the author: '. . . after her husband's death, Rammoni used to work as a maid servant for a [monthly] salary of two rupees and ten annas . . . after a few days of work, Rammoni found favour in a 'babu's eyes . . . as a result, first her maid servant's occupation came to an end, she was put up in a two-storeyed house in an alley, the 'babu' began to visit her everyday, he was also joined by one or two Brahmin and Kayastha friends and *mosahebs* (many Brahmins won't touch water in a lower caste home . . . but at Rammoni Baiti's home they went on guzzling mutton and luchi—thin cake of flour fried in ghee). Earlier, Rammoni used to be called 'Rami thakurani'. But once she reached the two-storeyed house, she became 'Rammoni'. Then, when the 'babu' gave her some ornaments, she assumed the name 'Rammoni bibi' . . . Within a short time, Rammoni managed to build a house of her own, acquire several sets of ornaments, put together a splendid wardrobe, and came to be regarded as one among the top demi-mondaines . . .'[55]

Here is a thumb-nail sketch of a self-made woman and of her rapid rise to the pinnacle of success in her profession. She is not the archetypal prostitute of the past—the innocent victim of seduction or desertion, reluctantly entering the profession, or forced to join it by a procuress. Rammoni's entry is voluntary, and the steps are chosen by herself in the ladder of professional success.

Rammoni brought up a girl called Channanbilashi, who was the daughter of a Bagdi (a lower caste community of cultivators) servant of hers. Trained by Rammoni, she succeeded in moving up higher. She managed to win the favour of one of the richest 'babus' of Calcutta, whose exploits are described in a satirical extravaganza in the pages of Bholanath's narrative, and which gives us an idea of the changing tastes of the new generation of clientele which patronized the brothels in the last half of the 19th century.

The 'babu' of this period seems to represent two types—one, the last generation of the descendants of the 18th century *banians* and *dewans*, whose fortunes were being steadily dissipated by their grandsons on entertainments which had declined from the lavish 'nautch' sessions and maintenance of expensive *baijis* as mistresses (which the grandees of the past indulged in) to orgies of drinking and gluttony and promiscuous whore-mongering; two, a rising generation of a retinue class in the tertiary sector of the commercial, administrative and judicial systems—clerks, lawyers, and a host of professionals like teachers, doctors, engineers, etc.

Bholanath, in his farce, brings together both the types. The 'babu' who is fond of Channanbilashi still seems to have enough money from his inheritance to entertain not only her, but the entire band of prostitutes living in the bordello run by Rammoni. Along with his retinue of *mosahebs*, he takes these women to his ancestral garden house on the outskirts of Calcutta to celebrate Christmas. He invites members of his peer group, hires *baijis* and other dancers and musicians for entertainment. But very soon, the songs are drowned by drunken revelry and the dances turn into an orgy of lechery, ending up with groggy men and women waking up the next morning in odd corners of the garden.[56]

Old Rammoni, however, keeps a watch. At the end of a similar orgy in Kalighat (arranged by the 'babu' at the request of Channanbilashi and her colleagues to offer puja to the goddess Kali!), Rammoni warns her foster child against getting swept off her feet by the fun and games, and advises her: 'We do not have any lasting relations with the 'babus', they are from outside; they are here today, but may disappear tomorrow. But, they have cash . . . Now is the time to fleece them; you'll never get this opportunity again. As long as the 'babus' fancy us, however learned they may be, they submit to one word uttered by a whore—the word is *aan* [Bring]. My darling! This word *aan* has to be cultivated in such a manner that once you utter it, no 'babu' can resist it . . . He will have to bring it to you, even if he has to steal or sell his wife's ornaments . . .'[57]

Rammoni advises Channanbilashi to secure her future by judiciously using her earnings. Recalling the experiences of her less-fortunate colleagues, she says: 'Many among the whores, even though they managed to acquire a lot of expensive ornaments, could not live wisely; some among them did not pay attention to the need for earning enough when they could. Some are now maid servants, others are working in granaries, wallowing in dust and earning somehow a handful of rice.'[58]

Rammoni's words hark back to the advice given some forty years ago by the old madam to her apprentice in Bhabanicharan Bandyopadhyay's *Naba-bibi-bilash.* Rammoni, however, is more explicit in her explanation of the motives of both the prostitutes and their patrons. Unlike her predecessor, she does not feel the need for disabusing Channanbilashi's mind of expectations of love—since such emotional attachments were assumed to have no place in what had, by now, become a full-fledged commercial deal.

New pretences and skills were being cultivated in the brothels of late 19th century Bengal to cater to the demands of the contemporary clientele. The six skills required to be acquired by prostitutes according to the old madam of *Naba-bibi-bilash,* were being modified—and new ones added to them. Bholanath, in his farce, quotes a prevalent saying which sums up the qualities of prostitutes of his age—*Thaat, thamak, chatak, chaal, mithya, maan, kanna, gaal.* In addition to the old devices of coquetry and deception (now termed as *thaat, mithya, maan* and *kanna*), the new skills necessary to cultivate are *thamak* (flaunting an affected gait), *chatak* (dazzling the customer with gaudy glamour), *chaal* (putting on airs and big talk) and *gaal* (use of abusive language).[59] The stress is obviously on marketing the product to a clientele which is more attracted by the glitter and the tinsel of the commodity which it is using. Although deceptive devices like *maan* (acting as if her pride has been hurt) and *kanna* (weeping) are still being used to appeal to the emotions of the customer, the main direction, evidently, is towards attracting the new 'babu's' taste for tawdriness, and catering to his limited desire for a veneer of 'fine feeling' to cover his actual act of consumption.

One might wonder how, in this strategy of wooing the 'babu', a device like *gaal*—the art of hurling the choicest abuses—could have found a place. Descriptions in contemporary literature indicate that such abuses were sometimes in the form of light-hearted raillery—direct enough to hit the target, but soft enough to retain the 'babus' as their customers. The abused 'babus' also seemed to enjoy the abuses. Meer Mosharraf Hossain's *Er Upay Ki?* (What's the Way Out?)—a farce written in 1876—describes a scene where an inebriated 'babu' takes a prostitute whom he fancies to his home and introduces her to his wife. When the wife insults the prostitute, the latter kicks the 'babu' and warns him: 'Look here, you scamp! Better be careful. Unless you leave this place immediately and come back with me, I'll flog you with my shoes and break your head!' The 'babu' promptly folds his hands and apologizes to her, promising her that he'll never again visit his wife![60] Dealings between prostitutes and their customers quite often opened up the space for such insults in what anthropologists call ritual joking relationships between certain types of acquaintances.

The art of *gaal* also offered the prostitutes an avenue of protest or letting off steam. A typical instance can be found in *Sachitra Guljar-nagar* (1871), where the author, Kedarnath Dutta, describes how a prostitute, when pestered by a customer in a crowded Calcutta street, lets off a volley of expletives: 'Accursed bloke! Can't you find a place to kick the bucket? Itching for a quick bash, aren't you?' The man, obviously a *bhadralok*, feels embarrassed by her shouts, which have drawn a crowd, pretends to be her husband and changes his tone: 'Please, my darling, don't get angry. Bhulu, our son, wept for you all night. How long can he suffer?'[61]

The farces reflected in a large measure the popular perceptions about prostitutes in 19th century Bengal. Sayings current among the common people and their songs suggest mixed feelings of fear and envy which took the form of contempt and ridicule. There was the fear of the power which the prostitutes were suspected of wielding over men. There was also the envy at their reported success in amassing wealth by using their sexual skills. Any attempts made by prostitutes to adopt the manners of 'respectable' society were, therefore, perceived as threats and invited sneers, like the following—*Khankir abar jateyr bichar* (What cheek! Even the whore is fussy about caste); *Ranri betir biyer shakh, unaye rasher kato thamok* (The whore wants to marry; how she flaunts her overflowing love!).[62]

The belief that all prostitutes were gold-diggers who made fortunes by exploiting men (which could have been the case with a few lucky ones, but surely not with the vast masses of prostitutes who remained poor), was fairly widespread at the level of popular thinking. The oral literature of 19th century Bengal abounds with complaints about prostitutes acquiring wealth from their male customers, while respectable people are denied their dues. A common saying was *Beshyar duarey tanka tanka, gurur belaye nabadanka* (Heaps of money at the doors of the prostitutes, and nothing for the guru).[63] The well-known folk-poet Dashu Ray (1805-1857) in one of his *panchali* songs deplores:

> '*Satider anno jotey na, beshyader jaroa gahona*'[64]
> (Chaste wives do not get rice to eat, while whores wear ornaments studded with jewels).

An anonymous 19th century Bengali poetaster's song evokes the feelings of fear that overwhelmed an unwary pedestrian in the red-light areas of Calcutta:

> *Kolikatar beshyader leela oti chamotkar,*
> *Maya bojhey sadhya kar?*
>
> *Jetey Nather Baganey bhoy lagey money,*
> *Chailey porey tader paney, haat dhorey taney,*
>
> *Jorabaganey geley, mishta katha boley,*
> *Agey bhulaye shesh-kaletey daye phanshi galey,*
>
> *Abar Sonagachhi thakey jara, kashayer maton byabhar.*
> *Dekhey shuney lagey bhoy, porey ba ki hoy.*'[65]
>
> (Amazing are the games that the Calcutta whores play. Who can make out their wiles? . . . One is scared of going to Natherbagan, where if you even cast a fleeting glance at them, they'll pull you by your hands . . . If you go to Jorabagan, they'll first charm you with sweet talk, and then sling the noose around your neck. . . And those who live in Sonagachhi behave like butchers. Watching and listening to them, one gets frightened, not knowing what'll happen next.)

Yet, prostitutes living in the red-light areas—however aggressive they might have been, as made out by the above song and other popular and official accounts—were, themselves, also victims of physical violence. The same popular press which encouraged the myth of their making fortunes and living in eternal bliss, also reported the numerous cases of murders of prostitutes—purely, of course, from the commercial motive of selling sensational stories. But from these reports, we can decipher the hazards that these women faced in their occupation.

VI

Contemporary Bengali newspapers and popular chapbooks (published by cheap presses in the Battala area of north Calcutta, which existed cheek by jowl with the brothels that spanned a wide zone from the then Cornwallis Street in the north-east to Chitpore in the north-west of Calcutta), abound with reports of sensational cases of murder of prostitutes. Most of these cases—if we go by these reports—stemmed from personal motives of the male customers who used to visit these prostitutes—if the motive wasn't burglary, it was vengeance by a jilted customer.

Interestingly enough, in these various reports of murder of prostitutes, both in official records and newspaper accounts of 19th century Bengal, we have not yet come across any homicidal maniac like Jack the Ripper who terrorized East London in the late 1880s with his serial killings of prostitutes. Explanations about his behaviour continue to be mired in modern socio-psychological controversies—as to whether the motive was some deep-rooted pathological perversion, or an evangelical zeal (to get rid of prostitutes)!

In 19th century Bengal, in most of the cases of murder of prostitutes, jealousy did play a part—if we go by the contemporary reports. It suggests the intense sense of possessiveness that gripped some among the male clients who were drawn to the prostitutes. The following excerpt from a report of a 'crime passionnel' that appeared in a contemporary Bengali journal may give today's readers an idea of the style and choice of descriptive epithets that marked reportage on prostitutes: 'There's no end to the variety of evils that are committed in brothels! A man maintained a prostitute as his kept in a brothel in Shyambazar in Calcutta, while it is rumoured that two other men also visited her, and when the man who kept her learnt about this, last Sunday he told her that he was going out of town and took leave of her; meanwhile, the prostitute invited her two *madhoopas* [literally, a pair of black-bees feeding on honey—meaning her two lovers], sat in a circle with them and began to be merry on wine and meat, when at that moment the man who kept her entered the room with a sword, and made a sacrifice of all the three . . .'[66]

It is interesting to note, as the above report suggests, that even from prostitutes, the male customer expected faithfulness to him alone—like the usual demand of fidelity from the wife. Any act of infidelity on the part of the 'kept' prostitute invited punishment (just as in the case of the adultress wife).[67] The term 'sacrifice' (*balidan* in the original Bengali report) used by the reporter (obviously a male) suggests the prevalent socio-religious sanction of the killing of a woman, if found unfaithful, as a necessary sacrifice to the altar of morality. The suggestive description of the prostitute getting 'merry' with her two lovers over 'wine and meat' (with the subtle hint of more merry-making to follow), builds up to the climax, where the 'man who kept her' (owning her, and therefore requiring exclusive sexual obedience to him by her) arrives on the scene, and delivers the retributive blow to his faithless 'kept'—as well as the two male lovers whom she apparently preferred to her owner!

Jealousy over prostitutes among Bengali aristocrats and *bhadralok*—which, quite often, led to acts of violence against these women—could have reflected the macho instinct of holding on to a much-sought-after prostitute (like a singer, a dancer or an actress) as a trophy, and resenting violently the trophy's choice of another man. It could have also reflected—in many cases—the possessive client's deep sentimental attachment to his 'kept' woman, with whom his relationship, which was physical to start with, had developed over the years into one of emotional dependence on her.

The well-known Bengali actress, Binodini Dasi (1863–1941), narrates in her autobiography how, during her career in the Star Theatre in Calcutta in the early 1880s, she was almost killed by a young jealous lover who kept her as a mistress for some time. Since he was not willing to allow her to continue to act on the stage, she decided to leave him for another man who promised to look after her and provide her with a home. On hearing this, her previous lover broke into her room early one morning, and offered her twenty thousand rupees in lieu of her promise to give up the stage. When Binodini scornfully rejected his offer (with the words: 'I have made money, but money cannot make me'), the infuriated lover took out his sword and struck at her, but missed. An alert and brave Binodini (hardly 20 years old) held him by his hand when he was about to lunge again and reminded him of his respectable *bhadralok* family background and the scandal that would blemish his family reputation if he was hanged for murdering a prostitute: 'Think of your fate, of your family prestige. Will you have to depart from this world with a stain on your character—all because of a despised prostitute?' The words had immediate effect, and the *bhadralok* lover threw away his sword and sat down hiding his face in his palms![68]

Having been exposed to Bengali *bhadralok* society through her involvement with the theatre as a young girl from 1874 onwards, and aware of the vulnerable spots in the *bhadralok* psyche, Binodini could show her presence of mind by immediately appealing to that sensitive spot in her jealous lover's mind that could dissuade him from murdering her. She did not weep or make pathetic appeals to him to spare her—as one would have normally expected from a threatened female in such circumstances. It was her experiences with the *bhadralok* lovers and her accumulated knowledge about the chink in their armour, that emboldened her—a virtuoso as she was in the contemporary Bengali stage—to extemporize a dialogue that happened to touch the right chord in the mind of her jealous lover, and save her life!

Unlike stage actresses like Binodini (who, although born of, and living in, the red-light areas of Calcutta, emerged into the limelight of publicity through sheer histrionic talent—and thus enjoyed a certain degree of protection from contemporary social and administrative norms, which could have also dissuaded her murderous lover from killing her), her sisters in the profession in her neighbourhood quite often failed to escape the fatal end that she evaded.

A contemporary chapbook celebrated in a typical sensational manner an actual incident—the murder of a prostitute in the red-light area of 'Sonagaji' (Sonagachhi) in north Calcutta sometime in 1875. It describes the victim, Golap, as a girl of 16 to 18 years of age, fair-skinned, with beautiful eyes and of medium height ('*Bachhor atharo sholo boyesh tahar, shubrabarna sulochona madhyam akar*'). Composed in verse, it then narrates how the then Deputy Commissioner of Police of Calcutta, Lambert, arrested the murderer—a man of about 30 years, dark complexioned and slim built, called Kali Rakshit. Without showing any trace of remorse, the murderer in a sportive mood departs with Lambert ('*Lamberter shongey rangey korichhey poyan*').[69] The author of this chapbook followed it up with another called *Sonagajir Khunir Phanshir Hukum* (The Sonagaji killer sentenced to death by hanging). It is an account of the trial proceedings, in the course of which we learn that Golap was hit twenty-four times, and that ten of her wounds were extremely serious. The doctor's opinion was that the murder was a deliberate act. But when the murderer heard about his death sentence, he appeared to look down upon it with scorn, and exclaimed repeatedly— 'Excellent! Excellent!' ('*Shuniya Kayedi jeno prakashia shlesh, kohilen bar bar besh besh besh*').[70]

It is significant that in neither of the two narratives has the murderer been depicted as a villain. Even after his arrest, he is in high spirits (*rangey*). At the end, he is almost elevated to the status of a hero—the second narrative showing him treating the death sentence with utter contempt (*shlesh*). One can discern a sneaking admiration for the murderer in the attitude of the poetaster. This was in keeping with the contemporary patriarchal society's perception of the prostitute as a villainess who deserved punishment—even death, if necessary.

The working people of 19th century Bengal, among whom the disparaging sayings and songs about prostitutes, or the chapbooks about them, were popular, did not appear to have any sympathy for the prostitutes, although the majority of the latter came from the same background of poverty and social exploitation that was shared by the other members of the labouring poor. Unwilling—and unable—to understand that prostitution was just another profession in the market where the prostitute sold her skills like any other wage worker or artisan, the lower orders, particularly the males, felt that she enjoyed an undue advantage over other workers. The general belief was that while others toiled to earn their livelihood, the prostitute made money the easiest way—by entertaining with her body. The moral stigma stamped by society on a prostitute's labour further reinforced the image of the prostitute as an inferior being in the hierarchy of the labouring classes in 19th century Bengal. While the poor prostitute was rarely recognized as a co-sufferer by other members of the labouring poor, the rich prostitute was denied the respect and prestige that were enjoyed by her sisters in the upper-class *bhadralok* society. Whatever her economic status, the prostitute always remained an exile.

V
Voices from the Pit

'. . . just because we expressed our disaffection with our husbands, and left them, are we to be treated as sinners?'

—Letter from prostitutes, uprooted from their brothels by an eviction drive .[1]

The responses of the prostitutes themselves to the various experiences involved in the practice of their profession in 19th century Bengal, open up a wide area for exploration, which, quite often, defies any single, hold-all explanation. The unidirectional postulate that poverty alone drove them to choose the profession, or assumption that they did not have any opportunity to exercise a rational control over their lives within the exploitative structure, may not be valid in all cases.

Poverty and male exploitation (like *kulin* polygamy, a sense of deprivation among widows, and seduction by philanderers) did, indeed, force the first generation of prostitutes in the early years of the colonial era—and continued to drive their successors later, too—to swell the ranks of the denizens of the red-light areas of Bengal. But a number of new socio-economic developments soon began to play an important role in the commercial relations that were being transacted in the red-light areas of Calcutta and other parts of 19th century Bengal, as well as in their cultural manifestations. As discussed earlier, a later generation of clientele with a different set of demands and tastes opened up new opportunities of upward mobility for those among the prostitutes who were hard-headed enough to exploit the 'babus' to their own advantage.

All through the 19th century, there was a continuous influx of poor women, mainly from the toiling cultivating and artisan communities of the depressed castes, into the red-light areas. As mentioned earlier, they were driven by famines to leave their village homes and move to places like Calcutta or nearby towns in search of a livelihood—only to end up in brothels. But, having been used to tough living and self-reliance for survival needs, these women in their new profession were quick to introduce unsqueamish norms in their dealings with their male customers. In driving a hard bargain with them, they carried out the transaction in terms which were quite often sexually explicit and down-to-earth—unlike the language of their submissive sisters who came from the sheltered upper caste *kulin* or middle-class homes.

One must also note the changing life-style of the descendants of the first generation of prostitutes—those who were described as 'hereditary prostitutes' in colonial officialese, and as *dobol khanki* in the slang of the Bengali underworld. These women were far removed from the nostalgic memories of the domesticity of 'respectable' homes nursed by their mothers, who were initiated into the profession in the late 18th–early 19th century period. These descendants of the first generation of prostitutes gradually reconciled themselves to the prevalent norms that were developing in the red-light areas, and acquired the behavioural pattern that was required of them, by the new generation of male clients.

The socio-cultural scene of 19th century Bengal was marked by certain other developments, which, although extraneous to their profession, helped the prostitutes, in a large measure, to become articulate. First, as a result of the establishment of cheap printing presses in Calcutta and mofussil towns, there was a flow of chapbooks, some of which publicized sensational events in the red-light areas, and also published songs of the prostitutes, and their autobiographies.[2] The Bengali press, which grew into a flourishing business during this period, also, occasionally, provided space to letters and interviews by prostitutes.

Another major avenue for articulation by prostitutes was the Bengali stage. A highly successful public theatre had come to dominate Bengali culture by the 1870s, when, for the first time, actresses came to be recruited from the red-light areas. (Since no women from 'respectable' middle-class homes were allowed to be seen in public—leave alone perform on stage—female roles till then were enacted by male actors.) This offered a large number of women in the profession the opportunity to come out and enter a cultural milieu which exposed them to the best in classical and modern literature, since the plays in which they acted were quite often adaptations from the works of ancient Sanskrit poets, or contemporary Bengali authors (like Bankim Chandra Chattopadhyay), or even Shakespeare. The experience of rehearsing, and delivering dialogues, in the course of staging these plays, gradually shaped the mode of literary expression of these women, some among whom took to writing.

It was thus a variety of influences—socio-economic (e.g. the influx of women from the traditionally assertive and more articulate poorer classes, the changing life-style of the new generation of prostitutes), as well as cultural (e.g. the flourishing of the printing press and newspapers, and the birth of the theatre)—that led to an amazingly wide diversity of outpourings by prostitutes in the different media of communication that were available to them at that time. Their voices expressed the whole gamut of their existential problems, ranging from the mundane dealings with their landladies (the *mashis*, or aunts, as they were known in the parlance of the red-light areas) to their choice of lovers; from their subjective preferences to the objective compulsions of their profession that often prevented them from exercising these preferences and choices; from their individual priorities to their more general grievances.

These voices can be rediscovered and heard from a number of sources—(i) songs and sayings current among prostitutes in the red-light areas of 19th-century Bengal; (ii) letters of prostitutes in contemporary newspapers; and (iii) reminiscences and writings of actresses who came from the red-light areas.

How do we tune our ears to the nuances of these voices? Far removed by both time and space from their experiences, which were recorded by some among them in their distinctive idiom in their songs and sayings, we, today, can at best try to decipher the half-forgotten coded messages and double entrende embedded in those cultural expressions of the red-light areas. It is much easier with the other two categories—the letters of prostitutes and their autobiographies—since they were written in a Bengali which emerged as the standard language of literary compositions at the end of the 19th century, and the idioms used there still remain in vogue and are, thus, more comprehensible.

The songs and sayings of the prostitutes were primarily about their customers—the rakes and false lovers, the seducers and gigolos, the old roués and young macho men. They were turned almost into characters in a merry strip-tease, watched and dissected by the bargaining eyes of these women. It was their way of turning the tables on their male customers. The idiom in most of these songs is sexually explicit, with a liberal sprinkling of four-letter words. The language is sinewy and robust.

The following song, for instance, plays on the imagery of the contemporary popular game of kite-flying to describe a prostitute's response to her lover:

> *Ketey diye premer ghuri*
> *Abar keno lotkey dharo?*
> *Ek tanetey bojha geloe*
> *Tomar sutor manja kharoe.*[3]
> (Why are you still hanging on after having snipped off the kite of love? One pull was enough to show that the glue had made your string sharp.)

One can discover two layers of meaning here, with the *suto*—the string raising up the kite in the air—evoking phallic associations. At one level, the woman could be complaining about her lover's libertinism—rousing the love-kite in her and then snapping it off by a sharp swing (like the kite-flier's, which cuts the string of his rival's kite, and brings it down). At another level, she might be laughing at her lover's inadequate performance—one pull of his string (one stroke?) was enough to prove that his *manja* ((the glue used to sharpen the edge of the string) was *kharoe*—a term which could be also interpreted as 'brittle', or that which crumbles fast. Such double entendre lent a nimble-witted twist to the songs and sayings of the prostitutes.

As today, in the 19th century also, policemen as customers were both feared and secretly derided by the prostitutes of Calcutta. The police wielded tremendous power over the city's underprivileged, including the prostitutes. A contemporary

Bengali newspaper once appealed to the Police Commissioner of Calcutta to treat the city's prostitutes as 'subjects of the government' and find out from them how the 'constables arrested them and handed them over to the police station inspectors who tortured them all through the night.'[4]

It is in this context that one can appreciate a popular saying current among prostitutes in these days :

> *Machh khabi to ilish.*
> *Nang dhorbi to pulish.*
> (If you want to eat fish, choose hilsa. If you want to take a lover, choose a policeman).

The insinuation is clear. A cop tastes better since he can protect the prostitute, who, in her turn, can also ensnare him in her net (like the hilsa) and fleece him to her advantage.

In a reversal of roles, prostitutes could also exploit some men by using them as studs. Following are the lines of an old song sung by a prostitute, addressed to another:

> *Sadhey ki hoinu, didi,*
> *Chhokra nanger boshibhuto ?*
> *Taka paisa daye na botey,*
> *Thapguli daye moneyr matoe."*
> (It's not for nothing, my dear sister, that I'm loyal to my young lover. Although he can't pay me, he's good in bed.)

Acceptance of customers was most often determined on religious grounds also. We come across one song which in a mock-regretful style relates a Hindu prostitute's discovery that the customer was a Muslim only after he was about to make love to her:

> *Agey jantam na, didi,*
> *Shey jey Musalman chhilo.*
> *Paan kheye, dhuti porey,*
> *Thik janoy Hindur chheley.*
> *Hatey niye sonar chhori,*
> *Buk-pocketey sonar ghari.*
> *Jakhon niye dhuklam gharey,*
> *Dekhlum tar kata chhilo.*
> (I didn't know, dear sister, that he was a Muslim. He was chewing *paan*, dressed in a dhoti and looked just like a

Hindu, with a golden stick in his hand, and a golden watch chain hanging from his breast pocket. Only when I took him inside, did I discover that he was circumcised.)[5]

The description of the sartorial habits of the customer in the above song throws light on the stereotypes of Hindus and Muslims that stuck in the minds of the prostitutes of those days. Unlike the dhoti-clad Hindu customers, the Muslims were associated with *chapkan* (loose upper garment) and pyjamas—among the richer classes—and with vest and *lungi* among the lower class Muslims.

Some of the songs available suggest the perpetual tensions between the prostitutes and their landladies (the brothel-keepers) known as *bariulees*, the latter hiking up their rents every now and then, and the former seeking shelter elsewhere. The following song, while complaining about the *bariulee*, replaces the conventional romantic images of flowers, rivers, moon, etc., with more substantial images of material things of daily use:

Amar bhalobasha abaar kothaye baasha bendhechey,
Piriteyr parota kheye mota hoyechey.
Mashey mashey barchhey bhaara,
Bariulee dichhey taara,
Goylaparar moyla chhonra praney merechhey![6]

(My love has taken me to set up home at another place. It has fattened upon the *paranthas* of past affairs. The room rent is going up every month. The landlady is threatening to evict me. But my soul is smitten by that dark lad from the milkman's colony).

The choice of the metaphor *parota* (or *parantha* in Hindi, which means layered fried bread) to describe her experiences of love is a marvellous bravura. Like the thin layers of fried bread in a *parantha*, the endless sheets of varied encounters with male customers, one piling upon another, make up the prostitute's portmanteau of memories—both physical and emotional. But from this reservoir, she chooses the 'dark lad from the milkman's colony'—which is a reconstruction of the Radha-Krishna legend in her own localized version, where her lover is imagined as a contemporary replica of that dark prince of the cowherd-milkman community of the ancient myths—Krishna.

The room of the prostitute—which was workshop-cum-residence—acquired a value of its own. Luck in business depended on its location, interior decor and rent. In one song, which is quite forthright and explicit, a prostitute complains about the poor room given to her by the landlady of the brothel:

> *Bariulee, hisheb metao,*
> *Kal jaboe utey.*
> *Emon baler ghar diyecho,*
> *Nang jotey na motey.*
> *Ebar jaboe Beleghataye,*
> *Nang jotaboe mota-shota,*
> *Kuli-mojur shob boshaboe,*
> *Baad deboe na motey.*[7]
>
> (Send me my bills, landlady, and let me clear them. I'm quitting your place tomorrow. Fuck your room! No lover ever comes here. This time, I'll go to Beleghata and pick up lovers who are beefy and chunky! I'll entertain everyone—porters and labourers—and refuse none.)

Some of the songs are sort of romantic, with bizarre images embedded in them. The following lines are from a song of a village prostitute, lamenting the departure of her lover:

> *Tamak kheye geley na, bondhu hey!*
> *Kato dukhho money je balo.*
> *Oi je chander pashey tara hanshey,*
> *Tentul pata shukolo.*
> *Mara gange kumir bhashey,*
> *Shukaye sundir phul.*[8]
>
> (Friend, you left without finishing the *hookah*! You can't imagine how sad I feel. Look at the stars smiling around the moon. But the tamarind leaves are drying up here. The crocodile is floating on the dead river. The water-lily is withering.) Is the lonely woman trying to discover shades of her own feelings in the dying rural landscape? She also weaves in the image of a familiar phrase—that of the crocodile in a dry river—which is used to describe the plight of a professional desperately looking for clients in a shrinking market.

But suddenly we come across another song which is as

surprising as a smile on the face of a sick child, like the following lines:

> *Abar ki basanta eloe ?*
> *Ashamoye phutlo kusum,*
> *Saurabhey pran, jadu amar,*
> *Saurabhey pran akul holo.* [9]
>
> (Has spring come again? The flowers have blossomed at the wrong time. I can smell the fragrance, my darling! It's the fragrance that makes my soul restless.)

Significantly, in none of these songs can one discover any sign of woe, self-pity, penitence or sense of guilt—characteristics that were to be attributes of the fictionalized prostitutes in the Bengali romantic literature authored by the *bhadralok* writers during the next century. In this type of literature, the prostitute came to be stereotyped as either a vamp waiting to be reformed by a generous male, or a snivelling crypto-Sati ready to sacrifice everything to help her paramour return to his 'respectable wife'. But the women who appear in these songs suffer from no false modesty and are in no mood to encourage any illusions about themselves or the trade they ply. In their songs—sung either in the intimate surroundings of their brothels, or as jibes at their customers outside—they seemed to seek relief in mockery, which made each day possible for them in their miserable profession.

The words and expressions used in the songs and sayings of the red-light areas of 19th century Bengal refute the common characterization of women as dependent and soft, diffident and submissive. It will be noted that certain terms keep recurring—sometimes in a humorous tone, sometimes in a pejorative sense (*gaal*). Words like *nang* (a customer who used to be treated as a lover and enjoyed special privileges); *holdey-bhatar* (a sarcastic term used to describe a favourite customer for whom the prostitute cooked rice in *ghee* which gave it a *holdey* or yellowish hue. It is a play on the two words—*bhat* or rice, and *bhatar* which meant 'a husband'); *khanki* (whore); *bandha-khanki* (a prostitute who was a kept woman); *korey-ranri* (a young widow, the term *ranri* being interchangeable, meaning both widow and prostitute, which suggests the influx of a large number of widows into the profession); *bariulee* (the madam, or landlady who ran the brothel); *boshanoe* (literally meaning making someone sit, but in the slang of the prostitutes implying entertaining the customer); *chhenali* (coquetry); *gormi* (syphilis)—all these terms came to constitute the language of trade in the flesh market of 19th century Bengal. Like the acronyms used in international trade today, they formed the glossary of terms necessary to distinguish preferences of both the suppliers and the buyers in trade negotiations and describe the various functions and categories of people involved in the trade. The slang of the red-light world of 19th century Bengal was essentially a code language used for commercial transactions. In speaking this language, as also in the uninhibited use of explicitly sexual expressions, the prostitutes were merely talking shop, drawing upon the daily experiences of their own trade.

II

Any account of the songs of the red-light areas of 19th century Bengal will remain incomplete if we leave out the *baijis*, or those who were described in the 1867 official despatch on the Calcutta prostitutes as belonging to the 'fourth category' consisting of 'dancing women, Hindoo or Mussulman, living singly or forming a kind of chummery . . . receiving visitors without distinction of creed or caste' living mainly on Chitpore road and adjacent streets and by-lanes. The Muslim *baijis* who lived in these areas of Calcutta, as well as in old cities like Dhaka, were usually descendants of the Muslim dancers and musicians of northern India, who, displaced from the declining Moghul court, gravitated towards these cities of Bengal (and other parts of eastern India—like Patna in Bihar—which were developing into commercial and administrative centres under colonial rule) from the end of the 18th century. They kept up the tradition of the famous singer Nikki, and other *baijis* of those days, whose 'nautch' performances were the talk of the town in the early decades of the 19th century.

We can get a glimpse of the code of behaviour that lingered on among this class of *baijis* even at the turn of this century from the reminiscences of Goniur Raja—the self-proclaimed libertine whose encounter with a Hindu prostitute in Dhaka in the late 19th century we have described earlier. During a visit to Dhaka sometime in the early 20th century, Goniur Raja was taken by his friends to a Muslim *baiji*. On his being introduced as a 'zamindar', the *baiji* (who was known as 'Kazi Sahib's daughter') came towards him and saluted him in the traditional Muslim style of *adaab*. She then requested him to place his order for the type of song that he might like to listen to. She said that she could sing in three languages—Persian, Urdu and Bengali.[10]

It seems that among the upper- and middle-class Muslim prostitutes, the commerce of sex was interwoven with cultivation of skills in north Indian classical music. The Bengali Hindu *baijis* also shared the same training in those skills. Muslim *baijis* were quite often employed by Hindu women in the red-light areas to train their daughters in classical music. For instance, the famous actress Binodini, when she was eight years old, was apprenticed by her mother to a Muslim *baiji*, through whom she was introduced to impresarios who recruited her for the theatre.[11]

But, while Binodini carved out her cultural space as an actress on the Bengali stage (helped, no doubt, in a great measure by her childhood training in classical singing), many among her contemporaries in the Calcutta red-light areas chose their cultural space in the area of music as *baijis*. These Bengali *baijis*—mostly Hindus—were either mistresses of rich 'babus', or daughters from middle-class homes which had seen better days, but were in dire straits. They lived in the red-light areas, and were patronized by the Bengali gentry. They got themselves trained in classical Indian music and kathak dancing. Some among them also sang the Bengali *kirtans*—songs about episodes in the life of the god Krishna. These women were in great demand in Bengali households during religious ceremonies.

Thanks to the introduction of the gramophone at the turn of this century, songs of some of these Bengali *baijis* (who had been operating in Calcutta since the last quarter of the 19th century, and had survived till the beginning of the 20th) were recorded, and can still be retrieved. Although not all of these songs can be proved conclusively as original compositions by the *baijis* (some are traced to contemporary, or even earlier male poets), they were so intimately associated with their rendering by the Bengali *baijis* in those days that in public memory these songs came to be attributed to those popular *baijis* who sang them—Ascharyamay

Dasi, Bedanabala Dasi, Saralasundari, Krishnabhamini, among others.

Unlike the songs of the prostitutes quoted earlier, these songs of the *baijis* rarely touched upon the hazards of the profession. They were cocooned in a certain life-style of luxury—maintained as they were by rich 'babus' in two-storeyed or three-storeyed houses in north Calcutta, or patronized by scions of old Bengali aristocratic families who came to listen to their singing or to watch their dancing.

Composed in the traditional romantic vein, the songs of these Bengali *baijis* usually spoke about the strong longings of the beloved for the lover, or the trauma of being neglected by the lover. Some of these songs strike us with a beautiful turn of phrase, or a typical homely metaphor, that in those days was peculiar to the speech pattern of Bengali women.

Here is an example:

Sada pran keno chaye?
Bhalobashar mukhey agun,
Shatru berey paye
Bhalobeshey khub jenechhi,
Hatey hatey phal peyechhi,
Sararat kendey morechhi,
Tomar dhorey duti paye.' [12]

(Why does my soul want it always? Fie upon love! It's an enemy that binds my feet with shackles. I've had enough of love. I've suffered the consequences. I've wept the whole night, holding on to your feet).

Or, take, for example, another song which describes in a typically contemporary domestic vein, the trappings with which the woman wants to adorn herself to seduce her lover:

Didi lo! Medipata nokhgulotey poriye de na;
Sonela alta guley, ranga galey makhiye de na.
Keora-khayer diye pane, pran-bodhua mojbey praney,
Benitey jhampta diye, lachpachani shikhiye de na.' [13]

(Dear sister—please anoint my nails with the *mehdi* leaf: mix the golden lac-dye, and put it on my rosy cheeks. The screw-pine flower and catechu in the betel leaf are sure to make my lover lose himself. Please teach me how to flip around my plait of hair.)

The *baijis* appeared to be free from religious prejudices. Hindu *baijis* learnt from Muslim musicians, and Muslim *baijis* took lessons in kathak dancing from Hindu 'gurus'. Gahar Jan, the famous *baiji* of Eurasian origins, who was born in the 1870s in Calcutta, was believed to have enamoured Hindu devotees with her song:

> *Hari boley dak rashona ei bela ray,*
> *Ar emon din pabey na rey*[14]
>
> (Take the name of Hari now; you will never get a better chance.)

But the *baijis* were perhaps marginal to the red-light area, which was primarily dominated by the exclusively professional, commercial sex-workers—the prostitutes who, in their songs, expressed their existential feelings in more direct, and often abrasive, fashion. The life-style of the *baijis* in the red-light area constituted a twilight zone—with some among them maintained as mistresses by rich 'babus', and others occasionally entertaining customers. Their main source of livelihood was their expertise in singing and dancing in the classical north Indian mode. It was this expertise that earned them a certain recognition from the Bengali gentry which allowed them access to the cultural arena—through *mehfil* performances in the houses of the old aristocrats, invitations from middle-class Bengali homes for singing *kirtans*, and later the Bengali stage (where some among the *baijis* were employed as singers).

III

Some of the earliest expressions of protest and assertion of rights by prostitutes in print are available from letters in contemporary newspapers. Unlike the oral expressions—in songs and sayings, quoted earlier, where the language was the patois current in the red-light areas—these letters were composed in the chaste Bengali language of *bhadralok* society. The letters indicate that the writers either had past training in reading and writing, or were assisted by some outsiders. One letter, written by a *kulin* Brahmin woman in the early 1840s, states how she was married off when she was less than three years old, but continued to stay with her parents since the husband, being a typical *kulin* polygamist, went off on his marital spree elsewhere. Then, when she was sixteen years old, 'one afternoon, a fifty-year old man appeared at our doorsteps . . . I was shocked by his uncouth appearance, his decrepit limbs and gnarled white hair. I had never knowingly accepted him, never met him ever since I had come of age, there had never been any harmony of minds or love between the two of us, and yet he was my husband . . . Like his ugly appearance, at night I got a taste of his equally rude behaviour. The next morning, he collected some money from my father and left, never to return. I cannot describe my disturbed feelings at that time, what with the anguish caused by this experience, what with my approaching youth and the dismal prospect of remaining denied the happiness of a life with a husband. I just wept for days together. Although I genuinely tried to remain chaste and maintain the honour of my family and religion, finally, out of sheer torment I chose to go astray, and I came to Calcutta and I am living independently now in Mechhobazar. Last year, my younger sister also, after discord and quarrels with her husband, joined me here. Further, I have located twenty of my childhood female companions who, like me, are living in different parts of Calcutta.' The letter was signed by 'A prostitute living in Calcutta'.[15]

Another letter, published a decade later in the 1850s, signed by 'Displaced Prostitutes' from the Midnapur district of Bengal, highlights the discriminatory attitude followed by the authorities in the treatment of prostitutes. The letter refers to a complaint made in the columns of newspapers by a correspondent against the location of a brothel near a school in Midnapur town, as a result of which the prostitutes (who wrote the letter) were evicted from the houses they occupied, and now 'like hinds separated from a flock of deer, are mourning; while some have found shelter in thatched huts, some are staying in stalls at fairs, and others under trees . . .' The letter then hits out at the school authorities and wonders by what yardstick they made a distinction between the *bhadra* (the respectable) and the *abhadra* (the disreputable) when 'every man—whether honest or wicked in this town—has become rich through earnings made by their women . . . The so-called respectable wives . . . even with their husbands around, are without fear indulging in adultery, and yet because of their pride of wealth and right to chastity due to their marital status, they are worshipped . . . As for us, just because we expressed our disaffection with our husbands, and left them, are we to be treated as sinners?' Continuing in this vein, the letter paints a devastating picture of the life-style of these *bhadra-kula-badhus* (the wives from the respectable households): 'When these powerful, so-called respectable women, in order to ensnare the males, expand the net of their swaying hips and with their slightly veiled side-long glances and smiles . . . move around near the school, do the students put blinkers on their eyes? Or, do they get struck by those arrows?' The letter then adds: 'These proud women from the prestigious and respectable families can never be stained by the dark stamp of ignominy like us . . . But, after they retire at night . . . they have to demonstrate love to their husbands whom they hate.'[16]

The letter quoted above is an excellent illustration of how a socially ostracized community looked at contemporary societal norms that operated against them, as well as of their perception of the behaviour of the privileged members of their own gender group, who could get away with anything just because they were protected by the socially respectable institution of marriage. That this appraisal of theirs was not a bias-induced exaggeration is corroborated by numerous contemporary newspaper reports and commentaries complaining about adultery among women in respectable middle-class Bengali homes. Typical is the following observation made by the editors of a Brahmo Samaj newspaper, who, while condemning adultery among these women, appeared at the same time to understand the logic behind their behaviour: 'When they [the wives in *bhadralok* society], leading a life of imprisonment, watch the prostitutes enjoying freedom, and observe their husbands carousing with the prostitutes, is it not natural that they would be inflamed with a similar passion for immoral deeds which they mistake for pleasure ?'[17]

What was felt at the gut level by the prostitutes of Midnapur in the 1850s was conceptualized with theoretical precision some thirty years later by Frederick Engels, when he wrote: '. . . marriage is determined by the class position of the participants, and to that extent always remains marriage of convenience . . . this marriage of convenience often enough turns into the crassest prostitution—sometimes on both sides . . . monogamy and prostitution in the modern world, although opposites, are nevertheless inseparable opposites, poles of the same social conditions . . .'[18]

IV

A major development in the Bengali cultural field in the 1870s helped the prostitutes in a large measure to articulate their grievances and assert their rights through the printing press. This was the recruitment of actresses from the red-light areas to perform in female roles in Bengali plays (since *bhadralok* families did not allow their women to perform alongside male actors on the public stage). Actresses like Golap, Jagattarini, Elokeshi, Tinkari and Binodini left a lasting impression on the contemporary Bengali audience. Their impact was not confined to Calcutta. The National Theatre and the Hindu National Theatre (the leading theatre groups of those days) took them along on tours of different districts of Bengal and outside, where they staged selected plays from their repertoire. This inspired members of their community in other parts of Bengal to join the burgeoning theatre movement. We learn from a contemporary newspaper of Dhaka in East Bengal that 'some Muslim prostitutes' were acting in plays staged in a hall called Purbabanga Rangabhumi in that city in November, 1880. [19]

These actresses learnt to communicate in the new literary Bengali idiom (fashioned by *bhadralok* society), by taking on roles in which they played heroines who often had to utter dialogues in high-flown, ornate Bengali. Some among them also learnt from their *bhadralok* patrons in the theatre world, or from those educated Bengali gentlemen who kept them as mistresses—a common practice in 19th century Bengal. Among them, Binodini left behind an autobiography, where the narrative of her own struggles and successes provides us with an insight into the travails of the members of her profession in contemporary Bengal. Although the entire portrayal of her life and events is bathed in the diffused glow of her grace and sense of dignity, it is shot through by memories of bitter experiences of persecution and humiliation that were the common lot of prostitutes. Binodini is unsparing in her denunciation of those responsible for the plight of women like her, and shows an unerring understanding of the socio-economic powers that operated in her society, as in the following passage: 'Is the life of a prostitute disgraceful and despicable? But then, how did she become disgraced and despised? Surely, she did not become a despicable creature the moment she came out from her mother's womb! . . . It is necessary to find out who made her life abominable. It is possible that some voluntarily choose to plunge into darkness and pave their way to hell. But many are lured by men, and by believing in their false promises end up by carrying on their heads the load of calumny and suffer hellish agony. Who are these men? Are not some of them members of the same male community who are admired and respected in society?' She speaks on behalf of her own self, as well as her sisters in the profession, when she adds: 'Only those women who have been cheated in this way and have been forced to turn their lives into a wilderness, can understand how agonizing is the life of a prostitute. Only they can feel deeply the poignance of the pain.'

Binodini gives a perceptive analysis of the pervasive powers of these men, who, by virtue of their position in society, tried to control the options and choices of the prostitutes: It is these men who deceive the women, who become the leaders of society, and administer the moral norms in order to crush these same unfortunate women. Just as they have ruined these women, they take the utmost care to prevent the children of these women from getting admitted to schools or vocational institutes, where the women might send their innocent sons and daughters in order to provide them with a path of virtue. Because of the sanctimonious moral ideas of these men, the miserable boys and girls are forced to take to the path of sin, and watch the world with venomous eyes.' [20]

That Binodini's allegations are not without foundation is evident from the case of the *baiji* Heera Bulbul's son whose admission to Hindu College was opposed by the Bengali *bhadralok* society in 1853 (as mentioned in Chapter IV).

Another interesting literary piece left by an actress of those days is the play *Apurba Sati* ((1875). It was written by Sukumari Dutta, formerly known as Golap, who was one of the first women recruited from the red-light area to join the stage in 1873 (to act in Michael Madhusudan Dutt's *Shormishta*). The plot of the play is melodramatic, but it gives an incisive picture of the manners and motives of an ageing prostitute, Haramoni. She tries to initiate her daughter into the profession, hoping that she will look after her during old age. But Nalini, the daughter, falls in love with the son of a zamindar, Chandraketu, who was introduced by Haramoni to Nalini as her first customer. The young couple elope, and escape to Benaras. Chandraketu is finally traced down there by his father who forcibly brings him back. Nalini breaks down, and after a hysterical outburst, commits suicide. A heartbroken Chandraketu follows suit soon after.

The author of *Apurba Sati* (the title, incidentally, means 'A Unique Chaste Woman', obviously used to describe the self-sacrifice of the daughter of a prostitute), left the red-light area after her marriage to a Bengali Brahmo *bhadralok* in 1874. But while writing the play a year later, she could not forget the environment and the trials and tribulations with which she grew up. Even though fictionalized, the story and dialogues of *Apurba Sati* reflected the lot of her sisters, who still continued to plod away in the red-light areas of Calcutta—the fears and calculations of an ageing prostitute like Haramoni, the dreams and efforts to escape by younger inhabitants, like her daughter, Nalini.

Haramoni is introduced in the first scene of the first act of the play through a soliloquy, delivered in familiar feminine terms, interspersed with typical women's idioms of those days. The soliloquy sums up her plight, and sets the tone for the course of action by the characters in the play—since she manipulates the course by trying to trap customers for her daughter, whom she wants to initiate into her profession.

Although a translation can rarely recapture the vivacity of the Bengali women's dialect, it is worth making an effort—just to convey the feelings of an old prostitute of 19th century Bengal, as observed by someone who was once a member of the profession. Haramoni speaks to herself:

> 'What am I to do now? I have now reached old age. After having passed the three stages of life (*tin kal*—a common

> term in Bengali, meaning childhood, youth and adulthood), I am now stuck at the final one. I haven't had any sons to feed me. There's this daughter only. But what can she do ? We don't have any property either, by selling which we can get food and clothing.' [21]

In Scene two of Act one, Haramoni decides to initiate the daughter, and dresses her up, daubing her face with thick make-up—lac-dye on her lips, and powder on her cheeks—the cosmetics that were popular among the prostitutes. She then asks her to stand at the door waiting for the customer.

At the end of Act IV, when Nalini confesses to her mother about her love for Chandraketu in a high-flown declamatory style, Haramoni lashes out at her:

> 'What a bother! Look at the hussy! Pretending to be a chaste lady! What will you do with your chastity? It butters no parsnips. Will chastity fill your stomach? Arrange for that first . . . Who will feed you?'[22]

Actresses like Binodini and Sukumari Dutta faced tremendous opposition from *bhadralok* society, in spite of their histrionic talents. Such resistance continued till the beginnings of the 20th century. When the famous actor and playwright, Girish Chandra Ghosh (who trained some of the best actresses from the red-light area in the 19th century) died in 1912, his pupils from among the actresses were not allowed to pay their homage to their master at the public condolence meeting held in the Calcutta Town Hall. They appealed to another famous actor colleague of theirs—Amarendranath Dutta—in the following words: 'We do not have the right to enter any public function in Town Hall, or any other place. But we hope that someone like you who had been dedicated to the task of presiding over the theatre, will not deny us—these miserable women—the opportunity of weeping in our homes, and of paying homage on bent knees on the stage, to our master and god, Girish Babu.'[23]

Amarendranath Dutta responded to their appeal by organizing a special condolence meeting at the Star Theatre that year, where he presided and invited the actresses to speak on Girish Ghosh. Addressing the 'respectable' ladies and gentlemen who had gathered there, one of the actresses, Susheelabala said

'We may be prostitutes, we may be ostracized by society—but we are human beings. You may not believe it, but like you people, we are also capable of feeling joy and grief. Like you, we also laugh when we are happy. Like you again, our cheeks also are flooded with tears when we are lashed by bitter sorrow. Surely you will not grudge these equal rights of humble women like us . . . If the sorrow of the disciples at the death of their master is natural, why should our tears, our wailings, our mourning, be considered crimes?' Another actress, Norisundari, paid homage to her teacher in the following words: 'After my birth, your respectable society said to me—Since you haven't been born in a family that is certified as virtuous, you will continue to commit sins all your life, and we, thanks to our power of virtue, will hate and abuse you. But Girish Babu wasn't that virtuous! He was [on the other hand] a great man. So, he could make a wretched woman like me utter the sweet dialogues of *Chaitanya-leela . . . Bilwa-mangal . . .*'[24]

The speeches of these actresses are lit with flashes of tongue-in-cheek remarks against the self-righteousness of a stodgy *bhadralok* society, and are dignified by their own self-confidence in their talents. Their sense of pride in performing with aplomb in the roles of religious saints in plays like *Chaitanya-leela,* obviously gave them the right to claim superiority over their lack-lustre sisters from among the respectable *bhadralok* society. They lost no chance to drive home the point that while members of this society were compelled to admire their enactment of the roles of these saints whom the Hindus worshipped, on the stage, it was these same *bhadralok* who determinedly sought to ostracize them in social life.

The oral songs and sayings of the red-light areas, the printed letters of prostitutes, and the reminiscences of actresses, reflect the different levels at which the profession was practised in 19th century Calcutta and mofussil towns. The songs—judging by their direct and uninhibited mode of expression—can be traced to the poorer prostitutes, those described in the British records as coming from the 'low castes', who were compelled to solicit in the streets and, therefore, often engaged in slanging matches with their prospective clientele, thus earning the displeasure of the authorities as 'the moral plague of our principle thoroughfares, where they exhibit their persons with a barefacedness unsurpassed in any other part of the world.' The 'barefacedness' comes out in their songs. Some of the songs were, perhaps, also composed by the slightly better-off, whom the official records described as 'Hindoo women living under a Bareewallah, either male or female' receiving 'Hindoo visitors only without distinction of caste.' The songs about fights with *bariulees*, or the particular one on the encounter between the Hindu prostitute and the Muslim customer, can be put in this category.

The two published letters, mentioned earlier, could have been written by prostitutes belonging to the other category, those described in official records as 'Hindoo women of good caste, who, being possessed of small means, live by themselves.' The chaste Bengali used in the letters suggest the high caste origins which could have provided them with access to some elementary education, or to ghost-writers from their peer group. Unlike the songs, where one hardly finds any signs of harking back to superior caste origins, the letter of the prostitute published in the early 1840s, harps on her *kulin* Brahmin background. The grouses voiced in the letter by the Midnapur prostitutes—ousted from their homes—again in chaste Bengali, in the 1850s, suggest the fears felt by them about being dispossessed of their possessions and reduced to street-walkers like the low-caste prostitutes who occupied the lowest level in the hierarchy of their profession.

The actresses were a class apart—although they shared to a large extent the social discrimination and humiliation and emotional deprivation experienced by those occupying the lower levels of the profession. Even if some among them came from the poorer lower castes, they succeeded in overcoming the handicap in the theatre world, which allowed them a space which recognized their talents, irrespective of their class and caste origins. They reached the position of those who, according to the official records, belonged to the upper category, those who 'live a retired life and who are kept or supported by rich Natives.' The *baijis*, also, could be put in this category. Binodini's memoirs (where she narrates how she learnt singing from a *baiji*) give us a glimpse of the life-style and manners, the aspirations and struggles of this class of women. They also reveal the extent of humiliation and persecution that they continued to suffer a every step, in spite of their acquiring fame as actresses, and proficiency in the language and literary forms, and norms of behaviour that made them hardly distinguishable from the *bhadramohilas* or the women of respectable society. Their social status as 'fallen women' (the term invented by society to imprison them in an untouchable pigeon-hole) remained a hurdle in the way of their acceptance by society at large.

The available literature, ranging from the songs to the letters of prostitutes and published reminiscences of actresses, opens up a huge gallery of life as lived by these women in 19th century Calcutta and surrounding areas, where we come across a variety of women who were forced to inhabit the condemned fringes of contemporary society. Against the murky background of low retreats, where alcohol and cheap perfume mingled, the poorest among them scrutinized everything around them with a cynical detachment. Their songs and sayings display an agressive assertiveness, making the best of a bad job to which they seemed to reconcile themselves without any hope of change. At another level, in surroundings which were slightly better, the middle-class prostitutes who could afford the leisure of reflecting on their present and future, wrote about the pains of their livelihood, harking back on their descent from the upper caste, respectable families from which they had fallen, and aspiring for their reincorporation into that society.

The impressions left by the prostitutes of 19th century Bengal—in their different manifestations, corresponding to their respective socio-economic positions—build up the image of a multi-dimensional life-style that was filled with trickery and combat, where each one sought to carve out a niche for herself—some by fighting their way from a lowly position into the sun of the footlights of the stage; some by asserting their right to be taken seriously as individuals with definite views; some by falling into attitudes of an audacity that invented a provocative mode of communication through witticism, double entrende and ribaldry by which they could laugh at their grim surroundings.

VI
The Burden of the 'Bhadralok'

> '. . . the prostitutes should by no means be allowed to enter the precincts of the 'Mela' (exhibition). If you want to do good for the country, anything that is visibly ugly must be kept out of public sight.'
>
> —Editorial in a 19th century Bengali journal.[1]

The attitude of the 19th century Bengali *bhadralok* to prostitution and prostitutes betrayed a peculiar ambivalence which can be traced to the dilemma that these members of the male gentry were facing in trying to reconcile certain traditional norms of behaviour and grudgingly accepted social practices in contemporary Bengali society, on the one hand, and a new set of moral values and code of duties that they were cultivating under a colonial administration, on the other.

As for the prevalent social practices, maintenance of mistressses (who usually came from the red-light areas, or the so-called 'disreputable' fringes of society) was quite often a common practice among male members of the old *sambhranta* or aristocratic feudal families. The habit of visiting brothels and consorting with actresses was not confined to the gauche, half-baked 'babus', but marked the life-style of even some educated *bhadraloks*. Given this situation, the leaders of the Bengali *bhadralok* society faced an extremely awkward predicament whenever required to take a position on prostitution. Their Victorian English mentors harped on the evils of prostitution (although back in their homeland, it thrived, thanks to the patronage offered by members of both the English aristocracy and the bourgeoisie).[2] 'Respectability' in society, according to the norms set by these mentors, implied avoidance of demonstrative displays of licentiousness (like advertisement of power and prestige by 'building a pucca house for a mistress', as indulged in by the first generation of 'babus' in the early years of the 19th century, or reckless whoring and drinking among members of the English-educated Bengali middle-classes in the later decades), and stress instead on a 'happy married life' based on the cultivation of genteel norms and domestic virtues by both the husband and the wife.

Yet, the *bhadralok* could not just sweep prostitution under the carpet, as members of their own society patronized the institution. The patronage, under the new norms, therefore, had to be carried out as discreetly as possible. But while the needs of these members of their society had to be accommodated, there was a fear looming large—the fear of their wives increasingly getting estranged from wayward husbands and leaving their homes to choose the independent life-style of prostitutes. The fear was expressed in no uncertain terms by the Brahmo Samaj journal *Tattobodhini Patrika* in 1846 (quoted in Chapter V).

In fact, the independent life-style of the prostitutes in 19th century Calcutta did allow some among them to dictate terms to sections of the *bhadralok* society. The rich prostitutes—although socially ostracized, as were their sisters in the profession—wielded enough financial power to hire the services of different sectors of the market, like those of lawyers (to fight their cases in the courts—particularly after the enactment of the Contagious Diseases Act), builders (to construct houses for them), doctors (whom they could pay to buy certificates that exempted them from the humiliating medical examination under the CDA), gold merchants (to buy jewellery), among many others. In the market economy of colonial capitalist society, where monetary transactions were beginning to override social taboos, *bhadralok* professionals and traders had no qualms about being hired by, and depending on, prostitutes for their income. Sections of the Bengali *bhadralok* society were, therefore, willy-nilly entangled with members of the 'oldest profession' in 19th century Calcutta and its suburbs.

Even the orthodox Bengali Hindu religious establishment

could not afford to ignore the rich and prosperous among the prostitutes, who became milch cows for the priests. The prostitutes were eager to observe religious rituals during sacred occasions like the various pujas. This stemmed from a desire to emulate their sisters in *bhadralok* households, as well as from a guilt complex that led them to appease the Hindu gods and goddesses (and Muslim saints) to atone for what society regarded as sins committed by them. The Brahmin priests were equally eager to get the best out of the prostitutes' earnings by presiding every now and then over some religious ritual or other in the brothels. Otherwise extremely puritanical in matters like pollution (of Brahminical purity by contamination with 'untouchables', among whom prostitutes were also included), these priests had no qualms about visiting brothels and accepting from the prostitutes cash and gifts—which, according to their religious principles, ought to have been rejected as 'tainted' by sin!

A contemporary 19th century account describes how the Brahmin priests used to rationalize their acceptance of prostitutes as their clients. While painting a typical evening scene in a lane (called Harkata Gali—which still survives in Calcutta today) in a red-light area, thronged by whore-mongers and rakes of all types, the author suddenly introduces a pair of characters who look totally out of place. 'From one house emerged an old Brahmin, with a tuft of hair springing from the back of his head, accompanied by his son. They were carrying bundles which held together a variety of goods. Both of them were chewing betel leaves. The old man addressed his son: 'Did you carefully watch, my boy, how I've gathered these clients of mine? They may be whores; but when it comes to giving gifts [to Brahmins] they are head and shoulders above all the kings and the nobility . . . I am introducing you to all these clients of mine. You never know how long I'll live. If you, therefore, can satisfy their whims, you'll live happily ever after! But be careful! Don't ever reveal this in your village home. The villagers will ostracize us and turn us into outcastes.'[3]

The acceptance of prostitutes by certain sections of the Hindu religious establishment of Calcutta could have been partly influenced by the traditional scriptural sanction (which we referred to in Chapter I), and partly by the purely commercial motive of exploiting the rich prostitutes by playing on their sense of guilt (and sin) and persuading them to shell out money, in expiation, for the construction of temples and maintenance of a retinue of parasites, supposedly looking after the various rituals. We come across a report—from the early decades of the 20th century—about a prostitute called Surat Kumari donating a house owned by her on Manicktollah Main Road (in north Calcutta) to a religious preceptor called Prabhu Jagadbandhu. Her house was turned into a temple called 'Maha-uddharan Math'.[4]

The question of legitimacy of earnings from prostitutes appears to be a bone of contention that troubled religious authorities in the past in other countries, too. The European counterparts of the Indian Brahmin clergy came up with their own canonical rules for accepting money or gifts from prostitutes for religious purposes. One medieval Christian priest, for instance, made the following curious proposition: ' . . . she does evil in being a prostitute, but she does not do evil in receiving the price of her labour, it being admitted that she is a prostitute.' He, then, added consoling advice for the prostitutes: '. . . it is possible to repent of practising prostitution while keeping the profits of prostitution for the purpose of giving alms . . .' Then, justifying the church's demand of money from prostitutes, the priest rationalized: '. . . if the prostitute perfumes and adorns herself so as to attract with false allures and give the impression of a beauty and seductiveness which she does not possess, the client buying what he sees, which, in this case, is deceptive, the prostitute then commits a sin, and she should not keep the profit it brings her. If the client saw her as she really is, he would give her only a pittance, but as she appears beautiful and brilliant to him, he gives a handsome sum. In this case, she should keep only the pittance, and return the rest to the client she has deceived, or to the Church . . .'[5]

I

The 19th century Bengali *bhadralok* leaders chose a via-media. Knowing well that prostitution could not be eradicated, they decided to sequester the prostitutes and render the institution as unnoticeable as possible. One of the first steps they took was to try to banish them from the *bhadra pallis* (the Bengali term for the areas inhabited by the 'respectable' and educated gentry). In Calcutta, in 1856, the Vidyotsahini Sabha, an association set up by Bengali intellectuals, and headed by a scion of one of the city's best-known aristocratic families—the famous author Kaliprasanna Sinha—appealed to the colonial administration to issue orders to the prostitutes to move out from the city to its outskirts and ply their trade there. It describes how the young men from Bengali respectable homes had ready access to the brothels in the heart of Calcutta. [6]

Ironically again, the same letter from these *bhadralok* leaders of 19th century Bengali society, complained that the houses from which the prostitutes were operating in the city, were being let out by members of their own community—the rich Bengali house-owners in north Calcutta and other parts of the city. The letter bemoaned that these Bengali landlords were polluting the 'social environs of the respectable parts of the residential area.'[7]

Similar demands for the ousting of prostitutes from 'respectable' areas were made by the *bhadralok* in other towns of Bengal, too. The *Dhaka Prakash* (brought out from Dhaka in East Bengal) in an editorial in 1865 asked the government to pay attention to the need for 'reducing whore-mongering and the inclination [amongst women] towards whoring.' It then came out with a three-pronged plan of action: 'First, let there be a system of exacting taxes at a higher rate from the prostitutes . . . so that they can just survive at a subsistence level and are denied any opportunity of enjoying any luxury. Secondly, it is necessary to put an end to the prostitute's right to dispose of her property through a will. A law should be enacted to empower the government to take away her entire property after her death. Thirdly, the prostitutes should be removed from the city to its outskirts, so that the minds of ordinary men are not polluted by their allurement.' The editorial, then added that if the three measures were carried out, '. . . housewives will not wish to become prostitutes after watching the hardship of the prostitutes.'[8]

In the *bhadralok* bid to curtail the movements and rights of prostitutes, pressures were brought upon them in various ways. In 1854, a Bengali judge, Rashomoy Dutta, succeeded in persuading the government to stop prostitutes from plaining against their customers in courts. Welcoming the decision, a Bengali newspaper observed: 'Calcutta's prostitutes used to approach the lower courts with false accusations against respectable gentlemen. Their complaints ran as follows: such and such person, a raja, or a rich man, kept me and agreed to pay me a certain amount as wages, but has not paid me for several months. Following this, the judges of the lower courts used to serve summons on these men. But the respectable gentlemen could not get embroiled in legal disputes with the prostitutes, and, therefore, opted for out-of-court settlements under which they were required to pay the money to the prostitutes. This provided the prostitutes with an excellent opportunity of earning money.' Hailing the government's decision to stop this practice, the newspaper added: 'Now, the respectable gentlemen have finally been able to extricate themselves from that net woven by the prostitutes.'[9]

Not all the *bhadralok* were so lucky. In 1872, we hear of a case that came up before the Calcutta High Court, where a Bengali Brahmin *bhadralok*, Goureenath Mookerjee, sued a prostitute, Modhoomonee, for not paying rent for a room which he let out to her on his premises in Krishnanagar, in which she lived and plied her vocation. While the plaintiff argued that contracts between prostitutes and people of other classes were recognized by the old Hindu legislation, and since the litigants were Hindus, the Hindu law ought to govern the disposal of the case, the court held that the plaintiff could not recover the rent, as a 'Court of Justice would give no assistance to the enforcement of a contract opposed to public policy . . .' It refused to grant judicial aid in enforcing a contract which 'infringed public policy and offended public morality.'[10]

In order to restrict the movement of the prostitutes outside their residences, the *bhadralok* sought to prevent them from attending public entertainments. Complaints about the presence of prostitutes at functions like theatrical performances or fairs were quite common in contemporary Bengali newspapers, which urged the organizers of such functions to bar the entry of prostitutes. Typical is the following comment by a newspaper brought out by the Brahmo reformer Keshub Sen, warning the organizers of 'Hindu Mela' (an annual fair exhibiting traditional Bengali crafts and skills, sponsored by enterprising *bhadralok*): '. . . the prostitutes should by no means be allowed to enter the precincts of the 'Mela'. If you want to do good for the country, anything that is visibly ugly must be kept out of public sight.'[11]

Sometimes, more drastic methods were resorted to in order to oust prostitutes from their homes. In the 1880s the Brahmos acquired a plot of land for building a temple in Chittagong town. The plot, however, happened to lie next to a colony of prostitutes. One night, the entire colony was razed by a devastating fire, after which, when the prostitutes tried to build their homes anew, the local municipality and the Brahmo Samaj raised objections. The prostitutes went to the court to assert their rights, but were defeated, and finally driven out.[12]

Even when some women from the red-light areas were invited to participate in cultural activities, like acting in the theatre, by a section of *bhadralok* society, other sections tried their best to prevent their entry into that area. Manomohan Bosu, a well-known literary figure of those days, lamenting the presence of prostitutes as actresses on the public stage, wrote: 'Young *bhadralok* carousing with prostitutes in their midst, dancing and acting on stage, in public with prostitutes—how can we see and listen to all this? How can we suffer this?'[13] Manomohan did not stop at this. When, in 1874, Goshthabihari Dutta dared to marry the actress, Golap, Manomohan composed a scurrilous song, which was meant to be sung as a *nagar sankeertan* (a popular urban form of street singing in procession). The song lampooned Golap, reminding her that when she was a public woman, she had had a hundred husbands and that fate brought to her a gem of a husband through the theatre greenroom. It described Golap as 'dressed as a chaste woman, but looking for sport.'[14]

Even the famous Brahmo reformer, Keshub Sen, denounced the marriage. A news journal edited by him came out with the comment: 'Where is the proof that a woman who had turned her soul into hell through years of dissoluteness, can overnight become a chaste woman?. . . We indeed regard every unchaste woman as a miserable creature. But then, so do we regard every drunkard . . . In order to show compassion to such miserable creatures, one should first try to reform their minds . . .'[15]

One must hasten to add that there were exceptions among the *bhadralok*. Some, in their attitude and behaviour towards the prostitutes, demonstrated considerable sympathy and understanding—an effort that needed a lot of courage in Bengali middle-class society in those days, which was increasingly controlled by prudish Victorian values.

The theatre in Calcutta, and elsewhere, provided an important space for interdependence on a different level between the *bhadralok* directors and actors on the one hand, and the actresses from the red-light areas on the other. It also offered ample scope for mutual understanding between members of two groups who, although divided along gender and class lines, shared the public scorn and ridicule of Bengali middle-class society. Like the actresses who were already rejected by that society as pariahs, the *bhadralok* who worked with them on the public stage were shunned by 'respectable' society, which denounced them as drunkards and womanizers (an attitude which persisted in this society till as late as the 1940s). It was this common plight which, in a large measure, helped in the creation of the space for their interdependence and mutual understanding.

At the professional level, collaboration between male theatre personalities like Girish Ghosh, Amritalal Bosu, Ardhendushekhar Mustafi, Amarendra Dutta and actresses like Binodini, Golap (known as Sukumari Dutta after her marriage with Goshthabihari Dutta), Tinkari, Tarasundari, in the course of producing the plays, often worked as a catalyst for members of both the groups. It led to the training and flowering of some of the most gifted actresses of the 19th century Bengali stage. When Binodini in her reminiscences spoke of her fruition as an artiste under the lovingly careful teaching of Girish Ghosh, she was faithfully recording the fascinating experience of the discovery of one's own creative talents under such training—an experience shared by Golap, Tinkari, and many others of her peer group.

The skills cultivated by these actresses from the red-light areas in the course of traditional trade thus found in the theatre an opening for artistic expression. This contiguity between the world of prostitutes and that of the theatre—which had marked the history of dramaturgy both in the West and the East, both in the ancient past and the early modern age—was best described by Baudelaire: 'What can be said of the courtesan can also be said, with reservations, of the actress; for the latter, too, is a manufactured confection and a thing of public pleasure. But where the actress is concerned, the conquest and the booty are more noble, more spiritual. Her business is to win general favour not only by her physical beauty, but also by talents of the rarest order. If on one side the actress is akin to the courtesan, on the other side she is akin to the poet.' Baudelaire's observations on his contemporary courtesan-cum-actresses of mid-19th century France move beyond spatial and temporal confines when he says: 'We must remember that, apart from any natural beauty and even from any artificial beauty, all human creatures are stamped with the idiom of their trade—a characteristic that can physically express itself in ugliness, but also in a sort of beauty of the profession.'[16]

The male participants in the Bengali theatre also underwent a change. Amritalal Bosu makes an honest self-appraisal when he speaks of his own transformation from an almost allergic misogynist into a sympathetic friend: 'I was under the mistaken belief that, considering the class of women the actresses would be chosen from, they were bound to be licentious and indisciplined, and even if able to sing and dance, would be quite incapable of doing justice to the roles of superior women . . . But this belief was thoroughly shaken within two weeks of their arrival. Their salary was extremely low compared to the present rate, but the five actresses who first came to us—their extreme desire [thirst] for proper instruction in all aspects of theatre, their commitment and respect for the sanctity of the workplace, has obliged many of us men, to take stock of our own "character". They [the actresses] have frankly told us "You have rescued us from inexpressible suffering by opening up this new path for the oppressed . . ."'[17]

Amritalal echoed the feelings of most of his male colleagues in the theatre when, at the death of Gangamoni Dasi, a famous singer and actress of those times, in a poignant moment he composed a poem describing her as *Shishya, sakhi, sahachari . . . rangamanchey baar baar samparka hoyechhey aar sukhey dukhhey sama sathi prabashey sadaney . . .*' (Pupil, friend and companion . . . our affinity deepened on the stage, and you were my comrade in happiness and sorrow, at home and abroad . . .)[18]

Recognition and appreciation of these actresses of the red-light areas came from an unexpected quarter of 19th century *bhadralok* society. Ramakrishna—the priest of Rani Rashmoni's Kali Temple at Dakshineshwar, near Calcutta, who, by the early 1880s, had become a sort of cult figure and worshipped as a saint among Calcutta's educated gentry—visited the Star Theatre in the city on 21 September 1884, to watch the actress Binodini in the role of the 16th century Bengali religious reformer Chaitanya in the play *Chaitanya-leela*. A high-strung mystic by nature, Ramakrishna was immediately overwhelmed by Binodini's acting and after the performance was over, was reported to have walked into the greenroom to give Binodini his blessing. The event created a sensation. While the highly-honoured Ramakrishna conferring his blessing on a prostitute-actress offered some respectability to the Bengali stage (damned till then by Bengali middle-class society, among whom the theatre was popular, but never respected), it initiated a debate among the *bhadralok* on the need to redefine their attitude towards prostitutes. As Ramakrishna continued to develop his friendship with the hitherto condemned theatre personalities—the famous playwright-director-actor Girish Ghosh, in particular—and shed his benign grace on actresses like Binodini, some among his *bhadralok* disciples started expressing their misgivings about him. The German Orientalist, Max Muller, who was an admirer of Ramakrishna's, tells us how he was pestered by 'a relative of Keshub Chandra Sen (who was Ramakrishna's disciple)' who brought charges against Ramakrishna relating to his permissive attitude towards prostitutes. Max Muller, defending Ramakrishna, says: 'If, as we are told, he did not show sufficient abhorrence of prostitutes, he does not stand quite alone in this among the founders of religion,' and then goes on to quote similar instances from the life of Christ.[19]

Differences among Ramakrishna's disciples on taking a position regarding prostitutes continued even after their master's death. One of them complained to Swami Vivekananda against prostitutes being allowed to attend religious festivals at the Dakshineshwar Temple, sometime in 1896. Vivekananda, of course, wrote back in his usual spirit of defiant irreverence: 'I pray to the Lord—let prostitutes come in hundreds to pay obeisance to Him. Even if not a single *bhadralok* comes to the temple, let it be. Let others come—prostitutes, drunkards, thieves, robbers—every one. His doors are open for all.'[20]

It would be worthwhile to analyse Ramakrishna's liberal attitude towards prostitutes. Did it stem from his social background of a rural society where prostitutes—even though outcastes—were offered a certain space? Did it have anything to do with his propensity towards eclecticism in religion, which he extended to social issues too? An investigation into this aspect of Ramakrishna's thoughts—still to be undertaken—is, however, beyond the scope of the present discussion.

Outside the circle of theatre artistes and Ramakrishna's disciples, there was another section of Bengali *bhadralok* who got involved with the problem of prostitution. They often empathized with the prostitutes, and tried to take initiatives to 'rehabilitate' them in society by arranging marriages of their daughters with liberal-minded *bhadralok*. The Brahmo reformer, Shibnath Shastri, tells us how he succeeded in marrying off Lakshmimani, the fourteen-year-old daughter of a Dhaka prostitute, to a young Brahmo. The news prompted a few other prostitutes to approach him. One of them—Thakomoni—called him over to her house in a red-light area, and offered her infant girl to him to save her from the profession which she would be forced to adopt if the daughter grew up in that environment. When Shibnath reminded her that she was still suckling her baby girl, Thakomoni replied, 'That's a problem. But I think she'll forget her mother if she gets a little affection and care. She'll get devoted to your wife, once she showers love on her.' Shibnath asked Thakomoni to wait a few months more, but then lost track of her. Recounting his experience with Thakomoni, Shibnath comments: 'Maybe she changed her mind. Or, maybe she could not trace me.'[21]

'Change of mind' among the prostitutes was an imponderable that the Bengali *bhadralok* reformers often encountered when they tried to help them with promises of 'rehabilitation'. Another Brahmo reformer, Nilmoni Chakravarty, narrates in his autobiography how, during his youth in Calcutta in the 1880s, he was approached one evening by a young medical student who sought his help to rescue a prostitute who wanted to escape from her profession. The next morning, when Nilmoni with another Brahmo friend of his, arrived at her house in a 'narrow lane in Burrabazar', and reminded her of her wish to be rescued, 'she started giggling'. Commenting on the unsuccessful venture, Nilmoni concludes: 'The woman's mind changed.'[22]

Why did the prostitutes 'change their minds', when given a chance to quit their profession? Was it 'caprice'—the quality usually associated with the stereotyped image fixed in the *bhadralok* mind? It is significant that Nilmoni Chakravarty was put off by the 'giggling' of the prostitutes whom he wanted to rescue, and did not feel it necessary to pursue her case. Even Shibnath Shastri, when he was first approached by Thakomoni one day on the streets of Calcutta, was revolted by her 'immodest behaviour and laughter' and by her using the intimate term of address, *tumi,* instead of *apni* (reserved for the respectable gentry and elders). Only when another Brahmo friend of his, Kedarnath Ray (who, at one time, was engaged in social work among prostitutes) persuaded him to visit Thakomoni, did he agree.[23] It thus seems that the *bhadralok* reformers, their well-meaning intentions notwithstanding, tended to treat the prostitutes as pathological cases, miserable creatures who could not exercise a rational control over their lives.

But there could have been rational choices behind these prostitutes' reluctance to follow up their initial attempts to break out from their profession. Was it a basic distrust in the promises of emancipation held out to them by a member of the male gentry? Members of this same group had initially been responsible for seducing many of them into the profession, and still continued to exploit them. How could they trust men? Binodini, in her autobiography, at times, explodes into bitter outbursts against men, like the following: 'We also crave the love of husbands. But where can we get it ? Who will exchange his heart for mine? There is no dearth of men charming us with talks of love, but out of lust. But who will wish to offer his heart and test us whether we also have hearts? Has anyone ever found out whether we were the first to deceive, or whether we learnt to deceive after having been deceived?'[24]

Binodini's stunning indictment shakes us up to the recognition of the stark fact that the terms of relationship in a hierarchically ordered society are dictated by those in power. These terms are replicated at the different levels of such a society. They percolate down to all the levels. In the descending order of the struggle for existence conducted on the principles of laissez faire, the art of deception becomes all pervasive. This art is crucial to the technology of power that enables those who wield power—at different levels—to control the ever-widening circle of human activities.

In the male-dominated hierarchically ordered society, among all strata of women, the prostitute continues to occupy the singular position of being a victim of male deception (representing those who are seduced and then deserted by men) as well as of a wielder of power over men through the same device of deception. It is in this context that one has to understand Binodini's perceptive observation: '. . . we learnt to deceive after having been deceived.'

In the 19th century Bengali society, the prostitute who had been deceived by her male seducer (like her predecessors in the past, and her successors today), adopted the same art of dissembling by devising her own skills to ensnare and fool her customer—the male who became defenceless once he entered her den, where she wielded power. It was her little empire, where she had the power to put her sexual prowess up for sale to the highest bidder, and dictate her terms.

The control that she exerted in this little empire of the brothel, was, of course, restrained by belligerent macho threats which occasionally led to killings in the red-light areas, and by frequent police interventions (like those following the enactment of the Contagious Diseases Act).

Notwithstanding this, she did enjoy a space in her miserable surroundings that allowed her access to the outer world—a freedom that her *bhadramohila* sisters in better surroundings missed in 19th century Bengal. Was it this sense of freedom which prevented many prostitutes from exchanging their life-style for a so-called rehabilitation in the form of marriage? Even those from among these prostitutes who found in the Bengali theatre an avenue for expressing their talents and thus asserting their power as individuals on an intellectual level, were quite often reduced to mere housewives once they got married (like Golap, who married and withdrew from the stage—only to return for a brief spell after a long lapse).

One wonders whether women who had grown up in an environment where they had been used to exercising their power, however limited at their petty level, would have opted for the alternative of 'rehabilitation' offered by *bhadralok* reformers like Shibnath Shastri. Such rehabilitation—in the form of marriage—implied constraints on the movements and rights (not necessarily sexual) which they had enjoyed in their professional career.

The history of *bhadralok* efforts to come to grips with the problem of prostitution in 19th-century Bengal suggests a complex mentality. It typified both the prevalent patterns of class and gender domination in contemporary Bengali society and the new requirements of a colonized educated middle-class to codify sexual relationships—within the family as well as outside—according to the norms set by the colonial rulers. Proposals for repressive steps (like forcible eviction of prostitutes from the cities, or imposition of taxes on them, or restriction on their movements in public) were quite often mooted by the *bhadralok* to protect their own families. They were particularly obsessed with the fear that their womenfolk might get ideas from what they thought was the footloose life-style of the prostitutes. Even when condemning the men who consorted with prostitutes, the *bhadralok* reformers significantly refrained from proposing any penal action against them. They were in agreement with the precept laid down by the Royal Commission that with the women 'the offence is committed as a matter of gain,' while with the men it was 'an irregular indulgence of a natural impulse.'[25] The 'respectability' of the *bhadraloks* and the reactions of the prostitutes to this remained insuperable barriers, even when the former tried to 'rehabilitate' the latter.

Curiously enough, even the *bhadramohilas*—the women of the respectable Bengali households—seemed to internalize the ambivalence of their male counterparts in their attitude towards prostitutes. One would have expected them to share with the prostitutes the common vulnerability of their sex to male oppression in a patriarchal society. But, thanks to the traditional norms of female submission to male dictates in social behaviour and economic choices, as well as the newly imported Victorian values (which reinforced those traditional norms in a new form in the homes of the educated Bengali *bhadralok*), the question of male exploitation of the prostitute completely escaped the attention of even those *bhadramohila* observers who chose to show sympathy for the prostitute. They tended to look upon her as a victim of her own folly. But instead of discarding her altogether (like the orthodox Hindus), the *bhadramohilas* displayed their generosity by taking a philanthropic pose—which they learnt to cultivate due to their education in convent schools, or under English governesses, or from their English-educated husbands. Their attitude was one of pity towards the prostitute's plight (without recognizing the male responsibility for it), and of a vague desire to rehabilitate her in society (without again any practical programme). A typical example of this attitude is available from a poem composed by a Bengali *bhadramohila*, and published in a Bengali women's magazine, towards the end of the 19th century. Entitled *Patita* (The Fallen Woman), it describes its heroine—a prostitute—as a 'half-blossomed flower bud' and tells her:

> *Korechhili bipathey gamone,*
> *Tai tore e dasha akhone*
>
> (You took to evil, and hence this is your fate now).

The poetess then asks her to abandon her profession and accompany her to her house where she promises to take care of her.[26]

Bhadralok from the theatre world, and people like Ramakrishna and some Brahmo reformers, did display a better understanding and a sympathetic attitude towards the prostitutes. They were perceptive enough to recognize economic and social factors like poverty and male oppression as responsible for the growth of prostitution. Instead of blaming the prostitutes and treating them as untouchables, they tended to take pity on them. Their efforts, therefore, were directed towards 'rehabilitating' them by training them to become acceptable in *bhadralok* society. The model held up before them was that of the ideal middle-class housewife. But in their well-meaning attempts to integrate them into respectable society, they ignored the individual prostitute's capacity to exercise a rational control over her life—a capacity that she enjoyed in her environment, however degrading and miserable it might have been. It is true that all prostitutes were not in a position to exercise this right. The initiate into the trade, the young rural girl newly sold to a brothel, and those caught up in extreme misery, remained trapped in the clutches of the *bariulee* or the male trafficker. Even when they learnt the ropes of the trade and sought to operate independently, they faced risks. Murders were quite common in the red-light areas, the victims mostly being prostitutes who refused to entertain unwelcome customers, or resisted demands from the *bariulees.* [27]

Yet, despite these hazards of the profession, the prostitute often seemed reluctant to give up the trade, when faced with the offer of a 'respectable' life as a wife, or a dependent, in a *bhadralok* house. It was this ambiguity in her attitude—her yearning for a home, and yet her unwillingness to accept the strictly ordained rules of domesticity (which she probably perceived as a threat to the comparatively free life-style that she enjoyed as a prostitute)—that baffled reformers like Shibnath Shastri.

VII
Official Laws versus Unofficial Needs

> Prostitution exists in all countries, as well as in all the climates of the world. It has been considered a necessary social evil which cannot be eradicated by repressive legislation any more than by moral influence and religious teaching.
>
> —C. Fabre-Tonnerre.[1]

Under pressure—primarily from concerns for the health of the British soldiers posted in India, and, later, from the reformist zeal of certain social and political circles in England in the 1860s and 1870s—the British administration in Bengal contemplated from time to time measures to restructure the system of prostitution, and bring it under some form of control.

These measures were influenced by the new definition of crime that was being shaped by the ideology and structures of colonial power and control in 19th century Bengal.[2]

In fact, as early as 1720, the British rulers had created institutions that enabled them to exercise tremendous powers and extend their criminal jurisdiction over the native inhabitants of Bengal, and Calcutta in particular. One such institution was that of the 'black zemindar'—a Bengali deputy to help his British bosses collect revenue and taxes from the native population. Gobindaram Mitra, the first 'black zemindar', earned notoriety for filling both his own coffers and those of his bosses, by extracting money from the people with the help of an armed force of *paiks*, *naiks* and *naibs* (who, in ascending order, approximately correspond to today's constables, head constables and investigating officers). By the first decades of the 19th century, this armed force of musclemen, recruited from both within and outside Bengal, had developed into a well-structured police force, operating under their British officers, in a Calcutta divided into several *thanas* or police stations. A government committee set up in 1829, headed by the chief magistrate, Charles Barwell, to examine police administration, approvingly noted the extension of criminal jurisdiction in the shape of the establishment of a house of correction, the town guard prison and—what is relevant for our present investigation—a female prison! There was thus an already officially sanctioned establishment for imprisoning women—an institution which later enabled the colonial administrators to herd prostitutes arrested under the CDA into jails. The colonial administration had thus armed itself with the necessary coercive machinery to apprehend and prosecute those who were defined as criminals in colonial jurisprudence. Prostitutes formed one such group.

In the pre-colonial era, the Moghul emperors based in Delhi, or their locally appointed administrators operating from provincial capitals (like Dhaka, and later Murshidabad in Bengal) rarely interfered with the value systems and social practices that were prevalent in rural society—as long as their demands for revenue and levies were met. Some of these indigenous value systems and practices were viewed as a challenge to the British style of rule—and often as crimes—by the new colonial administrators. The British notion of authority, which replaced the Moghul, was more centralized and—more importantly—combined both the concepts of administrative power (to coerce and effect changes) and moral prerogative (of assuming the sole right to lay down ethical norms in Indian society).

In the course of this clash between the pre-colonial value-systems, on the one hand, and the British administration's formal attempts to introduce institutionalized mechanisms of control, along with informal attempts to reform indigenous social networks along contemporary British moral notions, on the other, the practice of prostitution in Bengal underwent a reconstruction in terms of definition—from its earlier socio-religious interpretation as a 'sin' to the colonial socio-legal codification as a 'crime.'

In the hierarchically organized society of pre-colonial Bengal, where each social unit had its locus standi, the prostitutes—although branded as sinners—were an accepted part of society, like the scavengers (necessary to remove carcasses from the villages) or the *doms* (who were needed to burn the dead bodies of Hindus in cremation grounds). The Brahmin-dominated indigenous society invented explanations to accommodate these occupational groups as necessary evils within the socio-religious milieu, while, at the same time, stigmatizing them as untouchable outcastes. They were allowed to perform their respective occupations—whether the *dom* burning the dead body, or the prostitute satisfying the physical needs of the male customer. These tasks—considered rather distasteful by respectable society—were necessary, and, therefore, the Brahmin law-givers came up with the explanation that members of these professions were 'sinners', who, because of some sin committed by them in their previous births, were doomed in the present to pursue occupations which were considered 'shameful' by the Brahmins! Within this socio-religiously determined rural structure, the prostitute, although branded as a 'sinner', was permitted to pursue her occupation without being hauled up as a 'criminal'.

Under British colonial rule, however, prostitution became a 'crime'—as codified under the institutionalized mechanisms of control. Its codification as a 'crime' was shaped by the colonial perceptions of the occupation as practised in 19th century Calcutta and its suburbs, as well as the colonial concept of 'sin' which clashed with the indigenous concept that perhaps allowed the 'sinners' some space in society, albeit grudgingly.

The clash of perceptions becomes explicit in the observations made by a British police officer posted in India during the last decades of the 19th century. He acknowledged the prevailing indigenous societal norms when he said: 'Prostitution in India must be viewed from a different standpoint to that which we are accustomed. Prostitutes are treated with a degree of respect, are tolerated and even encouraged in India, to an extent incomprehensible to Western standards of ethical thought . . .' After having acknowledged this traditional indigenous perception of prostitution, the British officer presents the colonial perception: 'Prostitution . . . is the root cause, the source and mainstay of our brothels, opium dens and gambling saloons . . . The sexual element predominates in all such haunts of vice and crime and is such a fruitful source of income that I doubt if there is a single 'Night Haunt' in Calcutta, which does not harbour a few of these unfortunate women to cater for their regular customers, or by singing and dancing attract fresh trade . . .'[3]

While damning prostitution as 'vice and crime', the British officer, however, ignored the fact that the 'brothels, opium dens and gambling saloons' that fostered prostitution were fall-outs of the colonial order. The close association of prostitution with the new dens of crime in an urban metropolis like Calcutta reflected the economic changes that were altering land relations in the countryside, driving thousands of unemployed villagers to the metropolis and other towns, many among whom found means of survival through new, non-traditional channels like running distilleries or gambling dens—institutions that emerged in 18th century Calcutta, initially to cater to the needs of the British soldiers and civilians, and extended later to embrace the Bengali parvenu.[4]

The economic changes brought about by the colonial order also altered the gender composition of the ancillary appendages that used to accompany prostitution in pre-colonial Bengal. As mentioned earlier, pimping in the past was an informal machination, carried out by the female go-between, known as a *kutni*—who lured women from their homes and delivered them to their lovers, who, in their turn, after some time usually deserted these women, forcing them to enter the trade of prostitution. Bhabanicharan Bandyopadhyay's farces written in the early years of the 19th century—referred to in Chapter III—indicate the survival of the role of the female *kutni* in such brief liasions followed by the new commercial transactions that were developing in the red-light areas of Calcutta. But by the mid-19th century, the female *kutni* had apparently been replaced by the male *dalal*—the pimps who came to occupy a well-defined slot in the variegated organization that was developing in the red-light areas of 19th century Bengal. We hardly come across any female *kutni* or go-between in those farces that flowed from the cheap Battala presses that dealt with prostitutes and their clientele in the later decades of the 19th century. Instead, we find a crowd of male specialists hovering around the female prostitute—ranging from the *dalal* to the customer brought by him to her, from the flower-seller to the servant, from the *pujari* (the priest who used to come every day to conduct worship and offer obeisance to the pictures of the various deities that invariably decorated a prostitute's room) to the accompanists who played the musical instruments while the prostitute sang or danced to entertain her customer.

All these different components of the trade came under official surveillance at various times during the colonial regime, and were designated as 'crimes' according to the criminal code that was being fashioned by the authorities in different stages all through the latter half of the 19th century. Terms like 'obscene acts and songs' (in the Indian Penal Code of 1860) and 'public nuisances' (in Act V of 1898) became catch-all provisions for use against the prostitutes as well as their pimps and other associates involved in the trade.

I

Specific legislations enacted exclusively to cover prostitutes were the Cantonment Act of 1864 (to be followed by several amended versions in the late 1880s), and the Contagious Diseases Act, CDA, of 1868. We have already examined the working of the Cantonments Act, and its implications for the regimental prostitutes, as well as its failure to attain its objective—namely, to stem the spread of venereal diseases among the British soldiers (in Chapter III).

We have, earlier, briefly referred to the CDA, which was enacted following the failure of the Cantonments Act. It sought to bring the entire profession under strict state supervision and surveillance. Ironically, the CDA also suffered a fate similar to that of the Cantonments Act—ending up as a non-success, which had to be finally revoked after 20 years.

While repressive and restrictive laws of the colonial regime, like the Dramatic Performances Act, the Post and Telegraphs Act, the Arms Act, the Official Secrets Act (some of which still continue to be on the statute-book in India today) were strictly enforced by the authorities, the CDA was repealed by the colonial rulers themselves after they admitted their defeat in implementing it.

It would be worthwhile, therefore, to investigate more thoroughly the history of the 'rise and fall' of the CDA in 19th century Bengal. The episode—humiliating for the British administrators—illuminates various dimensions of contemporary socio-political history: the limitations of legal measures; the compulsions of both the rulers and the ruled that defeat such measures; the pressures and protests, both in the colony and the ruling country; and, especially, the agitation mounted by the fledgling feminist movement in the latter.

The main aim of the CDA was to counteract the spread of venereal diseases among British troops posted in India. The two main features of the Act that were to become controversial were, first, the provision of compulsory registration of all prostitutes, and, secondly, the compulsory treatment of all prostitutes in lock hospitals.

The net of registration, however widely cast, could not bring into its fold all the prostitutes. As one British official was to admit ruefully three years after the enactment of the CDA in Calcutta: 'The number of unregistered women who lived by prostitution is notoriously very large, but mere knowledge of this fact and of the persons and haunts of these women is not sufficient to decrease their number by securing registration.'[5] In Calcutta, the average number of prostitutes who were registered varied between 6000 and 7000 every year in the 1870s. Yet, according to an estimate made on the eve of the enactment of the CDA, by the then Lieutenant-Governor of Bengal, Sir William Grey, there were 30,000 prostitutes in the city.[6] In 1875, the then Lieutenant Governor, Sir Richard Temple, felt constrained to warn against assuming that 'with a male population of nearly half-a-million . . . the 6000 persons on the register even approximately represent the number residing within the town and suburbs who ought to be brought under the provisions of the Act.'[7]

The situation was no better in the suburbs and district towns. An officer visiting Berhampore, and going through the register in January 1870, commented in a sarcastic vein: 'It is preposterous to suppose that out of a population of 28,166 . . . there are but eight [registered] prostitutes; female virtue must be in the ascendant in this part of the world, in spite of which, however, gonorrhoea and syphilis reigns rampant among all classes.'[8]

Immediate reactions to the proposal of the CDA in Bengal—both among the Bengali *bhadralok* society and in the red-light areas of Calcutta—indicated the prevalence of a variety of social interests and concerns, sometimes converging, and at other times conflicting with each other. Those who supported the legislation felt that as a result, the number of prostitutes would come down, half would be removed to hospitals and the rest would flee from the cities and towns out of fear of examination.[9] Its opponents thought that it might indirectly encourage whore-mongering, since, if the diseased women were kept in hospitals and only the healthy ones were allowed to practise, men would visit them more frequently, their fear of imbibing venereal disease being removed. Another objection was the apprehension that the constables and *chowkidars* who were entrusted with the task of locating women who had not registered, might oppress them. It was felt that many prostitutes would bribe them and thus escape the law, while innocent poor women could be harassed by them and compelled to seek registration.[10] As it happened, the fears of police oppression and bribery (extortions from the prostitutes) turned out to be true.

In Calcutta's red-light areas, the CDA, or the *Choudda Ain* as it was known (the Bengali translation of the words 'Act XIV') among the prostitutes, created a furore. It sent the prostitutes scurrying for shelter outside the city's limits. According to one later day estimate, 'more than half the native public women had left the city and sojourned in the suburbs and further away.'[11]

This was confirmed by the contemporary popular songs and chapbooks that were published by the cheap presses in Battala in north Calcutta at that time. In these books, the Bengali poetasters—who were usually neo-literate people of humble origins, often living cheek by jowl with the prostitutes in the same neighbourhoods—documented the events in the wake of the CDA. Narrated in a droll style, these accounts remain an important source of contemporary popular perceptions of the CDA and its implications for society. Let us examine two typical chapbooks that were published on the occasion of the implementation of the CDA.

The first, written in prose—interspersed with two poems—came out on 31 March 1869, a day before the CDA of 1868 was actually implemented in Calcutta. The author, Prankrishna Dutta, entitled the book *Badmaesh Jabdo* (The Taming of the Profligate), and welcomed the CDA as a gift of the British government to punish both the prostitutes and the lechers who patronized them. In his narrative, however, we come across graphic descriptions of scenes in Sonagachhi and other red-light areas of Calcutta on the eve of the implementation of the CDA. To quote him (in English translation, which can never capture the waggish tone of the contemporary Calcutta street patois which the author used to describe, in a mock-heroic style, the plight of the prostitutes): 'The entire city is in a turmoil, the whores are upset, with their heads in their hands, sitting either inside their rooms, or on their terraces, or on their door-steps, and wherever in their locality the dandies gather they talk about examination and registration'—thus stressing the two main provisions of the CDA that were resisted by the prostitutes. The author, then, continues to describe the gradual evacuation of the red-light areas: 'Within minutes, the red-light districts emptied themselves . . . At night, the cries of the hawkers selling Bel flowers, ice, . . . and snacks [which were in demand among the clientele which thronged the brothels in the pre-CDA days] proved futile, with no one to buy them, leave alone anyone to haggle over prices. The cooked fish, mutton, eggs, vegetable snacks that were offered by the restaurants, stared at the streets in expectation, and began to weep and wither away, forcing the owners to put up the shutters . . .'[12]

A large number of the Calcutta prostitutes, in order to escape the CDA, apparently shifted to Chandernagore—a French-ruled enclave further north from Calcutta on the main arterial Grand Trunk Road on the banks of the Hooghly river, where the British-enacted CDA did not operate. Prankrishna Dutta, in his chapbook, describes the situation in the Calcutta red-light districts after the large-scale flight of prostitutes to Chandernagore: 'Almost all the whore-houses are empty, while Chandernagore is becoming a grand centre. Houses [in

Chandernagore] which used to be rented out for ten rupees [a month] are now fetching fifty rupees. Owners of whore-houses in Calcutta are striking their foreheads in dismay and weeping . . .'[13]

Prankrishna also reported the rumours about the medical examination that were doing the rounds of the town: '. . . some people are saying that they [the medical examiners] use syringe, others claim that it is a lath, and these rumours are making all shake in fear . . .' [14]

The second is a longer narrative, entitled *Panchali Kamal-koli: Choudda Ain* (A Poem about a Lotus-bud: Act XIV). The title is intriguing. The poet, Aghor Chandra Ghosh, never makes it clear whether the 'lotus-bud' represents the prostitutes about whom he writes, or the CDA which was victimizing them. It is a droll piece, moving from doggerel through comic songs to a mock-heroic climax. It opens with a light verse describing the plight of a prostitute called Sona:

> *Sarjon jamaddar*
> *phiritechhey dar dar*
> *Sonar darey amoni dhukilo.*
> *Baley key baritey achhey*
> *jaldi kargey ao hmiachhey,*
> *Thanamey abi janey hoga*
> *Monaguney maromey marey*
> *daktarkhanaye probesh karey*
> *Ain anusharey karjya dilo.*
> *Tikit dilen daktar*
> *heldi shoi koriye tar,*
> *Peye dhonee beriye eshey banchey.*[15]

> (Sergeants and constables are moving from door to door. They suddenly enter Sona's doorway. And shout—Who's there? Come here, fast. You have to come to the police station right now' . . . Given her nature, she is stung to the quick. (But) she goes to the doctor and submits herself [to the examination] according to the law. The doctor gives her the ticket and certifies her as healthy. Our young heroine comes out heaving a sigh of relief.)

The narrative, then, moves on to Sona's less fortunate sisters, who, to escape the law, abandon their old quarters in Calcutta and rush for seats in trains to take them to 'Farashdanga' (another name for the French enclave, Chandernagore). While Prankrishna Dutta in his book hints at the sudden emergence of Chandernagore as a flesh-pot due to the influx of prostitutes from Calcutta, Aghor Chandra Ghosh gives us tell-tale descriptions of developments in Chandernagore at that time. Apparently, once the Calcutta prostitutes set up shop in that town, they began to attract new customers ranging from the local 'babus' to the labourers:

> *Ekkhonetey nobyo babu achhen tatha jara,*
> *Dibya korey chul phiraye bahar diye tara,*
> *Pocketey pheley panch paisha, churut gunjey mukhey,*
> *Ranrey'r bari eyarkiti machhey mano sukhey*
> *Aat paishar mojur jara khajur chataye thakey,*
> *Khat palonkey khasha bichhanaye suchhey lakhey lakhey"*

> (The neo-rich 'babus' living there, curling up their locks in a swanky style, with five paisas in their pockets and cigars stuck in their mouths, are carousing at will in the houses of these whores . . . Labourers who earn eight paisa and sleep on coarse mats made of palm-leaves, are now in hordes moving over for a chance of sleeping comfortably on bedsteads and couches, in the houses of the prostitutes.)

As for the other prostitutes who decided to stay on in Calcutta, *Panchali Kamal-koli* describes how, to escape the *Choudda Ain*, they took to different guises—as milkmaids, as Vaishnavite singers—to serve their old customers, so that

> *Du dik bajaye roy pariksha na ditey hoy,*
> *Premer khelao nahi jaye boye.*

> (Both the needs are met—you don't have to pass the medical test, and yet you don't allow your game of love to go waste).

The narrative ends on a mock-heroic note with the King of Spring, Madan, anguished by the departure of his devotees (the prostitutes) from Sonagachhi, arriving in Calcutta and camping on the top of the (Ochterlony) Monument in the Maidan to investigate the causes. He is told by the 'cuckoos perching on the trees in Battala' (i. e. the Battala poetasters) about the *Choudda Ain* and how it drove the prostitutes from the city. Madan, however, approves of the provisions of the CDA, and shoots his 'darts of love' at both the prostitutes who left the city and those who are operating in different guises within the city's precincts, brings them together and makes them register with the police and undergo the medical tests. They, then, resume their old profession in the city.[16]

Panchali Kamal-koli, through the construction of a fantasy, represents the responses of a section of the colonized people to the colonizer's control of social and political power. In the tradition of folklore, where collective imagination deifies an unforeseen development in real life to justify its happening, here we find the invention of a new myth (through the appearance of Madan in Calcutta), which seeks to legitimize an unpleasant change (the introduction of CDA) which has to be submitted to.

Both these Battala chapbooks that were published on the occasion of the enactment of CDA in Calcutta and described its impact, interestingly enough, in their attitude towards the prostitutes hark back to the mood of the Bengali farces. Like the farces (which we discussed in Chapter IV), they look down upon the prostitutes as objects of distrust and ridicule, who deserve the punishment that is provided for by the CDA. Even when, occasionally, some sympathy for these women creeps in—as in the opening verses of *Panchali Kamal-koli*—it is soon drowned by the comic mood that dominates the narrative and targets the prostitutes and their customers.

It is obvious that the general public of Calcutta (whose views and tastes were reflected in some measure in the popular Battala chapbooks) were somewhat ambivalent in their reactions to the CDA, immediately after its introduction. To start with, they could not recognize the prostitutes as any other professional community working in a commercial set-up (like themselves) which deserved support when threatened by legal measures. Secondly, there was the in-built public prejudice—a combination of fear, envy, and distrust of prostitutes—which influenced popular response to the CDA.

As a result, the victims of the CDA remained isolated from the rest of the Bengali public, and bore the brunt of the punitive provisions of the CDA. The system of registration and medical examination under the Act provided for arrests for violation of these two regulations. All through the 1870s and till its repeal in 1888, at least 12 women on an average were being arrested every day for breach of the rules.[17]

Data collected from one year's report on the working of the CDA in Calcutta indicate the general trend of arrests. In 1874, the average rate of monthly arrests for non-registration varied from 22 to 63, reaching the highest—236—in September that year. The average monthly arrests for non-compliance with medical examination that year ranged from 122 to 381. The majority of those arrested all through the year were defaulters of the latter category, numbering 2572, against 802 arrests for non-registration. Arrests on this particular charge steadily increased from year to year.[18] It is evident—from other official reports, also—that the prostitutes resisted the medical examinations. Outsiders may attribute this to a superstitious fear of medical treatment, and blame them for having been highly irresponsible in spreading the disease. But there was a logic behind the prostitutes' resistance to such treatment—apart from their revulsion against the inhuman methods by which they were examined. If found diseased after examination, the prostitute was required to be confined to the lock hospital for treatment—which meant a long period of no work, and as a result, loss of income for herself, and lack of food and essentials for her dependants at home. As one prostitute defiantly stated her options: 'Arrest me, I shall only get a month in prison; but if I register I may have six months in hospital.'[19]

But not all prostitutes accepted the harassment without putting up a fight. We come across a few interesting cases where some among them ably defended themselves in the courts and managed to escape the penal provisions of the law. We hear of one Sukhimonee Raur, who was convicted under the CDA for not having presented herself for medical examination, as required by her registration. When produced before the Calcutta High Court on 22 September 1869, she said: 'I did not attend for examination twice a month as I have not been a prostitute . . . I had my name registered at the Thannah. The [police] Inspector registered my name. I did not voluntarily register my name at the Thannah.'[20]

Sukhimonee, however, did not disown the surname by which

she was described—'Raur'—which was the official English misspelling of the common Bengali term *ranrh* used for prostitutes. A petition presented by Sukhimonee to the Calcutta Commissioner of Police, suggests how some women like her plied their trade on a part-time basis under the protection of a male—as well as how the police in those days forced them to register to be able to prosecute them under the provisions of the CDA. In her petition, Sukhimonee said that she was not a 'common prostitute', but worked at one Mr Angelo's factory, and lived under the protection of one Mataoh, who was also employed in the same factory. She then proceeded to narrate how, in the beginning of May last, she was informed by the police that they had orders to arrest her and take her to the *thanna*, if she did not go. She accordingly went, and was asked her name, father's name, etc. By answering these questions, she did not know that she was rendering herself liable to registration under the CDA. Following this defence of hers, the High Court quashed her conviction. The two English judges felt that mere possession of a registry ticket would not necessarily make the holder of it a duly registered prostitute under the Act, for registration must be voluntary.[21]

Three years later, a prostitute called Mukta Bewa was convicted under the same section of the CDA for failing to appear for the required medical examination, in spite of registering herself as a prostitute under the Act. She appealed against the conviction. The judge quashed the conviction and sentence on the grounds that the evidence for the prosecution was insufficient, and that no evidence was heard for her when the sentence was passed.[22]

There were various other means also—ingenious and original—by which the prostitutes dodged the CDA. The medical officer in charge of lock hospitals, visiting Berhampore in 1869, found to his chagrin: 'A woman has only to say that she is attached to one man, and it is enough to have her name taken off the list [of registered prostitutes]', and mentioned one case where a woman 'attached herself to a servant of the Assistant Superintendent of Police'![23]

They also learnt by experience the weak points of the law, and many, as we have seen earlier, went to the courts and go acquitted. In 1873, a British official complained: 'They [the prostitutes] know to a nicety the evidence that is required by a court to establish the fact that they are public women. The difficulty of procuring such evidence is very great, and even when proof is forthcoming they prefer to undergo the penalties provided by law and still decline to register themselves.'[24]

As a result, very few arrests led to convictions. Of the 2359 women arrested in Calcutta in 1872 (a sample that was representative of the annual average), only sixty-nine could be finally imprisoned.[25] But since trials—as today, also—took a long time, these women continued to languish in jails as under-trials for a considerable period.

Some left their old places of operation to escape the CDA—as described in the chapbooks discussed earlier. In his report on Barrackpore (where the lock hospital treated women who served the soldiers in the cantonment) in 1869, the visiting Inspector stated: '. . . at times there have been as many as seventy-two women on the register, but they clear out and go to other places, and other women take their place in the Barrackpore bazaar, so that at the end of the year only thirty-seven women were on the registered list. Many of these women fail to attend for examination, and then they are fined, but they are so poor that they cannot pay the fines, and then they leave the bazaar and go elsewhere.'[26]

Even 15 years later things had not changed much in Barrackpore, as evident from the following remarks made by an official in 1885: 'Prostitutes Nos. 12, 32, 37, 38 and 40, Radhiab, Tahibjan, Manku, Janku and Woolfuth have been reported twice over and struck off as absconded. Prostitute No. 35 Bagum, reported thrice over and struck off as absconded. Eight women were apprehended, and each fined annas 8. One woman died; 4 struck off for not returning after the expiry of leave granted to them.'[27]

II

The lock hospitals were expected to be the lynchpins for the success of the CDA. Although, initially, it was proposed to establish four lock hospitals in Calcutta, till the early 1870s apparently two were functioning. One was at Alipore, and the other at Sealdah.[28]

Right from the start, treatment at the lock hospitals was marked by racial discrimination. A British police officer, writing in 1873, suggested the segregation of Indian prostitutes from European and Eurasian prostitutes during medical examination, since 'the annoyance caused to women of the latter class (Europeans and Eurasians) by detention among Natives on these days at the examining wards is certainly regarded by them as the most unpleasant part of registration under the Act.'[29] Following this, in November 1873, all 'Native patients were removed to the Alipore Lock Hospital, the accommodation at Sealdah being reserved for European and Eurasian women.'[30]

The annual average rate of infection among the Calcutta prostitutes was found to be 26 per cent, leading the Superintendent of lock hospitals to observe: '. . . the mere fact that nearly 400 [diseased prostitutes] are detained throughout the year and prevented from communicating disease to others, is, in my humble opinion, a sufficient justification for the introduction of the Act.'[31]

But, as pointed out earlier in the case of registration, the number of admissions to the lock hospitals, also, did not necessarily reflect the actual extent of the spread of venereal diseases—since a large number of prostitutes remained outside the scope of the lock hospitals. Official reports from the lock hospitals outside Calcutta—Hooghly, Berhampore, Dum Dum, Barrackpore and Darjeeling (where British troops were stationed)—repeatedly complained about the difficulty of making the prostitutes attend the lock hospitals twice every month, even under police pressure, and about prostitutes leaving the hospitals before completion of treatment.[32]

That there was no sizeable increase in admission rates among prostitutes is evident from the fact that, as a whole, the annual average ratio of admissions of women suffering from venereal diseases per 1000 women was 281 in 1863 (before the enactment of CDA), and more or less remained the same during the next 20 years.[33] Yet, around the same period, the incidence of venereal diseases among the troops in India rose from 196.8 per thousand in 1871 to 342.7 per thousand in 1885.[34]

The British administrators usually blamed the 'native' policemen for laxity in forcing the women to come to the hospitals.[35] In actual practice the 'native' policemen extorted money from the prostitutes in lieu of relieving them from attendance at the lock hospitals.[36] In fact, the provision for compulsory attendance became a weapon in the hands of the police, who could threaten any poor woman with detention and extort protection money from her. Some years later, a British official was to admit that the CDA had led to 'numerous daily arrests made without warrant, the risk of oppression of the very worst form to decent women . . . vast field which it opens for bribery and corruption . . .'[37] In 1883, inhabitants of north and south Barrackpore municipalities submitted a petition to the Lieutenant-Governor of Bengal, alleging harassment of ordinary people living in the vicinity of the cantonment by the police 'in their endeavours to detect cases of illicit prostitution.'[38]

By the early 1880s, it was becoming quite evident that the experiment with lock hospitals had not made any dent in the spread of venereal diseases among the British troops. In the heart of Calcutta itself, in the Fort William (where the soldiers were supposed to be the most protected, and the prostitutes serving them were regularly examined), the percentage of cases of venereal diseases was found to have risen to 14.5 in 1882—higher than it had been in any year since the introduction of the CDA.[39] An exasperated British official posed the query: '. . . are these lock hospitals worth keeping up; do the results repay or anything like repay the trouble and annoyance they cause to the people, or the labour of inspections and report-writing which they cause to the authorities?'[40] The government had spent about half a lakh of rupees on implementing the CDA in Bengal every year for 15 years—a total of seven-and-a-half lakhs; 'but all this has produced no permanent benefit.'[41]

III

In the face of the dismal failure of the CDA in checking venereal diseases among British troops in spite of heavy expenditure, the British authorities remained divided—one section demanding more stringent rules for registration and continuation of the lock hospitals, and another section seeking modifications in the rules, if not the total withdrawal of the CDA. The tussle between the two continued even after its repeal in 1888.

Meanwhile, in July 1880, the Government of Bengal proposed that the CDA should be made self-supporting by levying monthly fees upon the registered prostitutes, and that the provisions for registration be made more stringent. But there were moral objections from a section of the Government of India to the government raising revenue from prostitutes.[42]

With the rejection of its proposal, the Government of Bengal decided on the next best option—to curtail the operations under the CDA in order to reduce expenditure. In 1881, it decided to 'restrict the limits of the operation of the Act to those parts of the town [Calcutta] which are frequented by soldiers, and to withdraw it entirely elsewhere.'[43]

Several factors were cited by the administration in defence of narrowing down the scope of the Act to only a few areas. First, the then Governor-General of India, Sir Ashley Eden, felt that it was impossible to work the CDA as it existed any longer in Calcutta 'save at the risk of creating serious complications both of a legal and administrative kind.' On the administrative side, police operations had come in for a lot of criticism from 'a large portion of the public and of the Press'. As for the legal complications, the Calcutta High Court had declared the Act's rules of procedure illegal. Secondly, it was felt that unless its provisions were extended to the suburban town of Howrah, the Act could not be worked with perfect success. But Howrah, containing a population of 104, 908, was under a separate municipality. If the Act was to be extended there, the number of women required to be under inspection would be upwards of 18,000, which would also increase the expenditure to a very large amount.[44]

After deciding to restrict the operation of CDA, the Commissioner of Police of Calcutta identified certain spots in the city 'in which women who are visited by soldiers reside'. They were sections of Colootollah in the west, Bowbazar, Fenwick Bazar and Taltollah in the centre, and Watgunge and Bhowanipore in the south. Having identified these areas of residence of those prostitutes who were easily accessible to the soldiers of Fort William (they were within walking distance from the Fort area), the Police Commissioner then set out to spread his net around this core area, along with its neighbouring sections, so that the prostitutes could not escape by migrating into the outlying localities. Elaborate preparations were made to set up a sanitary cordon. First, a 'ring fence' was carved out—'a line commencing at Import Jetty No. 2 [in the dock area in the south] and following Canning Street, Colootollah and Mirzapore Street, as far as Circular Road [in the east]; thence along Circular Road to the south corner of Chowringhee; thence along [in the south] Russapugla Road to its junction with Peepulputti Road, along which the line runs back to Circular Road; thence along Circular Road as far as the Kidderpore Bridge, whence the line runs southwards along Diamond Harbour Road, Komedan Bagan Road, and Circular Garden Reach Road to Kootree Road, and along that road west to the River Hooghly, the bank of which it follows upto Import Jetty No. 2.'[45] Since most of these roads are still in existence, it is possible today to draw a map of this 'ring fence' and give our readers an idea of the wide area in the western, central and southern parts of the city that were encompassed by the modified CDA. It constituted more than half of the city's residential areas at that time. One can well imagine the plight of the residents living in this 'ring fence', if we recall the strict injunction issued by the government: 'Within this area (the ring fence) the Act must be worked with strict legality and the results watched.'[46]

Secondly, in order to take further precautions—in their efforts to protect their soldiers—the British administrators imposed the condition on the prostitutes who were residing within this 'ring fence' and entertaining British soldiers, that they could not leave this 'fence' and go elsewhere to pursue their occupation. Thus, the prostitutes living in this vast area of the city were sought to be turned into a captive group of sex-workers—sanitized by medical examination (that continued under the 1881 version of the CDA, which merely withdrew its area of operation from entire Calcutta to the 'ring fence' of central and southern Calcutta).[47]

Thirdly, it was proposed that 'if any of the women who receive soldiers are found hereafter to have migrated north of

Colootollah [the northeast boundary of the "ring fence"], it may be necessary to extend the operation of the Act to Cotton Street.' Cotton Street was the southern-most end of the northern division of Calcutta, which, thickly populated, led upwards to Sonagachhi, the traditional red-light area of the city. The Bengal Government proposal, however, felt that Cotton Street could be 'the furthest limit to which it is likely to be necessary to extend the Act, as the women will find it difficult to induce soldiers to follow them so far north . . .'[48]

Fourthly, the Brigadier General commanding the troops in the Presidency District in Bengal, issued an order 'prohibiting non-commissioned officers and soldiers from going beyond specified limits'[49] so that the British army personnel, in their search for women, confined themselves to the sanitized 'ring fence'!

But all these precautions proved futile. A report on the working of the CDA in its restricted form in Calcutta during the year 1882 complained: 'Even in the restricted area, and among the class for whose sole protection the Act was avowedly worked, the increase in the prevalence of disease seems to be as great as elsewhere.' The Lieutenant-Governor of Bengal expressed the opinion that the Act 'in its restricted form, could not be maintained.'[50]

The increase in the incidence of venereal diseases among the British troops even in the well-protected preserves of Fort William and its environs (58.14 per cent of admissions in 1884)[51] was not an isolated development. It was a part of a general trend in the Army in India in the 1880s. Admission rates of soldiers suffering from venereal diseases all over India rose from 249.7 per 1000 to 342.7 per 1000 between 1880 and 1885.[52] Ironically, however, the increase was indirectly caused by the policies of the colonial administrators. Explaining the causes for the increased ratios, an official report noted that they were for the most part a result of the short-service system introduced in the Army. Under this system, there was an increase in the recruitment of young 'unacclimatised and inexperienced men' who, according to the report, fell 'an easy prey to the lowest prostitutes of the country, among whom venereal disease is well-known to be rife.'[53] Their recourse to this class of prostitute was prompted by the dearth of registered prostitutes available in their environs. Due to the reluctance of prostitutes to register themselves, the number of registered women in most of the cantonment areas was absurdly inadequate. A comparison of the average strength of British troops in three major cantonments in Bengal with the average number of registered prostitutes in those areas in 1884, reveals a pathetic picture. In Barrackpore, every one from among the 36-odd registered prostitutes there was required to serve daily some seven soldiers on an average. In Dum Dum the ratio went up to one registered prostitute per 24 soldiers. In Darjeeling, there were only four registered prostitutes to cater to the needs of 241 British Tommies![54]

As a matter of fact, the paucity of registered prostitutes and the disproportionate demand made on the few available by the large number of soldiers in the cantonments, had been a headache for commanding officers in these cantonments ever since the enactment of the CDA in 1868, which sought to restrict the sexual access of the ranks to only the registered prostitutes. In a very candid report about the problems faced by his troops, a Commanding Officer posted in Jhansi in north India, as early as 1870, drew the attention of his seniors to the disproportionate ratio between his soldiers and the registered prostitutes available to them: 'There seems to be no doubt that in most stations the proportion of registered prostitutes is far too small compared with the number of unmarried soldiers . . .'

Under the given circumstances, calculating the possibility of 'each registered prostitute having connection with at least five men daily', the officer warned: '. . . such an arrangement, if carried out to the end, would probably reduce the registered prostitutes by degrees to a more or less diseased condition, and thereby tend indirectly to the spread of the disease . . .' He, then, proceeded to describe the mood of the soldiers under his command: '. . . owing to the facts stated above, the men, naturally disgusted at the indiscriminate nature of the connection suggested for their adoption, and finding many facilities for the private indulgence in pleasure, seek for variety whenever it can be found, whether in the sudder bazaar, the city, the neighbouring villages, or the coolie women working about the barracks, preferring to run the risk of infection to comparative immunity with the registered prostitutes of their Corps or Battery.'[55]

To come back to the 1880s, the increase in venereal diseases among the British troops in India was also attributed to another factor—which, ironically again, was caused by the policies of the colonial administration. The need to move the troops from Fort William and other cantonments (where they were supposedly protected by the CDA) to other parts of India during military operations made them vulnerable to infections from the unregistered prostitutes whom they might have frequented.[56]

IV

These various factors combined to render the CDA infructuous, and policy-makers at the top began to have second thoughts. The Governor-General, Lord Ripon, sent a despatch on 16 June 1882 to Lord Hartington, Secretary for India, where he expressed the opinion that the CDA could be abolished and the money spent in carrying out the Act might, with greater advantage, be devoted to the construction of sanitary works and other measures much more likely to benefit the health of the community at large than any system of lock hospitals. [57]

The pro-repeal lobby in Bengal was further emboldened in their efforts by agitations mounted in England by women's groups which attacked the CDA in their own country for its system of periodical examination of prostitutes as degrading to any female. In 1883, the British Parliament passed a resolution disapproving of the 'compulsory examination of women' under the CDA. With the suspension of the 'compulsory examination' clause, the entire abolition of the CDA in UK was inevitable, and in April 1886, the UK CDA was repealed.[58]

Attention soon turned to India. Josephine Butler, who led the Ladies' National Association in England, in the agitation against the CDA there, mounted a vigorous campaign among parliamentarians and social activists in the UK. A Liberal Party MP, James Stuart, collected information about harrassment of women in the Indian cantonments, and presented the data before the House of Commons. Another MP belonging to the same Party, Walter McLaren, obtained the copy of an application from an army officer heading the 2nd Cheshire Regiment which was posted in a north Indian town, requesting the cantonment magistrate to provide 'extra-attractive women' for his soldiers! Quoting extensively from this letter, McLaren, in a devastating speech in the House of Commons on 5 June 1888 said: 'The logical system is for the Government to send out English women to meet the demand (of the English soldiers)' and then added : 'You would not dare to send English women. Why? The reason is, because Indian women are black, and English women are white, and because they are a subject and inferior race, therefore you think they may be trodden upon . . .'[59]

Encouraged by the efforts made in England by the Ladies' National Association and MPs, the Bengali *bhadralok* politicians also began to voice their oppposition to the CDA and demand its repeal. In 1887, one of the major organizations in Calcutta, the British Indian Association, in a memorandum to the Secretary to the Government of Bengal, observed: '. . . the operation of the Contagious Diseases Act is wholly repugnant to the feelings of the entire Native community, and . . . it is attended with an incalculable amount of cruelty and oppression in this country.' Stating that out of the thousands of women hauled up for medical examination, only 14 to 34 per cent were found to be diseased in different years, the Association commented: 'No amount of sanitary benefit could compensate the outrage committed on the remaining women and through them on society. Nor is it at all a desirable state of things in a country where the police are virtually irresponsible as regards poor people . . .'[60]

At around the same time, the Calcutta Missionary Conference, in a memorial to the Governor-General of India, came out with stronger sentiments against the CDA: 'To pronounce a disease a grave national evil, which calls for such severe measures as the deprivation of personal liberty, without jury or any kind of trial, at the instance of a mere informer, in circumstances in which some of the women so treated prove to be perfectly innocent, while shrinking from placing any restraints whatever on licentious men, is not only . . . to be guilty of grave inconsistency, but also to sacrifice the liberties of one class of people to the license of another.'[61]

But the administration in India continued to dither on the issue, particulaly with the hawks in the Government of Bengal, with support from the Army top brass, opposing any effort to repeal the CDA. In a note to the Secretary of State for India in London, the Government of India claimed that the CDA had helped to check the spread of venereal diseases in the cantonments, and that 'at all events for the present, the maintenance of it in a country like India, in which the young British soldier is peculiarly exposed alike to temptation and to the risk of contagion, is essential for his protection.'[62]

The Army's need to maintain the system of regimental prostitutes—a captive group of women exclusively serving British troops—came into conflict with the demands of the pro-repeal groups (both in England and India) which wanted an end to that system. The demand for repeal of the CDA posed a threat to the British army in India. In England, during the campaign against the UK CDA, there was no noticeable opposition from the British military establishment, since there was no system of captive 'bazar' prostitutes in cantonments there against which the repealers could have protested. But in India, the British army over the years had institutionalized the residence of registered prostitutes inside the cantonments. It was the treatment of these regimental prostitutes that was being highlighted in the debates in the House of Commons in London, and in the campaigns by the Ladies' National Association there.

But the humanitarian concerns about ill-treatment of the regimental prostitutes, and the racial overtones involved in the system (as was being stressed by British MPs like Walter McLaren in the House of Commons) completely escaped the attention of the top brass in the Army. The latter, determined to stick to the old system, sought to meet criticisms about the failure to stem the spread of venereal diseases among British troops in spite of the CDA, by resorting to devious means. The Army authorities in Bengal, for instance, in order to mitigate the hazards of venereal infection among their troops while on the march outside their cantonments (a circumstance which officials mentioned as a cause for the spread of venereal diseases among the British soldiers), took recourse to the clumsy arrangement of taking along the regimental registered prostitutes with these troops on the move, along with the ordinary 'bazar' following. These women, thus, became camp followers in the British Army—a phenomenon accepted as normal by the Army brasshats. [63]

This military applecart got a little upset in mid-1888. A written order about regimental prostitutes accompanying troops on the march, issued by the Quartermaster-General in India (circular No. 21, dated 17 June 1886) somehow came to the notice of the authorities in London belatedly—at a time when they were facing tremendous pressure from the anti-CDA lobby in Parliament and the women's groups outside, to repeal the Act in India. The Secretary of State for India, in London, having come to know about the order, felt apprehensive that this information could be yet more grist to the anti-CDA mill of the Opposition, which might raise a hue and cry about 'bazar' prostitutes riding in carts provided by the British tax-payer! He hastily shot off a telegram to the Government of India office in Calcutta on 8 May 1888, asking it to stop at once the system of provision of prostitutes in regimental bazars.[64] In another despatch a few days later (17 May 1888) to the Governor-General of India, he instructed: 'No examination should be imposed upon women compulsorily . . .' Obviously under pressure from various groups and individuals in England who denounced the CDA as sanctioning organized sexual vice among the soldiers, he stated in the despatch, '. . . the principle should be steadily borne in mind that the efforts to control prostitution, and to mitigate its attendant evils, should not be developed into anything that can assume the appearance of the encouragement of vice by the Government and its officers. There should be no regulations which can be justly construed into a legislation of prostitution.'[65]

It was a cleverly worded despatch, which, instead of dealing with the basic question of whether the British soldiers should be given license to whore-monger or not (a question which was being turned into a moral issue by Josephine Butler and other social activists in England at that time), advised the government in India to avoid any officialese that could be construed by the agitators in London as 'encouragement of vice by the Government' and 'legalisation of prostitution.'

The responses to the message from the Secretary of State by the military establishment in India were mixed. While grudgingly accepting his advice, the British Army officers, at the same time, sought sanction from his ambiguously worded despatch in order to continue their tradition of maintaining the much-needed regimental prostitutes.

The immediate response was a fresh circular (No.3, dated 12 May 1888—obviously to meet the instructions of the Secretary of State in his telegram of 8 May) issued by the Quartermaster-General cancelling his office circular of 17 June 1886, and prohibiting 'the residence of registered prostitutes in bazaars of British Corps in cantonments', and ordering that 'no public prostitutes should be allowed to accompany regiments on the line of march, or to standing camps.'[66]

But behind this military officialese, the British Army officers, in their official correspondence, made no bones about their misgivings with regard to the liberal policies moving towards repealing the CDA. They, however, sought to continue their system of regimental prostitution by surreptitious means. We come across an interesting note from one such Army officer on the issue of regimental prostitutes living in the cantonments and accompanying the troops during their march. He was frank enough to state: '. . . There should, I think, be no "circulars" on the matter whether confidential or otherwise. Any instructions necessary should be of the nature of private unofficial instructions, as little formal as verbal instructions.' Aware of the risks of exposure through officially documented records that were being used by the anti-CDA campaigners in England at that time, he warned: 'The issue of any printed circulars will probably lead to further agitation on the part of the busybodies interested.'[67] The same officer, describing the government's move to ban the system of regimental prostitutes, and their accompanying troops on the move, as a 'come down', stated that 'by tact and discretion . . . we may be able to protect the British soldiers . . .'[68] Yet, another officer was more forthright in his reactions: '. . . many Commanding Officers would prefer that prostitutes should reside in the regimental bazaars, rather than their men should have to resort to the sudder bazaar. . .'[69]

Meanwhile, in London, on 5 June 1888, the House of Commons passed a resolution stating that 'any mere suspension of measures for the compulsory examination of women, and for licensing and regulating prostitution in India, is insufficient, and the legislation which enjoins authorities, or permits such measures, ought to be repealed.' This meant that the CDA itself would have to be revoked. Following this, a Bill repealing Act XIV of 1868 (CDA) and Act XXVI (Municipal Lock Hospitals Act) of 1868, was introduced and passed at the meeting of the Legislative Council of the Governor-General on 5 September 1888.[70]

The old Cantonments Act was also amended to incorporate the new policies, and, in 1889, a new Cantonments Act (Act XIII) was passed. It did not mention venereal diseases specifically, but provided for the enactment of rules for 'the prevention of the spread of infections or contagious disorders within a cantonment, and the appointment and regulation of hospitals or other places within or without a cantonment for the reception and treatment of persons suffering from any disease.' New rules were added in 1895 (under Act V), since it was found that the old system (of regimental prostitution and compulsory examination) 'had not been wholly discontinued in some cantonments'. The new rules, therefore, specifically emphasized: 'No person known to be a prostitute shall, under any circumstances, be permitted to reside within the limits of any regimental bazaar.'[71] However, two years later, yet another Cantonments Act was enacted—Act XV of 1897—repealing the old one. This new Act empowered the Commanding Officer of a cantonment with the right to issue notices to any person suspected of suffering from any disease, to appear for medical examination, and to expel that person from the cantonment within twenty-five hours if he or she refused to submit to the examination. Although the words 'prostitutes' and 'venereal diseases' were never mentioned in the main text of the Act, official correspondence regarding the new Act made it amply clear that the objects of the medical examination were the same regimental prostitutes believed to be suffering from venereal diseases. In fact, the new Act of 1897 had to be introduced in 'pursuance of the recommendations of the Secretary of State', since 'Her Majesty's Government cannot acquiesce in the continuance of the present state of things which has led to a disastrous increase in venereal disease among the British troops in India, and requires the immediate adoption of remedial measures.'[72]

The Cantonments Acts that were drafted from 1889 onwards are classic pieces of the art of imperialist hypocrisy in which the British law-makers and officials were past masters. They had to placate the critics in England, and yet could not afford to give up the old system of regimental prostitutes (who were necessary for the Tommies). While, in the provisions of the Acts, they scrupulously tried to keep out the terms 'prostitutes' and 'venereal diseases', both, apparently, continued to thrive within the cantonments. Otherwise, surely it would not have been necessary for the Secretary of State to recommend remedial measures in 1897, that were specifically targeted against these two villains! Euphemisms like 'anyone residing in a cantonment', or 'infectious or contagious diseases' were used in the provisions of the Acts to cover up the actual happenings inside the cantonments, and assure English women's groups and social activists that since under the law no prostitutes could live in the cantonments any longer, the medical examination was being conducted on residents suffering from infectious diseases like cholera, small-pox, etc. As a matter of fact, it was through the backdoor of these euphemisms that the notorious system of compulsory medical examination of prostitutes was legitimized in the cantonments. That the prostitutes were still living in the cantonments—in spite of the 1895 Cantonments Act which specifically banned their residing 'within the limits of any regimental bazaar'—was indirectly acknowledged by no less a person than the Secretary to the Government of India (Military Department). In an official letter on the subject of treatment of venereal diseases in cantonments, he issued the instruction: 'If a prostitute is suspected of being diseased and of being a source of danger to other persons, she may be required to be examined, and if she refuses to be examined, she may be required to quit the cantonment.'[73]

Thus, at the end of the 19th century—after almost 200 years of strenuous official exercise to protect the health of the British privates in India—the cantonments were back at square one. They were still coping with the rise in venereal diseases among their troops, and desperately experimenting with one legal measure after another.

V

The certitude and self-righteousness of one generation of British bureaucrats (of the 1860s, who thought that they could restrict prostitution in the straitjacket of the CDA) gave way to the abandonment of all such hopes by the next generation, which reconciled itself to its inability to bring under its surveillance prostitutes all over Bengal, and opted, instead, to confine its regulatory attention to prostitutes and British soldiers only in the cantonments. The Cantonments Acts of the 1880–90 period represented the colonial policy of a 'grand retreat' from the earlier ambitious strategy of the CDA.

A similar change was perceptible among the Bengali *bhadralok* during this period. In marked contrast to the attitude of their predecessors (expressed in the 1850–70 period in newspaper columns, where they demanded extreme measures against prostitutes), the new generation of vocal *bhadralok* leaders (of the 1880–90 period) appeared to back-pedal on such virulent demands. At times, they even came out in protest against official steps against prostitutes, as evident from the memorandum sent to the Secretary to the Government of Bengal by the British Indian Association in 1887 (referred to earlier). In 1893, when a Calcutta Missionary Conference on 'social purity' railed against prostitutes, the journal *Reis and Rayyet* (edited by a well-known Bengali journalist, Shambhu Chandra Mukhopadhyay), of 2 December 1893, accused the 'Puritywallahs' of hypocrisy in choosing to attack the 'feeblest interest in the community'—the prostitutes.[74] Still later, when the Calcutta Police authorities sought to empower any police officer above the rank of a native constable with the right to arrest a prostitute, even without independent evidence, two Bengali political leaders—Surendranath Banerjee and Lal Mohan Ghose, opposed the proposal, stating that it would be an opening to blackmail, and succeeded in getting it amended.[75]

Thus, the convergence of interests between the colonial authorities and the Bengali *bhadralok* community, which encouraged the enactment of the CDA in 1868, was replaced two decades later by a convergence of realization, among both, that the Act had not worked. The colonial authorities were reconciled to the reality by abandoning the earlier intentions of bringing the entire spectrum of prostitution under state control. The Bengali *bhadralok* society also appeared to realize not only the futility of the Act in curbing prostitution, but also the dangerous implications of its empowering the police with rights which could be exercised indiscriminately against poor and innocent women from their own community. Besides, the catch-all provisions of the Act could also entrap the richer practitioners of the profession living in the red-light areas, many among whom were known to be mistresses of some of the leading Bengali *bhadralok* social and political personalities of the late 19th century!

But even before withdrawing the CDA, the British government officials in India made another effort to control prostitution—with the same disappointing results! In 1872, the government came up with certain proposals for forbidding prostitutes from bringing up small girls, who might join the profession once they grew up. Registration of these children, imposition of penalties on prostitutes who possessed such children, and taking these girls away from the prostitutes, were some of the measures proposed. But here, also, the administration ran into difficulties, when a host of objections were raised by the Bengali *bhadralok*.

Gour Das Bysack (Basak)—a friend of the poet Michael Madhusudan Dutt—who was at that time the Deputy Magistrate of Howrah, summed up the Bengali objections to the administrative proposals in an official despatch: '. . . In the first place it will be difficult to distinguish between the natural and foster children of prostitutes; secondly, there is no registry of births, nor certificates of birth, among them. Hindu widows on quitting their families and proceeding to distant mofussil towns to practise as prostitutes take their infants along with them, and for these people to prove the birth of their children is simply an impossibility. The result will be that they will be unjustly deprived of the custody of their children.' He was, therefore, convinced that 'while the proposed law would fail to do any good, it would provide a prolific source of injustice and oppression.'[75]

The British officials also appeared to accept the arguments, and one of them went to the extent of stating that such a 'strong measure, devolving very delicate duties upon the police' recalled the 'kind of scrutiny which aroused the Wat Tyler rebellion in England.'[76]

Although such exaggerated apprehensions were totally unfounded, the government deemed it wise to drop the proposal. Instead of bringing in a package plan against trafficking in children, the authorities chose to take action against brothel-keepers, whenever cases of abduction of children were brought to their notice. Thus, we hear of one Kulsum Raur and her relatives being prosecuted in March 1894, for abducting girls from homes in Calcutta suburbs and Midnapur. The police raided her brothel and found fourteen Hindu girls between the ages of seven and fourteen. Sentences of seven years' rigorous imprisonment were awarded to Kulsum Raur and her associates. What happened to the girls? Most of them were restored to their homes, but the families of four refused to take them back, because they had lived in a brothel owned by a Muslim![77]

It was not the opposition from the *bhadralok* only that compelled the colonial administration to drop the several legal measures that it had initially proposed to control prostitution. Much fiercer opposition came from the *bhadralok* to the Dramatic Performances Control Act (1876) and the Vernacular Press Act (1878), and yet the authorities persisted in implementing these repressive legislations. As in the case of repealing the CDA, the decision to abandon the measure to prevent children from growing up into prostitutes was also dictated by the realization that the financial burden to be incurred in implementing the proposals (like providing official custody for the girls taken away from the brothels) was out of all proportion to the success likely to be achieved by their implementation. Besides, prostitution was far less a threat to the administration in the late 1870s than the more menacing developments that were developing in Bengal during that period—an increasingly aggressive Bengali press and a popular Bengali stage, both of which were being used by the nationalist *bhadralok* to hit out at the colonial administration. The Dramatic Performances Act of 1876 was introduced in retaliation against political plays like *Cha-kar Darpan* (about the brutal treatment of the Assam tea plantation workers by the English planters), *Gaekwar Darpan* (about the victimization of the Maharaja of Baroda by the English resident there), and Bengali farces that lampooned Prince Edward—Queen Victoria's son—who visited Calcutta in 1875.

The history of the colonial administration's attitude towards prostitution and attempts to bring it under control through legalistic measures indicate certain interesting dimensions of colonial policy. Initially, the policy was dictated by the need to protect the men of the ruling race—the European soldiers and sailors, the East India Company's officers and clerks, the traders and businessmen—from excessive indulgence in affairs with 'native' women. But right from the beginning, the policy was marked by a certain amount of ambivalence. Prostitutes were grudgingly accepted as necessary for the physical needs of the British privates and other British underlings in the network of the colonial administrative and commercial interests. Yet they were also considered a threat because of their deadly capacity to infect these underlings with a disease that would incapacitate them.

This threat was sought to be neutralized by a series of measures that allowed the continuation of prostitution, and at the same time tried to segregate sections of its practitioners under official care in order to provide adequate protection for the numerous segments of the European population who needed them. These administrative measures progressed in various stages—from the enactment of the Cantonments Act to the Contagious Diseases Act.

That the official measures were not inspired by any reformist zeal, but by sheer pragmatic considerations, was made very clear by the British Health Officer, C. Fabre-Tonnerre, who, while drafting the CDA, was frank enough to state: 'Prostitution exists in all the countries, as well as in all the climates of the world. It has been considered a necessary social evil which cannot be eradicated by repressive legislation any more than by moral influence and religious teaching.' After having acknowledged the inevitability of the continuation of the trade in every society, he suggested the remedy in the Indian colonial society in the shape of the CDA, justifying it on the ground that 'Society has a right to protect its own interests by the best means in power.'[78]

For Fabre-Tonnerre, 'society' was the British society in India, in whose interests the Bengal Government abandoned the attempt to work the CDA throughout Calcutta, and decided instead to limit its jurisdiction to prostitutes frequented by Europeans only, in 1881.

VI

In the European society of 19th century Calcutta, apart from the British soldiers seeking out Indian prostitutes either in their cantonments or neighbouring areas, there were also others who appeared to prefer women from their own racial stock to the black 'natives'. Their demands gave rise to the emergence of what was known as the 'white slave trade'. Calcutta, as a flesh-pot that served a wide range of customers from the Bengali 'babus' to the British Tommies, also hosted these white prostitutes in different parts of the city.

The history of these prostitutes, mainly European—concentrated first in Kalinga Bazar in central Calcutta till the end of the 19th century, later dispersing to Kareya Lane and its environs in south Calcutta, where they survived till the years 1930–40—offers us a glimpse into the international dimensions that the trade had acquired in colonial Bengal.

According to a British official, who was involved in crime detection in colonial India in the early years of this century—and in researching about the history of crime in the 19th century—European prostitution developed in the maritime cities of India after the opening of the Suez Canal in 1869. Describing the development of European prostitution in maritime cities like Calcutta, he then proceeds to give the details : 'The male procurers, who belong largely to the Jewish faith and are mainly responsible for the preponderance of Jewesses in the brothels of the Indian coast cities, acted also . . . as information agents, advising women in Cairo, Alexandria and elsewhere of vacancies in the Indian and Far Eastern brothels . . .' As for their living conditions, he adds: 'The houses are usually confined to a particular area and are sometimes distinguished by a red lamp hanging in the porch or verandah; a few poorer women live in single rooms, often opening directly on to the street, and live a more sordid and miserable life.'[79]

These prostitutes (outside the cantonments) who were frequented by the Europeans, appeared to be a thorn in the flesh of the English administrators. Most of them were Europeans and Anglo-Indians (offspring of liaisons between the Euopean settlers or visitors and Indian women). Their concentration in Kalinga Bazar in central Calcutta and their high-profile presence in the city—thanks to the regular visits to their haunts by the English soldiers and settlers—were a source of embarrassment for the colonial administrators as well as the Christian missionaries who were bent on proving the superiority of their European civilizational norms over the 'degenerate' habits of the natives! And yet, here, right in the heart of the capital of the Indian empire of Queen Victoria, a 'degenerate' business was thriving due to a convenient complicity between the European commercial sex-workers, who had converged on Calcutta out of their own needs, and the European soldiers and settlers looking for fun.

The sense of shame and repulsion felt by the English administrators at the continuation of European prostitution in Calcutta comes out clearly in the comments made by a later-day English official about Kalinga Bazar as it was at the end of the 19th century. Describing it as 'the headquarters of European immorality,' he painted a lurid picture in the following words: 'It was a stagnant pool of repulsive vice, far more disgraceful in its flaunting character than the Indian Vice Areas. On Saturday and Sunday nights there was a shameful disregard of public morals. Its women, European, Anglo-Indian and Indian, were bold, its pimps were aggressive. The number of young girls and even children concerned went into hundreds, and that traffic was carried on every night within sound of the chimes of Christian churches, the bells of boys' schools, and the call to prayer from Moslem Mosques.' Some two decades later, in the 20th century, a bit battered by punitive police measures, 'European prostitution' acquired the character of a 'wounded snake—dragging its slow length along.'[80]

These observations betray the old colonial ailment—the oozing of the pus of shame from the running sore of the 'sahib', caused by the 'repulsive vice, far more disgraceful' than the Indian variety, in which the 'sahib's' European sisters and Anglo-Indian descendants had been indulging. The comments of this early 20th century English administrator on 'European immorality' in Calcutta hark back to those made by one of his predecessors, Dr C. Fabre-Tonnerre, who reserved his deadliest comments for the 'women of pure European parentage . . . who have fallen to the lowest degree of degradation,' and who were described as the 'moral plague of our principal thoroughfares.'[81]

But while these European prostitutes could have suffered a decline at the turn of this century, their Indian sisters serving the indigenous clientele continued to enjoy their earlier popularity in the Calcutta flesh market. The 1901 census report recorded 14,370 registered prostitutes from among the city's 1,99,072 women over 10 years of age. It was estimated that each of the twenty-five municipality wards of Calcutta (into which the city was divided) on an average could claim 575 registered prostitutes—leaving out the unregistered ones. A contemporary Bengali newspaper, referring to the expansion of brothels on main roads like Chitpore, Cornwallis Street, College Street, Amherst Street and Corporation Street, complained that these brothels were housed in buildings owned by respectable people who earned more by renting them out to prostitutes.[82]

Like the cantonments, the *bhadralok* society in Calcutta, also, was back to where they had started in the early and mid-19th century, when they complained about the spread of prostitution, and the renting out of houses by members of their own community to prostitutes in 'respectable areas.'

By the beginning of the 20th century, the colonial administrators in India had already reconciled themselves to the admissibility of prostitution as a permanent institution—both among its soldiers, and the 'native' society. In the *chuklas* or cantonment brothels, which continued to function even after the enactment of the supposedly altruistic Cantonment Acts, the local British officers in charge of their troops went to a ridiculous extent to recruit prostitutes to meet the desperate demands of the privates. We hear of an SOS sent by a British quartermaster to a local city magistrate to call for Indian female 'volunteers' to join the *chaklas*, with the added remark: 'better looking ones this time, please.'[83] The source of this piece of information—a British Army general posted in India—blames the reformist elements in his country for the repeal of the CDA, thereby 'condemning English lads (in India) to syphilis run riot'. Although writing in the 1930s—six decades after what the British Health Officer, C. Fabre-Tonnerre wrote in his official despatch—this British general expresses the same sense of helplessness: '. . argue as you will, denounce what you like, you cannot get away from the fact that a proportion of our young men will not be continent.'[84]

In the ideology of the colonial administrators there seems to be a continuity of the notion that certain societal groups—whether British privates recruited from the lower classes, or Indian prostitutes recruited for their satisfaction—are genetically doomed to incontinence. Although, in certain official correspondence, these bureaucrats occasionally refer to the socio-economic causes of the growth of prostitution in colonial Bengal, the general tendency is to stereotype the prostitutes as pathological examples of congenital deviants, criminals or nymphomaniacs, just like the fixed image of their counterparts, the lower class British Tommies, is that of having been endowed with ingrained and insatiable concupiscence.

This mood comes out clearly in the reminiscences of the above-quoted British Army general, who, describing the cantonment after the repeal of the CDA, laments: 'The environs of barracks became the haunt of loose women of the type so well known in Ireland in days gone by as the "Curragh Wrens". They were in the bushes and thickets o' nights and their pimp men haunted the road to show the soldiers where to find them . . .'[85]

The pimps apparently could not—or did not—make any distinction between the white plebeian private and his boss. The latter, quite often, had to face awkward situations like the one described by the British general in his memoirs, when he 'shortly after becoming Quarter-Master General in India,' walked into one of the largest cantonment barracks after dark, and 'found an anxious gentleman accosting him with alluring descriptions of the beauty awaiting him in a neighbouring thicket!'[86]

Epilogue

The debates over prostitution in 19th century Bengal among the *bhadralok* and the colonial administrators; the latter's attempts to bring it under state control; and the responses of the prostitutes themselves to these exercises, reveal a variety of attitudes and needs that were locked in irreconciliable conflicts fought out with ambiguous gestures.

The irreconcilability was rooted in certain basic socio-economic positions from which these three main participants—the *bhadralok*, the administrators and the prostitutes—were operating. At the crux of the problem were the differing attitudes to prostitution.

In pre-colonial Bengali society, prostitution, at its worse, was considered a sin, but never a legal offence. By harnessing it to the colonial concept of crime, and putting it under penal laws, the British administration opened up a Pandora's box. The initial idea of revamping this pre colonial institution was basically motivated by the need to protect the British soldiers. But the administrators were trapped by the need of a moralistic justification for their penal measures (prodded by the Christian and other social reformers both in England and in India, who tended to take an abolitionist stand with regard to prostitution), on the one hand, and the compulsion of allowing prostitution—in a controlled form—in order to meet the requirements of their men, on the other. The series of measures for control (the Cantonments Act, the Contagious Diseases Act, the Lock Hospital Act etc.) provoked controversies in England around the suspicion that the administration, by enacting these legal measures, was legalizing prostitution. This, the British social reformers felt, went against the colonial power's professed moral claim that it was in

India to carry out the mission of 'civilizing' the natives!

In order to morally justify the regulations that allowed prostitution to continue—but under official guidance and supervision—the colonial authorities in India quite often conveyed the impression that the prostitutes were not coerced, but voluntarily registered themselves. But whether any obligation is voluntary or compulsory depends on whether the obligee and the obliger are equal in education, position and other matters, or whether the former is superior to the latter. In the case of the prostitutes of 19th century Bengal, these women were clearly in an inferior position, and the local administrators could resort to various devious methods to make their coercion appear voluntary. Practices which the colonial masters chose to speak of as 'voluntary' (like extortion of rack rent or taxes) were regarded by their colonized subjects as 'compulsory', and they usually deferentially submitted to them, since they knew that a frown of the local *naib* was as good as a warning of dire consequences if they refused to oblige.

The prostitutes faced similar pressures—operating under duress from the local police *chowkidar* or other similar petty personnel. As one contemporary English official report commented on the plight of the Indian prostitute under the punitive rules: '. . . the question whether any particular action can be said to be voluntary, presents two entirely different aspects according as it is looked at from the point of view of the official, or from that of the woman. The action of the officer may be merely persuasive, and entirely free from any tinge of compulsion. But for countless generations the *marzi hakim* or pleasure of the governor, and the *hukm hakim* or order of the governor, have been equivalent terms in India . . . There is still a strong tendency to receive the expression of his wish by one in authority as equivalent to a command.'[1] The pre-colonial tendency among the weak and the powerless to equate *marzi hakim* with *hukm hakim* was reinforced by the British colonial administration, which saw to it that its wish was translated into command through a network of loyal subordinates, ranging from the Bengali junior officials and English-educated *bhadralok* (the latter attempting to implant the moral values of the contemporary Victorian English establishment into Bengali society, under the delusion of *marzi hakim*) at the top of the colonized community down to the local minions at the ground level—the rent-collectors and their musketeers in the villages, and the police station officer and his constable in the cities—who spread the message of *hukm hakim*.

In trying to come to grips with prostitution in 19th century Bengal, the British administrators also sought to project it as an Oriental phenomenon to be treated differently from its counterpart in their homeland. Typical is the following observation about the Calcutta prostitutes made by a contemporary British official: 'They differ very much from the prostitutes of Europe. Their life in the eyes of their countrymen has not so much of the deep degradation attached to the European prostitute. This may be accounted for from the fact that the principal causes which induce the European woman to become a prostitute are so very different that there is not the slightest similitude between them. Whilst in our countries the primitive causes of prostitution are mainly due to want of religious and moral feeling, defective education, vanity, laziness and in very few instances to extreme misery, in India the principal causes of prostitution are the religious and social prejudices of caste and utter destitution.'[2] The colonial understanding seems to be based on the assumption that, while in Europe prostitution was more of an exception than a rule, caused by individual aberrations (like 'vanity , laziness', etc), in India it was almost a rule caused by the all-pervading socio-religious habits.

Significantly, like the colonial administrators, the Bengali *bhadralok* (both those who demanded penal measures against prostitutes at the beginning, and those who opposed such measures later), never for a moment thought of penalizing the men who patronized the prostitutes. Since prostitution was a trade (sale of sex for cash or payment in kind), it could not obviously survive without the active participation of the (male) purchaser. If it was to be considered a crime, both the participants—the seller and the buyer—should have been brought under penal measures by the yardstick of the principles of the so-called 'fair' justice of British jurisprudence. But, the seller in this case—the prostitute—was doubly damned. She was poor and socially ostracized to start with. Secondly, she was a female operating in a male-dominated, patriarchal market. It was she, therefore, who became more vulnerable to the penal measures than her male clients.

I

In the debates over prostitution in 19th century Bengal (and England also), the arguments—whether in favour of its abolition, or its regulation—revolved around three issues: one, allegations of 'immoral' habits of prostitutes, who were accused of seducing men and ruining their homes; two, the public outrage caused by their residing, and openly soliciting customers, in the 'respectable' areas of Calcutta and other towns; and three, the danger of contracting venereal diseases from them—a concern which, from the mid-19th century onwards, was to become almost an obsession with the British civilian and Army officials in India.

The colonial concern over venereal diseases at this particular juncture in the 19th century needs to be examined in some detail. It cannot be interpreted as an expression of the colonial administration's anxiety to protect its subjects from occupational diseases in general. While venereal diseases were peculiar to the particular profession of prostitution, there were other new diseases which were being caused by several trades and commercial establishments that had cropped up under the patronage of the British administration in 19th century Bengal—the coal mines and tea plantations, where labourers, including women and children, working under extremely unhealthy and unhygienic conditions, suffered from tuberculosis and other diseases; the proliferating factories on the banks of the Hooghly, spreading environmental pollution threatening the health of the residents in the neighbourhoods. Curiously enough, these occupational hazards were totally ignored both by the British administrators and the Bengali *bhadralok*—since they were confined to the restricted zone of the workplaces and the neighbouring residential quarters of the workers, and thus affected only the poor and oppressed labourers who toiled there, and were less visible in public than the Calcutta prostitutes. The latter made their presence felt in society on a wider scale, by virtue of their accessibility to the public. Unlike the factory workers or plantation labourers, they were serving a larger and more variegated clientele—a substantial section of which consisted of British troops. Unlike other diseases generated by oppressive working conditions in industries, venereal diseases not only affected the labourers in the trade—the prostitutes—but infected the customers, due to the physical nature of the transaction between the sex-workers and the clientele. The colonial administration, therefore, had to be more worried about venereal diseases than other occupational ailments. Its soldiers were more important than the industrial workers.

The colonial authorities' attitude towards venereal diseases in India was also shaped by the 19th century European aetiology and views of body and mind. There was a tendency to trace most of the diseases in the human body to syphilis. One British medical practitioner noted: 'In questioning patients as to their previous history, how often is it found that the first link of the chain dragging them to the grave is syphilis !' He then proceeded to attribute almost all physical disorders to this particular disease: 'Diseases of the eye, especially iritis, often ending in blindness; diseases of the spinal cord terminating in paralysis; diseases of the brain ending in a similar condition; diseases of the heart, the forerunner of dropsy—all result from syphilis . . . In short, disease of most internal organs has been fully traced to those degenerations and formations which result from venereal.'[3]

In the mind of the colonizer, syphilis assumed a more monstrous form in the context of India, where mortality among soldiers from various types of diseases (till then unknown to the European mind) was very high. The same aetiology traced all these ailments to syphilis. Take, for instance, the following statement: 'I believe that much of the anomalous or undefined fever soldiers suffer from in India, is rather syphilitic than true ague or other form of so-called malarious fever . . . Similarly, I believe that a considerable amount of the liver disease, from which European soldiers suffer, is either purely syphilitic or greatly aggravated by syphilis . . . an attack of sun-stroke is more likely to end in permanent disability when there is a syphilitic taint.'[4]

The colonial aetiology betrayed a typical patriarchal bias by blaming the woman primarily for the increased virulence of syphilis in the port towns of England, in the 1880s. The following comment is a revealing instance: 'The fact is, that the slight irritation caused in the female by the early stage of venereal rather excites than dulls the sexual appetite. As would naturally be expected from so many women with excited sexual appetites being suddenly allowed to disseminate disease, there was a large increase of syphilis among the men.'[5]

It was this aetiological bias against women that gave birth to the much-hated system of forcible medical examination of prostitutes—a system which was condemned by contemporary women's groups as the male doctor's infringement of female privacy and liberty. Besides resenting this form of medical rape of their bodies, the prostitutes were, also, mortally fearful of the treatment that they had to undergo, if found diseased. Antibiotics had not yet appeared on the scene, and the therapy used was often quite excruciatingly painful, what with the application of mercury and caustic salve on the sores.

II

But it was the prostitute who had the last laugh, notwithstanding the administrative measures to control her vocation, and the Bengali *bhadralok* efforts at social reforms along with their acquiescence in the administrative measures to a limited extent. Like the proverbial phoenix, she rose from the ashes every time, to the embarrassment of both the colonial administration and *bhadralok* society.

Prostitutes in 19th century Bengal survived not merely because of the demand in the market, and the sheer tenacity of their self-preservation, which fed on the sexual needs of the males—factors which have operated with various degrees of elasticity in every society and every age. What was peculiar to the 19th century Bengal situation was that prostitutes, for the first time, occupied centre stage in society, drawing upon themselves the spotlight from a wide variety of sources—successive generations of new clients from all classes, popular versifiers and farce-writers, producers and playwrights of the Bengali stage, Bengali *bhadralok* reformers, as well as hostile orthodox puritans,

English administrators caught between pressures and pulls from their minions in India, on the one hand, and social reformers in their own country, on the other.

Judging from contemporary accounts in newspaper reports and reminiscences in the early part of the 19th century, it seems that in those years, the emergence of prostitution from its pre-colonial rural form of a marginal occupation to a widespread and better organized profession in the market of colonial economy, roused Bengali society to recognize it as a force to reckon with. Bhudeb Mukhopadhyay (1827–1894), in his reminiscences recalled: 'In the past, one or two houses of prostitutes could be found at the margins of a village. Today, the number of prostitutes in the villages is undoubtedly increasing. Even among school children, this sin (whore-mongering) has assumed powerful proportions.'[6] The high-profile presence of prostitutes in Bengali social life—and in the new centre of socio-economic development, Calcutta, in particular—made prostitution an axis around which Bengali society revolved. News of dissolute descendants of old zamindar families going bust over some *baiji*, or of the exploits of the parvenu 'babus' in the red-light areas, continued to provide salacious staple for the Bengali popular press, and the new class of farce-writers—both thriving on the expansion of the cheap printing press establishments (initially concentrated in the north Calcutta area of Battala, but later extending to district towns like Dhaka, from where several such farces came out).

From being objects of farces, prostitutes soon emerged as cynosures of attention in a more serious cultural enterprise—the Bengali stage. Resisting social opprobrium and ostracism, they made their presence felt not only on the stage, but also in Bengali social life. Their regular communion with the *bhadralok* producers, playwrights and actors, created a variety of tensions in Bengali middle-class society. Till the entry of prostitutes onto the Bengali stage, they were regarded as a threat to those male members of Bengali *bhadralok* society who were vulnerable to their seduction, and to their wives and sisters who, it was feared, might opt for the free life-style of prostitutes. These concerns were repeatedly expressed both in the farces, and in newspaper editorials and articles by *bhadralok* intellectuals. But once members of the red-light area entered the cultural scene, and demonstrated that they could be equal to any leading *bhadralok* actor in enacting challenging roles and earning plaudits, prostitutes came to be regarded as a threat to the cultural domain that was carved out by the English-educated Bengali *bhadralok* for their exclusive use, the Bengali theatre, which was shaped as a distinct entity by these *bhadralok* intellectuals, who drew upon both the traditional indigenous *jatra* form and the contemporary English stage. Their entry created a division among the ranks of the *bhadralok*—even among the practitioners of the Bengali theatre. Thus, while Amritalal Bosu, Girish Ghosh and other luminaries of the Bengali stage chose to defy social criticism and stuck to the principle of discovering potential talents from Calcutta's red-light areas, and training them (which led to the emergence of some of the best actresses on the Bengali stage), other contemporaries like Manomohan Bosu (who was also a leading theatre personality), vehemently opposed the entry of prostitutes to the Bengali stage on moral grounds.

The Bengali middle-class audience also were caught up in a conflict. On the one hand, they remained hidebound by their moral prejudices against the prostitute-actresses. On the other hand, they could not but express their spontaneous emotional appreciation of the authentic rendering, by the same actresses, in the roles of characters (like that of Chaitanya, or of Hindu mythological heroines) whom they had been worshipping. They were, thus, torn between repulsion and admiration. Their mental conflict was further aggravated by the unusual gesture made by their guru—Ramakrishna of Dakshineshwar—when he went up to the greenroom and blessed Binodini. It was a sort of legitimization of not only the much-damned occupation of those Bengali deviant *bhadralok* who were involved in the theatre (which, although popular in middle-class society, was not regarded as quite respectable), but also of the participation in this occupation of those who were considered even worse than the *bhadralok* actors—the prostitute-actresses.

The prostitutes, thus, challenged both the traditionally-held moral prejudices of the *bhadralok* as well as their monopoly over their newly acquired intellectual occupations—like the theatre. They also invaded other areas of the *bhadralok's* cultural domain—the newspapers (where they vented their grievances through letters) and different genres of Bengali literature (poetry, drama and autobiography). These literary forays—although few and far between—were perceived as threats by the *bhadralok*, whenever they were published. When *Kamini-kalanka*—the autobiography of a prostitute, Nabinkali Debi, appeared in 1873, a journal of the progressive Brahmos came out with bitter comments: '. . . imagine a public woman depicting in her peculiar language the scenes of her early life and the strange vicissitudes which a career like hers necessarily presented . . . The repentance was all a sham for we are told the authoress was still pursuing her ignominous course . . .'[7]

By graduating from social sin in pre-colonial Bengal to a legal crime under a colonial administration, prostitution, ironically enough, acquired the distinction of becoming a subject of national debate. The prostitute's body became the site of numerous controversies both among the English administrators and the *bhadralok*. At one level, in the debates on women's education and emancipation, the prostitute was held up as a negative example to warn the *bhadralok* against neglect of their womenfolk, who were always suspected of getting enticed by the allure of the independent life-style of the prostitutes. At another level, prostitution was recognized as a 'necessary evil'—necessary because it was expected to act as the safety valve of respectability. Adherents of this view argued that prostitutes provided an outlet for the passions of certain types of male 'deviants', who, otherwise, would have ravished virgin daughters of respectable families! That this was a fallacious argument was evident from the numerous cases of seduction of daughters from Bengali upper-class and upper-caste families all through the 19th century, despite the prevalence—and expansion—of prostitution during the same period. Prostitutes, therefore, could never be guarantees against the deflowering of their 'respectable' sisters.

But Bengali *bhadralok* society, in its usual efforts to gloss over the 'irregular' or surreptitious sexual escapades of its 'respectable' male members, found it comfortable to fix prostitutes in the role of guardians of the virtues of their respectable sisters. They were depicted—in some of the contemporary Bengali plays (written by *bhadralok* playwrights)—

as paragons of virtue, who sacrificed their own chastity to satisfy the lust of dissolute *bhadralok*, but ultimately persuaded these lovers of theirs to return to their respective spouses (who, no doubt, were shown as ever-faithful wives waiting for their 'prodigal' husbands to come back!)[8]

Unlike other professions, in 19th century Bengal prostitution yoked disparate responses—repulsion and fascination, abhorrence and sympathy, acceptance and resistance. It never lost its relevance—whether as a negative example for errant wives, or as a positive need in the role of the safety valve of respectability—in the discourse of the *bhadralok* and *bhadramohilas*.

By their resilience, the prostitutes could demonstrate that human subjects were not wholly subsumed by oppressive systems. Although victims of the patriarchal and colonial structure, they could still carve out a certain space in the structure for manoeuvring. This was possible because the structure itself had to depend on them.

In this curiously shaped symbiotic relationship, the prostitutes succeeded in defeating the half-hearted attempts of the administrators and the *bhadralok*—both paralysed in an ambivalent position. Prostitution was spawned by a socio-economic system which, in its turn, became dependent on the institution, however unsavoury it might have been to those who shaped the system. Neither the colonial administrators, nor the *bhadralok*, were in a position to do away with the basic motivations and requirements, embedded in the system, that promoted prostitution and resisted every attempt to abolish or regulate it.

The prostitute, thus, succeeded in surviving all odds, and continued to practise the 'oldest profession' in colonial Bengal. In her own miserable way, she struggled to survive, now by exploiting the system, now by resisting encroachments by the system on her rights, through getting around laws like the CDA.

Of all the exploited sections in colonial Bengal, it is the prostitute who, somehow or other, appears to have been denied till now the serious attention that she deserves from modern historians who are attempting to reconstruct history from below. It may be because of the socially equivocal role attributed to her by Bengali society, which has remained divided and ambivalent with regard to her position. At times, some members of this society had regarded her sympathetically as a victim of exploitation. According to others, she was perceived as a manipulator and exploiter of male concupiscence, and a threat to domestic bliss in respectable Bengali homes. Both the sympathetic and the suspicious attitudes co-existed in the Bengali psyche—as is evident from the fascination for the prostitute expressed in a variety of literary genres, ranging from the 19th century farces lampooning them to poems by *bhadramohilas* weeping over their plight, from newspaper editorials urging their expulsion from respectable areas of the cities to reformist tracts recommending their rehabilitation.

This divided psyche seems to have affected the historians and critics—both in the past and the present—who, also, have sprung from the same *bhadralok* society. Their responses to the cultural representations of the prostitutes give us interesting clues.

The most vehement reaction of *bhadralok* society—both in the past, and today—has been against the oral cultural representations of the prostitutes (the songs and sayings which we have discussed in Chapter V). There are two reasons. One, these representations involved public display—the jaunty *khemta* dances and songs in the streets, the open haggling between the prostitutes and their customers in the marketplace (which gave rise to the invention of popular sayings and peculiar argot in the red-light areas). Two, they were often marked by scatological expressions that offended the refined tastes of the *bhadralok*!

The sympathetic liberal-minded *bhadralok* (like the 19th century Bengali theatre directors and actors, and a few Brahmo social reformers) did, indeed, acknowledge the talents of the actresses who came from the red-light areas. But while trying to appreciate their art, or attempting their 'rehabilitation' (either by giving them away in marriage, or by taking them under their own protection as mistresses), they tended to fix their female identity as that of a submissive domestic creature, to be trained under benevolent and civilized male patronage. They failed to recognize the strivings for an independent status that some among these women might have been fighting for.

It may be unfair to judge the 19th century Bengali *bhadralok* social reformers and liberal intellectuals by today's standards of feminist discourse, given the limitations of their views about, and attitudes towards, women in general, which were influenced in a large measure by contemporary Victorian values imported by the colonial rulers, and the traditional Brahminical norms, that equally shared the view that women were inferior to men and needed their protection.

Inspite of these limitations, the fact that a few among the 19th century Bengali *bhadralok*, even while adhering to this view, dared to defy the contemporary societal ban on prostitutes by welcoming them to the Bengali stage, and giving them their due recognition as artistes, in the midst of widespread social disapproval in Calcutta at that time, says a lot about their courage—and ardent sympathy for these downtrodden women from the red-light areas of Calcutta. Even today, in the supposedly progressive and permissive *bhadralok* society of Calcutta, one wonders how many among the radical middle-class Bengali youth have the guts of a Goshthabihari Dutta (who, coming from the same class in 19th century Calcutta, fell in love with Golap—an actress recruited from the red-light area—and married her, knowing well that the inevitable result would be disinheritance by his father and a life of poverty). One can, today, of course, dismiss Goshthabihari's decision as the romantic adventure of an individual. But, judging by the public attention that it received in contemporary newspapers and public discourse (both sympathetic and contemptuous), one has to admit that it did reflect an alternative—although weak—stream of dissidence that flowed through Bengali society in the 19th century.

But their flawed idea of female identity reinforced among the theatre actresses the binary concept of femininity being aligned with ignorance and subservience, and masculinity with knowledge and mastery. In Binodini's autobiography, for instance, there is a constant refrain of her being 'ignorant', 'a weak female', 'a wretched prostitute', etc., and her dependence on her teacher Girish Ghosh, and, later, on the unnamed aristrocrat who took her under his protection. Through all this apologetic discourse, however, her protest against male exploitation breaks out in occasional indictments.

The contemporary *bhadralok* liberals also faced another dilemma when trying to intervene in helping or 'rehabilitating' the prostititutes. The question of the individual woman's volition or the socio-economic coercion behind her practice of the profession quite often puzzled them. Nilmoni Chakravarty, for instance, was bewildered by the behaviour of a prostitute who, at first, agreed to escape from the brothel, but then later backed out.

Today, looking back at the dilemma, we feel the need to break up the binary thought pattern and to break out of the oppositional concept of volition/coercion that shaped the thinking and behaviour of the male liberal intellectuals. We should recognize the fluidity and complexity in the mentalities of the prostitutes who were coping with, and manoeuvring in, extremely complicated working and living conditions. The same prostitute who might have been compelled to join the profession under socio-economic pressures, could have—after a certain period—developed the free will to prefer it to the unknown evil of domesticity in a *bhadralok* home. Or, even when harking back nostalgically to their socially respectable origins and toying with the idea of renewing old ties through marriage, some could have retreated at the last moment when it came to the crunch, not knowing whether they would be accepted by *bhadralok* society. The plight of Sukumari Dutta (nee Golap Sundari) could have acted as a deterrent . . .

Interestingly, even some among the later-day historians and critics appear to have inherited the ambivalence and the binary thinking, the suspicion and the revulsion, that marked the attitude of their predecessors in the 19th century. One veteran historian, for instance, has expressed the view that Sukumari Dutta could not have written the play *Apurba Sati*, without providing any valid evidence to disprove her claim.[9] Obviously, the assumption is that a prostitute could not have acquired literary skills like an educated Bengali *bhadramohila*. It again looks like an attempt to fix the prostitute into a stereotype of a flippant and ignorant woman who can be proficient only in the skills of sexual entertainment.

A similar attitude of disdainfulness creeps into the assessment made by another modern historian about Binodini. According to him, she was full of 'self-conceit and arrogance' because she was the 'favourite companion of the owner of the theatre' and newspapers were 'profuse in their praise for her acting.'[10]

One should, however, hasten to add that a group of young modern Bengali historians and critics are engaged in reassessing the works of these 19th century actresses, and have come out with able rejoinders against the insinuations quoted above.[11]

But while such research has, indeed, paved the way for an alternative approach to the cultural representations of the actresses and their lives, there is an almost deafening silence in academic discourse about the oral culture of the less privileged poor inhabitants of the red-light areas. As in the past, today also, there seems to be a sense of revulsion against such cultural representations. The revulsion is often concealed by a dismissive attitude that refuses to acknowledge their cultural value, or by a tendency to suspect that the songs and sayings, the ribald jokes and bawdy terms attributed to the 19th-century prostitutes were actually coined by men. Such suspicion, again, seems to have been fuelled by the same *bhadralok* assumption that women are not expected to speak in such an earthy and sinewy style. In the perception of the *bhadralok* intellectual, it appears, while a sexually explicit abuse or remark befits a man—or may even improve his macho image—it is unbecoming for a woman, even if she is a prostitute!

Curiously enough, the oral cultural tradition of the peasantry and the working class is increasingly being recognized today as an important source of historical research—although these cultural records can also be suspected as products of dubious authorship. Since many of them have been collected by urban middle-class researchers, one cannot rule out the possibility of dilution and distortion. But modern researchers in folk culture have found ways of examining their authenticity—often by the 'regressive method' [12] of using contemporary survivals of popular culture and practices in order to go back in time to compare them with their earlier recorded versions, and, thereby, get a better understanding of their historical forms and evolution.[13] Needless to say, the methods are also necessary to sift the wheat from the chaff in the tortuously recorded history of popular culture.

A judicious selection and flexible combination of these different methods in examining the history of prostitution and evaluating its various forms of cultural representations in 19th century Bengal in the present work, have unrolled an unexpected panorama of a variety of patterns of socio-cultural behaviour among the practitioners of a profession which had so often been imagined as a homogeneous entity. Following from this, the present author would like to see a more searching approach to, and a rigorous analysis of, the history of prostitution in other parts of India in the colonial era. Such a search can yield more historical evidence—as well as promote fresh analysis—to enrich our understanding of the sufferings and the struggles of members of an exploited profession.

Since the exploitation of a prostitute was, in a certain sense, more encompassing—including the more compelling needs of the prostitute, the social ostracism that she was condemned to, and, in the sphere of gender relations, her total dependence on the sexual needs of the male customer—what is required on the part of modern researchers is closer empathy with the gut-level responses of the prostitutes who operated in a colonial setting.

The present study, therefore, should be seen essentially as a starting point for further research in one of the most exciting areas of interdisciplinary research, which can encourage the introduction of unconventional sources and their examination—whether in the realm of oral tradition or printed records.

Notes

Prologue

1. The few serious scholarly studies touching upon the subject of prostitution in the colonial context of 19th century Bengal which have come to my notice till now are: (i) Kenneth Ballhatchet's *Race, Sex, Class under the Raj* (St. Martin's Press, 1980); (ii) Judith R. Walkowitz's *Prostitution and Victorian Society* (Cambridge University Press, 1980); (iii) Antoinette Burton's *Burdens of History* (University of North Carolina Press, 1994); and (iv) Ratnabali Chatterjee's on-going research into the subject, published so far in the form of articles in journals (e.g. 'The Indian Prostitute as a Colonial Subject: Bengal 1864-1883' in *Canadian Woman Studies/ Les Cahiers De La Femme*, vol. 13, no. 1).

The other publications which have dealt with the topic are primarily of a documentary nature (both in English and Bengali), to some of which I have acknowledged my debt in the course of the present study, as major sources of information relating to the subject.

2. Michel Vovelle, *Ideologies and Mentalities* (Polity Press, 1990), p. 91. Notwithstanding their different perspectives, other historians who had been exploring alternative sources in the oral tradition of early modern Europe and the later period are: (i) Mikhail Bakhtin, *Rabelais and His World* (MIT Press, 1968); (ii) Peter Burke, *Popular Culture in Early Modern Europe* (Temple Smith, 1978); (iii) Jacques Le Goff, *Time, Work and Culture in the Middle Ages* (University of Chicago Press, 1980); (iv) Aron Gurevich, *Medieval Popular Culture: Problems of Belief and Perception* (Cambridge University Press, 1988); and (v) Piero Camporesi, *Bread of Dreams* (Polity Press, 1989).

3. Sukumar Sen, *Women's Dialect in Bengali* (Jijnasa, 1979), p. III.

4. Sushil Kumar Dey, *Bangla Prabad* (A. Mukherjee & Co. Pvt. Ltd., 1986), p. 128.

5. For a critical account of women's speech patterns and ribaldry

in 19th century Bengal, see Sumanta Banerjee's 'Bogey of the Bawdy: Changing Concept of Obscenity in 19th Century Bengali Culture,' in *Economic and Political Weekly*, 18 July 1987.

6. Veena Talwar Oldenburg's *The Making of Colonial Lucknow* (Princeton University Press, 1984) gives an excellent analysis of the decline of fortune of the courtesans of north India, and their replacement by, and transformation into, prostitutes, to meet the demands of the new ruling elite.

7. Prankrishna Dutta, *Kolikatar Itibritta* (Pustak Bipani, 1981), p. 20. Pramathanath Mullick, *Sachitra Kolikatar Katha* (Juno Printing Works, 1935), pp. 134–35.

8. Such strivings for accomplishment in the fine arts among this class of prostitutes need not be traced to the detailed instructions for the cultivation of artistic skills among prostitutes by Vatsyayana in his *Kamasutra*, written probably in the Gupta period. Such texts were not a part of the collective memory of the prostitutes of 18th–19th century Bengal, who, in that particular historical context of colonial rule, represented a new generation of converts to the profession. The need for cultivating the fine arts among certain classes of prostitutes of this period was dictated by contemporary demands.

9. Certain critics link the development of the *khemta* dance form in 18th century Bengal with the tradition of the folk dance form of *jhumur* that was current in the western parts of Bengal; cf. Ashutosh Bhattacharya, *Banglar Loknritya*, vol. II (A. Mukherjee & Co. Pvt. Ltd., 1982), p. 89.

10. In Calcutta, they spanned the middle belt of the three main arterial roads of the city—Chitpore in the west, on the banks of the Hooghly river; Cornwallis Street on the east; Bowbazar in the central part of the town, where the north Indian *baijis* and their descendants lived; and the south-eastern part called Colinga—including today's Kareya—which used to be a settlement of Eurasian and European prostitutes even till the beginning of the 20th century. In Dhaka, the red-light areas were situated in Jindabahar and pockets of Shankharipatti.

11. A journal from the year 1811 till the year 1815 . . . by Maria, Lady Nugent. London. 1839. Excerpted in P. Thankappan Nair (ed.), *Calcutta in the 19th Century* (Firma K. L. M. Pvt. Ltd., 1989), p. 144.

12. An anonymous British author's book entitled *Sketches of India* (London, 1816). Excerpted in P. Thankappan Nair (ed.), *Calcutta in the 19th Century*, p. 192.

13. Ibid., p. 299.

14. *Samachar Darpan*, 16 October 1819. Quoted in Brojendranath Bandyopadhyay (ed.), *Sangbadpatrey Sekaler Katha*, vol. I (Bangiya Sahitya Parishad, 1970), p. 121.

15. Let us not again rush to the conclusion that all those who were known as *baijis* in the red-light areas were 'blue-blooded' descendants of the elegant courtesans, dancers and singers of the Moghul era. The craze among the Bengali parvenu—who wanted to imitate the life-style of the members of the old Bengali aristocracy—led to the proliferation of ersatz *baijis* in 19th century Calcutta to meet their demands.

16. *Bangadarshan*, Kartik, 1280 (Bengali era; approx. 1873). Contrary to the opinion expressed by the author of the abovementioned article in the journal, the *baiji* tradition had nothing to do with the Hindu 'puranas', but originated in the Muslim courts. For a more exhaustive analysis of the two forms of dances—the *khemta* and the *baiji* dances—see Sumanta Bandyopadhyay's 'Bai-nach banam khemta', in *Baromash*, vol. VIII, no. 1, 1986.

17. *Sadharani*, Agrahayan 21, 1281 (Bengali era; approx. 1874).

18. Bijit Kumar Dutta (ed.), *Sukumari Dutta Ebong Apurba Sati Natak* (Paschim Banga Natya Akademi, 1922), pp. 8-9.

19. Binodini Dasi, *Amar Katha o Anyanya Rachana* (Subarnarekha, 1394; Bengali era; approx. 1987), p. 15.

I Introducing Phulmoni and Her Sisters

1. Published in *Madhyastha*, a 19th century Bengali periodical. Quoted in 'Madhyastha Patrika o Kolkata Pourasabha' by Sunil Das in *Purashree*, 29 December 1979, p. 1009.

2. Frederick Engels, 'Origin of Family, Private Property and State' (1884) in Karl Marx and Frederick Engels' *Selected Works* (Progress Publishers, 1970), p. 499.

3. Karl Marx, *Economic and Philosophic Manuscripts of 1844* (Progress Publishers, 1977), p. 68.

4. Cf. D. D. Kosambi, *The Culture and Civilization of Ancient India in Historical Outline* (Vikas Publishing House, 1977), p. 156. Also, A. L. Basham, *The Wonder that Was India* (Fontana, Indian edition, 1971), p. 185.

5. Quoted by Niharranjan Ray in his *Bangalir Itihash: Aadi Parba* (Dey's Publishing, 1993), p. 311.

6. Donagaji Chowdhury— 'Saiful-Muluk-Badiujjamal'. Quoted in Ahmad Sharif, *Madhyajuger Sahitya Samaj o Sanskritir Roop* (Muktadhara, 1977), p. 335.

7. Shukur Mahmud—'Gopichand Sannyas' (1705). Quoted in

Ahmad Sharif, *Madhyajuger Sahitya Samaj,* p. 401.

8. *Kamasutra*; i. 3. Quoted in A. L. Basham, *The Wonder that Was India,* p. 185.

9. A. L. Basham, *The Wonder that Was India* , pp. 185-86.

10. Cf. 'No Israelite woman shall become a temple prostitute, and no Israelite man shall prostitute himself in this way.' (Deuteronomy—23; v. 17). Also—'You shall not allow a common prostitute's fee . . . to be brought into the house of the Lord your God in fulfilment of any vow. . .' (ibid., v. 18).

11. Cf. Joshua—2. 1–21. Jeremia—3–1.

12. She is equated with tax collectors in Luke—15. 30.

13. 'Padma-purana Srishtikhanda': 23. 86 ff. Quoted in *Encyclopaedia of Puranic Beliefs and Practices,* vol. IV. Compiled by Sadashiv Ambaday Dange (Navrang, 1989), pp. 1129–33.

14. 'Padma-purana Srishtikhanda': 16. 107. *Encyclopaedia of Puranic Beliefs and Practices.*

15. 'Bhavishya-purana Uttarakhanda': 104. 31. *Encyclopaedia of Puranic Beliefs and Practices.*

16. 'Bhavishya-purana Uttarakhanda': 137. 18. Also, 'Agni-purana': 218. 16. *Encyclopaedia of Puranic Beliefs and Practices.*

17. Cf. '*Pujadrabyam samalokya beshya ramanamichchata*
Chaturvarnodvabha ramya sa beshya prikeertita.'

—Niruttaratantra. Pata 64.

('Watching the implements of prayer, she wants to make love. Coming from one of the four castes, she is known as 'beshya,' or 'prostitute'.) Quoted in Upendra Kumar Das, *Shastramoolak Bharatiya Shakti-sadhana.* (Vishwabharati, 1395; Bengali era; approx. 1988), p. 667.

18. *Tantrism* in Bengal can be traced to the later Buddhism. Marked by strong anti-Brahminical and anti-Vedic sentiments, *Tantrism* drew into its fold people from the lower castes, and the ostracized communities, who were looked down upon by the upper-caste Bengalis. Cf. Upendra Kumar Das, *Shastramoolak Bharatiya Shakti-sadhana,* and Panchkari Bandyopadhyaya, *Banglar Tantra,* (Bengal Publishers Pvt. Ltd., 1389; Bengali era. approx. 1982).

19. Ambapali in old age became a Buddhist nun—foreshadowing a practice common among Bengali prostitutes, who, after retirement, often become Vaishnavite nuns.

20. A. L. Basham, *The Wonder that Was India* , p. 187.

21. *Bharatchandrer Granthavali* (Basumati Sahitya Mandir, no date), p. 15.

22. The well-known Bengali historian and literary critic, Dinesh Chandra Sen, in his autobiography, quotes from a letter from his father, Ishwar Chandra Sen, describing a *khemta* performance in the early decades of the 19th century at a wedding ceremony in a rich Bengali household; cf. *Gharer Katha o Juga Sahitya* (Jijnasa, 1969), p. 34.

23. Among many other contemporary admirers of these female *kirtan* singers, who had left behind their reminiscences of the 19th century cultural scene in Bengal, the famous art critic, Ardhendra Kumar Gangopadhyay (better known as O. C. Ganguly), tells us about Panna Bai, whose *kirtans* on Radha Krishna he had heard as a child (cf. *Bharater Shilpa o Amar Katha.* 1969), pp. 43–44.

24. *Dooti-bilash* (1825), a narrative poem composed by Bhabanicharan Bandyopadhyay (1787–1848), describes, among other things, the plight of such abandoned women who drifted into prostitution.

25. 'Indian Recreations, V. III', p. 283 (published in 1808), quoted in Pramathanath Mullick's *Sachitra Kolikatar Katha,* (Calcutta, 1935), p. 122. Some among the girls born thus, in the absence of better employment, became prostitutes operating in Calcutta. In 1806, for instance, among prostitutes in the city, there was one Eurasian identified as John Bibi; re: S. N. Mukherjee, *Calcutta: Myths and History* (Subarnarekha, 1977), p. 99.

26. *Samachar Darpan,* 16 October 1819. Quoted in Brojendranath Bandyopadhyay (ed.), *Sangbadpatrey Sekaler Katha,* vol. I, p. 121.

27. *Calcutta Gazette,* 15 August 1831. Quoted in Anil Chandra Das Gupta (ed.), *The Days of John Company—Selections from Calcutta Gazette, 1824–32* (West Bengal Government Press, 1959), p. 655. We get another interesting account of such slavery, involving the famous 18th century British traveller and chronicler of old Bengal, Mrs Eliza Fay. A girl called Kitty Johnson—born of a 'free woman, half-cast (*sic*)'—accused Mrs Fay, who had employed her in Calcutta, of selling her, in 1782, into slavery in the island of St. Helena, where she was stranded. The Governor of the island summoned Mrs Fay, who was forced to shell out £60 (which included £10 for purchasing Kitty's freedom, £40 for her passage with her babies to Bengal—where she wanted to return—and £10 for maintenance on her arrival there). Re: Notes appended to E. M. Forster (ed.), Eliza Fay, *Original Letters from India (1779–1815)* (London, 1925), p. 285.

28. Cf. Niharranjay Ray, *Bangalir Itihash: Aadi Parba,* p. 466.

29. Home-Judiciary. No. 14. 25 November 1859.

30. *Maharashtra-puran,* composed in 1751 by Gangaram Dutta, gives

a graphic account of the *bargi* invasion of Bengal.

31. Report by Sir Williams Jones written in 1785, quoted in Pramathanath Mullick, *Sachitra Kolikatar Katha*, p. 36.

32. Cf. Arun Mukherjee, *Crime and Public Disorder in Colonial Bengal* (K. P. Bagchi, 1995), p. 67.

33. *Dewan Kartikeya Chandra Ray-er Atmajeeban-charit* (1st edition: 1904; Pragmya Prakashan,1990)), p. 33.

34. Shibnath Shastri, *Ramtonu Lahiri o Tatkalin Banga Samaj* (1st edition:1903; Signet Press, 1955), p. 43.

35. Nishachar (pseudonym of Bhuban Chandra Mukhopadhyay), *Samaj Kuchitra.* (1st edition: 1865). Reprinted in Brojendranath Bandyopadhyay and Das, Sajanikanta (eds.), *Hutom Penchar Naksha o Anyanya Samaj-chitra* (Bangiya Sahitya Parishad, 1384; Bengali era; approx. 1977), p. 186.

36. Ibid. pp. 186–87.

37. Reverend James Long, *Selections from Unpublished Records of the Government of India* (1st edition: 1869; Firma K. L. M. Pvt. Ltd., 1973), p. 52.

38. Quoted in Sunil Das, *Purashree..*

II British 'Sahibs' and 'Native' Women

1. Calcutta Annual Register, 1822.

2. Hundreds of such travelogues poured forth incessantly from the end of the 16th century (one of the earliest British travellers to India being Ralph Fitch, who spent eight years in the country from 1583 to 1591). The most important among them were written by Jean Baptiste Tavernier in the 1640s, Francoise Bernier from 1656–68, Francois Martin from 1670–94.

3. A typical example of this genre is the travelogue of Abbe Carre, who visited India during 1672–74, and narrated salacious stories about the debaucheries indulged in by his host, a Portuguese 'fidalgo' (gentleman) with Indian 'nautch girls', and boasted that the cloistered nuns in French monasteries enjoyed more freedom than women in Indian seraglios!

4. Byron, *Don Juan*, I. l xiii.

5. Cf. P. Thankappan Nair, *Calcutta in the 17th Century* (Firma K. L. M. Pvt. Ltd., 1986), pp. 423–30.

6. Ibid., p. 426.

7. Ibid., p. 425.

8. Ibid., p. 429.

9. Ibid., p. 425.

10. Ibid., p. 430.

11. Ibid., p. 435.

12. Re: Benoy Ghosh, *Kolkata Saharer Itibritta*; vol. I (Bak Sahitya, 1981), pp. 151–56; pp. 165–68; pp. 171–72.

13. P. Thankappan Nair, *Calcutta in the 19th Century* (Firma K. L. M. Pvt. Ltd., 1989), pp. 194–95.

14. C. R. Wilson, 'Early Annals of the English in Bengal'. 1895. Reproduced in Amarendranath Mookerji (ed.), *Glimpses of the Old Times* (Eastlight Book House, 1968), p. 124.

15. Quoted in Raja Binay Krishna Deb, *The Early History and Growth of Calcutta* (1st edition: 1905; Riddhi India, 1977), p. 199.

16. Re: P. Thankappan Nair, *Calcutta in the 19th Century*, p. 196.

17. Reminiscences of Umesh Dutta, as narrated to Bepin Behari Gupta in the latter's *Puratan Prasanga* (Vidyabharati Sanskaran, 1373; Bengali era; approx. 1966), p. 166.

18. Quoted in Major H. Hobbs, *John Barleycorn Bahadur: Old Time Taverns in India* (Calcutta, 1943), pp. 118–20. We come across another early 18th century description of a Calcutta suburb, indicating the growth of prostitution there to cater to the needs of the European settlers: 'Baranagul (Baranagore) is the next village on the River's side, above Calcutta, where Dutch have an House and Garden, and the Town is famously infamous for a seminary of female Lewdness, where numbers of girls are trained up for the destruction of unwary Youths, who study more how to gratify their brutal passions, than how to shun the evil consequences that attend their Folly, notwithstanding the daily Instances of Rottenness and Mortality that happen to those who most frequent those Schools of Debauchery'. Alexander Hamilton, 'New Account of the East Indies 1727'. Reproduced in P. Thankappan Nair, *Calcutta in the 18th Century* (Firma K. L. M. Pvt. Ltd., 1984), p. 11.

19. Letter to Court, 31 January and 24 March, 1766. Quoted in Rev. James Long, *Selections from Unpublished Records of the Government of India*, p. 580.

20. Cf. An advertisement put in by the auctioneers, Faria, William, and Hohler, some time in the early years of the 19th century: 'A garden house and ground situated at Taltolah Bazar, which to any gentleman about to leave India, who may be solicitious to provide for an Hindoostanee female friend will be founded a most desirable purchase.' Quoted in W. Carey, 'Good Old Days of John Company', reproduced in Santosh K. Mukherjee's *Prostitution in India* (Das Gupta and Co. 1935), suggests that some among these Company officials, on the eve of their departure from Calcutta, were willing

enough to buy garden houses to settle their Indian mistresses.

21. Letter to Court, 10 December 1767. Quoted in Rev. James Long, *Selections from Unpublished Records,* p. 643.

22. Quoted in F. C. Denver, et al, *Memorials of Old Haileybury College* (London, 1894), pp. 244–45.

23. From the speech by W. S. Seton-Karr at a Haileybury Dinner in the Calcutta Town Hall, on 23 January, 1864. Quoted in F. C. Denver, *Memorials of Old Haileybury College,* p. 93.

24. For an analysis of this change in the social attitude of Englishmen in 19th century Bengal following changes in the East India Company's administrative policies, see Sumanta Banerjee's *The Parlour and the Streets: Elite and Popular Culture in Nineteenth Century Calcutta* (Seagull Books, 1989), pp. 34–45.

25. Victor Jacquemont, 'Letters from India', 1829–32. Reproduced in P. Thankappan Nair, *Calcutta in the 19th Century,* p. 508.

26. Emma Roberts, 'Scenes and Characteristics of Hindostan, with Sketches of Anglo-Indian Society', 1835. Excerpted in P. Thankappan Nair, *Calcutta in the 19th Century,* p. 590.

27. Major H. Hobbs, *John Barleycorn Bahadur,* p. 195.

28. A modern British writer, in this context, stresses the role of British women in bringing about the change in the sex-habits of their men folks who were posted in India in the 19th century: 'British women—and the opening of the Suez Canal—have been, with some justification, blamed for the change. In all societies, women have ever been the conservators of culture. When British women began to arrive in India in numbers, they brought with them British attitudes, British fashions, and British morality; they were soon imposing their ideas, standards, and customs upon their new environment.' Byron Farwell, *Armies of the Raj: From the Mutiny to Independence, 1858–1947* (London, 1990), pp. 59–60.

III White Mars and Black Venus

1. Dr Fernando Henriques, *Stews and Strumpets. A Survey of Prostitution,* vol. I (MacGibbon and Kee, 1961), p. 204.

2. Major H. Hobbs, *John Barleycorn Bahadur,* p. 17.

3. J. MacMullen, *Camp and Barrack-room, or the British Army As It Is. By a Late Staff-sergeant of the 13th Light Infantry* (Chapman and Hall, 1846), p. 141. According to a survey contained in this book, in the 1840s, out of 120 soldiers, it was found that 80 were labourers and mechanics out of employment, 16 had been idle and considered a soldier's life an easy one, and 19 were 'bad characters', 'criminals', 'perverse sons' and 'discontented and restless'.

4. Re: Major H. Hobbs, *John Barleycorn Bahadur*, p. 100

An idea of the behaviour of the British soldiers in Calcutta can be had from the observations made by a Bengali newspaper in the 1820s. Referring to the arrival of fresh British troops and their initial stay in Fort William in Calcutta, the paper commented: 'Since the Fort was very near to the city of Calcutta, the newly arrived soldiers took leave and went to the city, moved around in the sun, boozed and indulged in debauchery and similar acts, as a result of which many among the soldiers kicked the bucket even before joining their respective regiments' (*Samachar Darpan*, 3 November, 1827. Excerpted in Brojendranath Bandyopadhyay (ed.), *Hutom Penchar Naksha*, vol. I, p. 180.

5. Rev. James Long, *Selections from Unpublished Records.*, p. 365.

6. Ibid., p. 194.

7. Victor Jacquemont, quoted in P. Thankappan Nair, *Calcutta in the 19th Century*, p. 500.

8. J. MacMullen, *Camp and Barrack-room*, p. 137

9. Ibid., p. 142.

10. Proceedings, 22 September, 1766. Quoted in Rev. James Long, *Selections From Unpublished Records*, pp. 601–02.

11. Santosh K. Mukherjee, *Prostitution in India* , p. 103.

12. Re: Kenneth Ballhatchett, *Race, Sex, Class under the Raj*. Also, Byron Farwell, *Armies of the Raj*, pp. 65–66.

13. Report of the President of the Sanitary Commission dated 21 March, 1864, quoted in a letter from the Government of India to Her Majesty's Secretary of State for India. Calcutta. 27 March, 1888. Home-Sanitary, 1888 A. June. Nos. 102–129

14. Letter by Dr T. Farquhar, dated 10 February, 1868. Home-Public. 20 February, 1869. Nos. 112–115.

15. Report of the Special Commission appointed to inquire into the working of the Cantonment Regulations regarding Infections and Contagious Disorders. London, 1893, p. 4.

16. Memorandum by W. J. Moore, CIE, Surgeon-General. October 1886. Home-Sanitary. June 1888

17. Home Department. Provision of public women for the Port Blair Free Police. No. 221. Dated Port Blair, 25 August 1873.

18. Ibid.

19. Report of the Special Commission appointed to inquire into the working of the Cantonment Regulations, pp. 12–16.

20. Report of the Committee appointed by the Secretary of State

for India to inquire into the Rules, Regulations and Practice in the Indian Cantonments and Elsewhere in India, with regard to prostitution and the treatment of Venereal Diseases. 1893. Reprinted with Explanations, notes, and c. by the British Committee for the Abolition of State Regulation of Vice in India and throughout the British Dominions. London. 1893. Paragraph 30.

21. Two American women, Mrs Elizabeth Wheeler Andrew and Dr Katharine (Kate) Bushnell, who visited India in 1891–92, on behalf of the London-based Ladies' National Association, reported that Indian men were not allowed to enter the brothels used by European soldiers in the cantonments. (Re: Report of the Committee appointed by the Secretary of State). This never changed, as is evident from the reminiscences of Private Frank Richards, who served in India in the years just before World War I, and wrote: 'Our Regimental police relieved one another in patrolling the small street which the Rag [the brothel] was in. Natives who passed through were not allowed to stop and talk to the girls; if any of them did, the policeman would give him such a thrashing with his stick that he would remember it a long time'. Quoted in Byron Farwell, *Armies of the Raj*, pp. 149–50.

22. Report of the Special Commission, p. 23.

23. Quoted in paragraph 9 of the Report of the Committee appointed by the Secretary of State.

24. Ibid.

25. Journal of Kate Bushnell, quoted in Antoinette Burton's *Burdens of History*, p. 158.

26. Re: Kenneth Ballhatchett, *Race, Sex, Class under the Raj*, p. 11.

The first 'lock hospital' was established in London in 1746. The term 'lock' is believed to have originated from the French word *loques* meaning rags, bandages, lints, etc. associated with lepers. London's first 'lock hospital' was founded on the site of a medieval house of lepers who were kept in restraint.

27. Letter from A. Mackenzie, officiating Junior Secretary to the Government of Bengal, to E. C. Bayley, Secretary to the Government of India, Simla. No. 1894. Dated 29 March, 1869. Home-Public proceedings. 8 May, 1869.

28. Reports on the working of the lock hospitals for the year 1885. Home-Sanitary. June 1887. Nos. 34–58.

29. Letter from the Government of India to Her Majesty's Secretary of State for India, dated Calcutta. 27 March 1888. Home-Sanitary. 1888 A. June. Nos. 102-129.

30. Reports on the working of the lock hospitals for the year 1885.

31. Re: William S. Sanger, *The History of Prostitution* (1st edition: 1897; Inter-India Publications, 1986), p. 354.

32. James Boswell, *London Journal of 1762–63* (Heineman, 1950).

33. *Samvad Prabhakar,* 15/2/1264 (Bengali era; approx. 1857). Excerpted in Benoy Ghosh (ed.), *Samayik Patrey Banglar Samajchitra,* vol. I. (Papyrus, 1962), p. 214.

34. From Dr C. Fabre-Tonnerre, Health Officer, to Stuart Hogg, Esq., Chairman of the Justices of Peace for the Town of Calcutta. Dated 16 September, 1867. Home-Public. 20 February 1869. Nos. 112–115.

35. Letter from G. H. M. Ricketts, Esq., C. B. Offg. Commr. of the Jhansie Division, to C. A. Elliott, Esq., Offg. Secy. to the Government. of the North-Western Provinces. No. 598, dated Jhansie, 6 July 1870. Home-Public. December 1870.

36. Letter from M. H. Court, Esq., C. S. I., Commr. of the Meerut Division, to C. A. Elliott, Esq. Offg. Secy. to the Govt. of the N. W. Provinces. No. 405, dated 25 August 1870. Home-Public. December 1870.

37. Letter from Surgeon-Major Arthur Payne, M. D., Superintendent, Lock Hospitals, to the Commissioner of Police Calcutta. Dated Calcutta, 4 March 1875. Home-Sanitary. June 1875. Nos. 32–34.

38. Reports of the working of the lock hospitals for the year 1885.

39. Report of the Special Commission, pp. 7–8.

40. Journal of Kate Bushnell, quoted in Antoinette Burton, *Burden of History,* p. 160.

41. Ibid. Also, cf. Letter from Surgeon-Major Arthur Payne to the Commissioner of Police, Calcutta. 4 March 1875.

42. Report of the Royal Commission on the Administration and Operation of the Contagious Diseases Acts, 1866–69 (1871). Quoted in Judith R. Walkowitz, *Prostitution and Victorian Society,* p. 71.

43. See Chapter II.

44. For Victorian attitudes towards gender relations and attempts at codification of sexual practices, see Judith R. Walkowitz, *Prostitution and Victorian Society.*

45. For a detailed account of the campaign against the CDA in England, see Antoinette Burton, *Burdens of History.*

46. The impact of the CDA, and the various Cantonment Acts, and the controversies surrounding them, are dealt with in greater detail in Chapter VII of this book.

IV. The 'Beshya' and the 'Babu'

1. Quoted in Bhabanicharan Bandyopadhyay's *Naba-bibi-bilash* (1822). Reproduced in *Rasarachana Samagra* (Nabapatra Prakashan, 1987), p. 202.

2. S. N. Mukherjee, *Calcutta: Essays in Urban History* (Subarnarekha, 1993), p. 32.

3. Ibid., pp. 12–13.

4. For an analysis of the various interpretations of the term 'babu', see Sumanta Banerjee's *The Parlour and the Streets*, pp. 179–82.

5. According to legends, Gazi Sonaullah Shah Chisti Rahamattullah came from Iran—probably in the 17th–18th century—and settled down in this part of north Calcutta, which was a village in those days. Even today, both Hindu and Muslim prostitutes leave offerings at his grave. The name of the area has changed into 'Sonagachhi'.

6. With the gradual expansion of industries in Bengal and the migration of workers from outside into the industrial belt along the western bank of the Hooghly river towards the end of the 19th century, a new class of clientele emerged from among these workers who had left their wives in the villages and whose needs gave rise to the sprouting of brothels adjoining the workers' slums and quarters, inhabited by the poorest prostitutes, some among whom often worked during the day as maid-servants.

As for the *rajahs* and rich *banians*—who were the leaders of early 19th-century Bengali society, their extra-marital sexual proclivities usually found avenues in secret liaisons with individual women who were kept by them as mistresses. Some of these women were Muslim *baijis*, like Anar Bai, the mistress of Kaliprasad Dutta, who ran into trouble in his upper caste Hindu society (discussed earlier). Raja Rammohan Roy was also reported to have had a liasion with a Muslim woman who bore him a son.The controversy over the rumour is reported in Brojendranath Bandyopadhyay (ed.), *Sangbadpatrey Sekaler Katha*, vol. II (Bangiya Sahitya Parishad, 1384; Bengali era; approx. 1977), pp. 772–74.

7. Bhabanicharan Bandyopadhyay, *Rasarachana Samagra*, p. 45.

8. Ibid., p. 202.

9. Ibid.

10. Report of the Chief Magistrate of Calcutta, and Calcutta Municipal Corporation Health Report, quoted in Usha Chakravarty, *Condition of Bengali Women around the Second Half of the Nineteenth Century* (Calcutta, 1963), p. 97

11. Kaliprasanna Sinha, *Hutom Penchar Naksha* (1st edition: 1862; Bangiya Sahitya Parishad, 1384; Bengali era; approx. 1977), p. 89.

12. *Dhaka Prakash*, 26 May 1864. Quoted in Muntasir Mamun, *Unish Shatokey Bangladesher Sangbad-Samayikpatra*, vol. IV (Bangla Academy, 1991), p. 458.

13. *Sangbad Bhaskar*, 1 May 1851. Quoted in an article by Maya Bhattacharya in *Anandabazar Patrika*, 19 August 1984.

14. Ibid.

15. Ibid.

16. Ibid.

17. I am grateful to Ms Ratnabali Chatterjee for drawing attention, in this connection, to a report on the principal causes of prostitution, prepared by the famous Bengali novelist Bankim Chandra Chattopadhyay, when he was posted in Berhampore in Murshidabad district of Bengal in 1872, as a deputy magistrate.

18. Quoted in Dinesh Chandra Sen, *Brihat Banga*, vol. II (Dey's Publishing, 1993), p. 775.

19. For an amusing account of how the daughter of a Srotriya Brahmin outwitted her father, see *Samachar Darpan*, 10 November 1821. Excerpted in Brojendranath Bandyopadhyay (ed.), *Sangbadpatrey Sekaler Katha*, Vol. I, pp. 240–41.

20. Usha Chakravarty, *Condition of Bengali Women*, p. 97.

21. Note by Deputy Commissioner of Hazaribagh, Col. H. M. Boddam. Home-Judicial, July 1873. Nos. 151–205.

22. Despatch by Dr C. Fabre-Tonnerre, Health Officer, to Stuart Hogg, Esq., Chairman of the Justices of Peace for the Town of Calcutta, 16 September 1867. Home-Public. 20 February 1869. Nos. 112–115.

23. Home-Judicial. 17 October 1872. No. 156.

24. Letter from S. Wauchope, C. B. Officiating Commissioner of Police, Calcutta, to Secretary to the Government of Bengal, Judicial Department. Home-Sanitary A. February 1876. No.19.

25. Reports on the working of the CDA in Calcutta and its suburbs during the year 1882. Home-Sanitary. 1885. January. No. 91.

26. Durgacharan Ray, *Debganer Martye Agaman* (1st edition: 1886 Dey's Publishing, 1984), pp. 453–54.

27. Ibid., p. 539.

28. Ibid., p. 558.

29. Despatch from Dr C. Fabre-Tonnerre. Home-Public. 20 February 1869.

30. Annual Report of the Superintendent of Lock Hospitals, dated 4 March 1875, on the working of the CDA in the town and suburbs of Calcutta during the year 1874. Home-Sanitary. June 1875. Nos. 32–34.

31. Letter from Surgeon-Major Arthur Payne to the Commissioner of Police, Calcutta. Dated Calcutta, 4 March 1875.

32. Ibid.

33. Ibid.

34. Despatch from Dr C. Fabre-Tonnerre. Home-Public. 20 February 1869.

35. Letter from Surgeon-Major Arthur Payne. Home-Sanitary. June 1875.

36. Despatch from Dr C. Fabre-Tonnerre. Home-Public. 20 February 1869.

37. Despatch from Deputy Commissioner of Police, A. H. Giles. 17 October, 1872. Home-Judicial. July 1873. Nos. 151–205.

38. Despatch from A. Abercrombie. Home-Judicial. July 1873. Nos. 151–205.

39. Despatch by H. Hankey from Chittagong. Ibid.

40. Despatch by Colonel J. C. Haughton. Ibid.

41. *Goniur Rajar Dhaka Bhraman.* Excerpted in Muntasir Mamun's *Smritimoy Dhaka* (Pallav Publishers, 1992), p. 92.

42. Wakil Ahmed, *Unish Shatokey Bangali Musalmaner Chinta Chetanar Dhara*, vol. I (Bangla Academy, 1983), pp. 32–36.

43. Descriptions of Saraswati Puja festivals in the red-light areas of 19th century Calcutta can be found in contemporary accounts (e.g. Bhabanicharan Bandyopadhyay's *Naba bibi-bilash*, published in 1830 and Bhuban Chandra Mukhopadhyay's *Samaj Kuchitra*, published in 1865).

44. *Sulabh Samachar*, Magh 15, 1280 (Bengali era; approx. 1873).

45. Re: Sudhir Chandra Mitra, *Hughli Jelar Itihash* (Mitrani Prakashan, 1962), p. 919. Also, *Samvad Prabhakar*, 11/11/1259; 16/11/1259; and 7/4/1260. Excerpted in Benoy Ghosh (ed.), *Samayik Patrey Banglar Samajchitra*, vol. II, pp. 59–65.

46. Re: G. O. dated 14 May 1877. No. 200. Educational Department. Quoted in Proceedings—November. Nos. 16–21. Subject: Admission of children of prostitutes into Government and aided schools. Home-Education. 1878.

47. Ibid.

48. Ibid.

49. R. Palme Dutt, *India Today* (People's Publishing House, 1947), p. 106.

50. Re: Despatch from the Magistrate of Dinajepore. Home-Judicial. July, 1873. Nos. 151–205.

51. Despatch from Asst. Magistrate of Serajgunge, Pubna. Ibid.

52. Ibid.

53. Karl Marx could have discovered in these developments in late 19th century Bengali society enough examples to illustrate his formulation about the changes brought about in social relations by the capitalist system: 'The bourgeoisie has torn away from the family its sentimental veil, and has reduced the family relation to a mere money relation . . . All fixed, fast-frozen relations, with their train of ancient and venerable prejudices and opinions, are swept away . . .' (*Manifesto of the Communist Party*, written by Marx and Engels in December 1847–January 1848).

54. Pyarichand Mitra, *Alaler Gharer Dulal* (Reprint: Bani Prakash, 1389; Bengali era; approx. 1982).

55. Bholanath Mukhopadhyaya, *Aponar Mukh Apuni Dekho* (Reprint: Pragmya Bharati, 1389; Bengali era; approx. 1982), pp. 66–67.

56. Ibid., pp. 93–97.

57. Ibid., p. 83.

58. Ibid.

59. Ibid., p. 37.

60. Meer Mosharraf Hossain, *Er Upay Ki?* Reprinted in *Pandulipi*, vol. III (Bangla Sahitya Samiti, 1380; Bengali era; approx. 1973), p. 188.

61. Kedar Nath Dutta, *Sachitra Guljar-nagar* (Reprint: Pustak Bipani, 1982), p. 118. The bulk of these farces indulged in titillating accounts at the expense of the prostitutes. A prurient interest in the red-light areas masqueraded as moralistic intervention. Typical are the following lines from the introduction prefixed to a farce called *Beshyasaktinibartak Natak* (a play on ending whore-mongering) by Prasannakumar Pal in 1860): 'This book describes, in the form of a play, how respectable women get excited by the pangs of separation, leave their homes and become prostitutes, and how they suffer the consequences; how lechers longing to taste the nectar of wives of others, bring about disasters and suffer from excitement, pain and humiliation. My only objective is that after reading the book, the people of this country may rid themselves of the habit of whore-mongering.'

62. Sushil Kumar Dey, *Bangla Prabad* (A. Mukhejee and Co. Pvt. Ltd., 1392. Bengali era; approx. 1985), p. 59 and p. 197.

63. Ibid., p. 160.

64. Haripada Chakravarty, *Dasharathi o Tanhar Panchali* (Calcutta, 1960), p. 375.

65. Baishnabcharan Basak, *Bharatiya Sahasra Sangeet* (Basak & Sons, no date), pp. 468–69.

66. *Samachar Sudhabarshan*, 23 January 1856.

67. One such incident which created a sensation in Calcutta in the 1870s was the murder of Elokeshi by her husband Nabin Chandra Banerjee as a punishment for allowing herself to be seduced by the head-priest of the Tarakeshwar Temple!

68. Binodini Dasi, *Amar Katha*, p. 42.

69. Akhilchandra Dutta, *Sonagajir Khun* (Chitpur Road, Calcutta, 1282; Bengali era; approx. 1875).

70. Akhilchandra Dutta, *Sonagajir Khunir Phanshir Hukum* (Chitpur Road, Calcutta, 1282; Bengali era; approx. 1875).

V Voices from the Pit

1. Published in *Sangbad Prabhakar*, September, 1854. Excerpted in Benoy Ghosh (ed.), *Samayik Patrey Banglar Samajchitra*, vol. I.

2. In the early 1870s, a book was published entitled *Kamini-kalanka* (The Disgrace of a Woman) by one Nabinkali Debi, which purported to be the autobiography of a prostitute. It was reviewed in a Brahmo journal in unfavourable terms. Still later, around 1929, a book entitled *Shikshita Patitar Atmacharit* (The Autobiography of an Educated Prostitute) by one Manada Debi, created a sensation in Calcutta. A flow of autobiographies (?) of prostitutes—mostly salacious—continued unabated from the cheap Battala presses of Calcutta, all through the 19th century. As in other genres of popular culture, we have to learn to distinguish the authentic from the commercially ersatz in the literature of prostitutes.

3. Meghnad Gupta, *Rater Kolkata* (Hemanta K. Ray, 1923), p. 10.

4. *Sangbad Bhaskar*, 9 August 1849.

5. The above three quotations are from private collections.

6. Meghnad Gupta, *Rater Kolkata.*

7. From private collections.

8. Dinendra Kumar Ray, *Palli Baichitra* (Ananda Publishers, 1389; Bengali era; approx. 1982), p. 102.

9. Durgacharan Ray, *Debganer Martye Agaman*, p. 560.

10. Muntasir Mamun, *Smritimoy Dhaka*, pp. 93-94.

11. Binodini Dasi, *Amar Katha.*

12. Attributed to Basanta Baiji. Quoted in Somnath Chakravarty, *Baiji Bilash* (Bookland Private Ltd., 1991), p. 128.

13. Attributed to Saralasundari. Ibid., p. 124.

14. *Gato Shatoker Gaan; Pratham Parba*, HMV pre-recorded cassette/ STHV 2448.

15. *Vidyadarshan*, No. 5, 1842. Excerpted in Benoy Ghosh (ed.), *Samayik Patre Banglar Samajchitra*, vol. III (Papyrus, 1980), pp. 20-21.

16. *Sangbad Prabhakar*, September 1854.

17. *Tattobodhini Patrika*, vol. 36. 1846. Excerpted in Benoy Ghosh (ed.), *Samayik Patre Banglar Samajchitra*, vol. IV, p. 106.

18. Frederick Engels, 'The Origin of the Family, Private Property and the State,' in *Selected Works* (Progress Publishers 1970), pp. 499-503.

19. *Dhaka Prakash*, 28 November 1880. Excerpted in Muntasir Mamun, *Unish Shatokey Dhakar Theatre* (Bangladesh Shilpakala Academy, 1979), p. 78.

The appeal of the talents of some among these actresses—like the famous Binodini—cut across cultural and linguistic barriers, as is evident from the following comment by a British army officer who watched her performance in the role of the 16th century Bengali Vaishnavite preacher, Chaitanya, in the then popular play *Chaitanya-leela* as stated in Calcutta in 1884: '. . . The poor girl who played Chaitanya may belong to the class of unfortunates . . . but while on the scene she throws herself into her role so ardently that one only sees the Vaishnava saint before him.' Colonel H. S. Olcott, quoted in Binodini Dasi, *Amar Katha,* p. 158.

20. Binodini Dasi, *Amar Katha*, pp. 61-62.

21. Sukumari Dutta, *Apurba Sati* (Nutan Bharat Jantra, 1875), p. 8.

22. Ibid., pp. 32-33.

23. Published in *Natyamandir*, Ashwin-Kartik, 1319 (Bengali era; approx. October-November, 1912). I am grateful to Ms. Rimli Bhattacharya for drawing my attention to this report and making available a copy of it.

24. Ibid.

VI The Burden of the 'Bhadralok'

1. *Sulabh Samachar*, 10 Falgun 1277 (Bengali era; approx. 1870).

2. Cf. Judith R. Walkowitz, *Prostitution and Victorian Society.*

3. Durgacharan Ray, *Debganer Martye Agaman*, pp. 539-40.

4. Re: Santosh Kumar Mukhopadhyay, *Amar Smriti* (Institute of National Culture, 1974), p. 92.

5. Quoted in Jacques Le Goff, *Time, Work and Culture in the Middle Ages*, pp. 66-67.

6. *Sangbad Prabhakar*, 19 November 1856. Excerpted in Benoy Ghosh, *Samayik Patre Banglar Samajchitra*, vol. II, pp. 244-45.

7. Ibid.

8. *Dhaka Prakash*, 20 January 1865. Quoted in Muntasir Mamun (ed.), *Unish Shatokey Bangladesher Sangbad-Samayikpatra*, vol. IV, p. 464.

9. *Sangbad Prabhakar*, 31 January 1854.

10. *Weekly Reporter* (Civil Rulings), vol. XVIII, 1872, pp. 445-46.

11. *Sulabh Samachar*, 10 Falgun 1277. A letter written in a similar vein appeared in *Sangbad Bhaskar*, 30 March 1849.

12. Re: Nilmoni Chakravarty, *Atmajeebansmriti*, (Sadharan Brahmo Samaj, Calcutta. 1382; Bengali era; approx. 1975), pp. 222-23.

13. *Madhyastha*, 1873, pp. 621-23.

14. *Manomohan Geetabali* (Calcutta. 1886), pp. 241-42.

15. *Sulabh Samachar*, 12 Falgun 1281 (Bengali era; approx. 1874). But, to be fair to Keshub Sen, it was he who, as early as 1870, wrote to the English social reformer and feminist Josephine Butler, detailing the horrors Indian women suffered as a result of the compulsory medical examination under the 1868 Contagious Diseases Act. (Re: Antoinette Burton, *The Burdens of History*, p. 131).

16. Charles Baudelaire, *The Essence of Laughter and Other Essays, Journals and Letters* (Meridian Books, 1956), pp. 57-58.

17. Arun Mitra (ed.), *Amritalal Bosur Smriti o Atmasmriti* (Calcutta, 1982), p. 198. Quoted in Rimli Bhattacharya, 'Public Women: Early Actresses of the Bengali Stage—Role and Reality', in Geeti Sen (ed.), *The Calcutta Psyche* (India International Centre, 1990-91).

18. Arun Mitra (ed.), *Amritalal Bosur Jeeboni o Sahitya* (Calcutta, 1970), pp. 316-17.

19. Quoted in Naliniranjan Chattopadhyaya, *Sri Ramakrishna o Banga Rangamancha* (Calcutta, 1978).

20. *Swami Vivekanander Bani o Rachana*, vol. VII (Udbhodan Karyalay, 1371; Bengali era; approx. 1964), pp. 324-25.

21. Shibnath Shastri, *Atmacharit* (Signet Press, Calcutta, 1359. Bengali era; approx. 1952), pp. 122-23 and 134-36. Shibnath's efforts to rehabilitate prostitutes, made at the end of the 19th century, were remembered with respect by the next generation of prostitutes in the early years of the 20th century, as is evident from the following

reminiscences of a prostitute in the 1920s: 'When we were staying in a house [a brothel] in one of the rooms of a woman I found her decorating a portrait with flowers. The woman was a bit elderly—but she was still beautiful. I asked her, whose portrait is this? The woman said—it is the portrait of Shibnath Shastri . . . I asked her—why have you kept Shibnath Shastri's portrait in your room? She said, When I was around seventeen or eighteen years old, a middle-aged fallen woman gave me shelter . . . She took me in order to support herself by earnings from the sale of youth and beauty. She was the daughter of a carpenter from Champatala [in Calcutta]. She became a widow when she was seven years old. [Ishwarchandra] Vidyasagar and Shibnath Shastri wanted to get her remarried. But because of various reasons, it couldn't take place. In her childhood, she used to address Shibnath Shastri as *dada* [elder brother]. Finally, due to circumstances, she was forced to become a prostitute . . . A few years before she died . . . she bought a portrait of Shibnath Shastri and used to worship it every day with flowers. She gave me this portrait before her death and asked me to decorate it with flowers like this all through my life.' Manada Debi, *Shikshita Patitar Atmacharit* (Calcutta, 1929), pp. 78-79.

22. Nilmoni Chakravarty, *Atmajeebansmriti,* pp. 17-18.

23. Shibnath Shastri, *Atmacharit,* pp. 135.

24. Binodini Dasi, *Amar Katha,* p. 41.

25. Report of the Royal Commission on the Administration and Operation of the Contagious Diseases Act (1871). Quoted in Judith Walkowitz, *Prostitution and Victorian Society,* p. 71.

26. Sarojini Debi, in *Antahpur,* March 1889.

27. See Chapter V.

VII Official Laws versus Unofficial Needs

1. Home-Public. Home Department. Proceedings. 20 February 1869. No. 139.

2. For an interesting analysis of the new concept of crime as shaped by the British colonial administration in India, see Anand A. Yang (ed.), *Crime and Criminality in British India,* The Association for Asian Studies Monograph no. XLII (The University of Arizona Press, 1985).

3. Augustus Somerville, *Crime and Religious Belief in India* (1st edition: 1929; Thacker Spink and Co., 1966), p.1.

4. Drunkenness and disorderly behaviour in public—about which we hardly find any complaint in pre-colonial official records or contemporary literature in Bengal prior to the arrival of the British—

appeared to have become widespread in Calcutta from the 18th century, when British settlers established taverns and punch houses which attracted British soldiers and sailors who, in their state of inebriation, created a law and order problem in the streets of the city, as decribed in Chapter III.

5. Letter from S. Wauchope Esq., C. B., Officiating Commissioner of Police, Calcutta, to the Secretary to the Government of Bengal, Judicial Department. Home-Sanitary A. February 1876. Nos. 19-21.

6. Letter from S. C. Bayley Esq., Officiating Additional Secretary to the Government of Bengal, to E. C. Bayley Esq., Secretary to the Government of India, dated 20 June 1868. Home-Public. 20 February 1869. Nos. 112-115.

7. Comment on the report of the Superintendent, Lock Hospitals, by R. L. Mangles, Officiating Secretary to the Government of Bengal. By order of the Lieutenant-Governor of Bengal. Home-Sanitary. June 1875. Nos. 32-34.

8. J. White, M. D., Medical Officer in charge of Lock Hospitals, 15 January 1870. Home Public. 26 November 1870. No. 67.

9. *Prabhakar*, 17 April 1865. Translated in *Report on Native Papers*, 1864-68.

10. *Dhaka Prakash*, 26 April 1868. Ibid.

11. Memorandum from Babu Peary Mohan Mookerjee, Honorary Secretary to the British Indian Association, to the Secretary to the Government of Bengal. 17 November 1887. Home-Sanitary. 1888 A. June. Nos. 102-129.

12. Prankrishna Dutta, *Badmaesh Jabdo*. Reprinted in *Dushprapya Sahitya Sangraha*, vol. II (Reflect Publication, 1992), pp. 5-11.

13. Ibid., p. 10.

14. Ibid., p. 9.

15. Aghor Chandra Ghosh, *Panchali Kamal-koli* (Calcutta, 1873).

16. Ibid.

17. Letter from A. Mackenzie Esq., C. S., Secretary to the Government of India, Home Department, to the Secretary to the Government of Bengal, dated 20 February 1883. Home-Sanitary. 1884. Nos. 76-97.

18. Letter from Stuart Hogg, Commissioner of Police, Calcutta, to the Secretary to the Government of Bengal, Judicial Department, dated 18 March 1875. Home-Sanitary, June 1875. Nos. 32-34.

19. Quoted in the report of the Superintendent of Lock Hospitals, 29 March 1870, in the letter from the Chief Secretary to the Government of Madras to the Secretary to the Government of India.

Home Department. Dated 17 February 1888. Home-Sanitary. 1888 A. June. Nos. 102-129.

20. *The Weekly Reporter*, Vol. XII, 1869, pp. 55-58.

21. Ibid.

22. Ibid., vol. XVII. Criminal Rulings, p. 12.

23. Report on the Barrackpore Lock Hospitals for the year 1869. Home-Public. 26 November 1870. No. 67.

24. From S. Wauchope Esq., C. B. Officiating Commissioner; Home-Sanitary A. February 1876.

25. Ibid.

26. Inspection Report on the Lock Hospital at Barrackpore, Home-Public, 26 November 1870. No. 67.

27. Report of W. Hopkinson, Lieut. Col. Cantonment Magistrate, Barrackpore. 9 January 1886. Home-Sanitary. June 1887. Nos. 34-58.

28. Home-Sanitary A. June 1875. Nos. 32-34.

29. From S. Wauchope. Home-Sanitary A. February 1876.

30. From Stuart Hogg, Esq., Commissioner of Police, Calcutta, to Secretary, Government of Bengal, Judicial Department. 27 March 1874. Home-Sanitary A. February 1876. Nos. 19-21.

31. Report of the Working of Act XIV of 1868 and of the Lock Hospitals during 1872. Home-Sanitary A. February 1876.

32. Home Public. 26 November 1870. No. 67.

33. Home-Sanitary, 1884. December. No.129.

34. Home-Sanitary. June 1887. Nos. 34-58.

35. Home-Public. 26 November 1870. No. 67.

36. Home-Sanitary A. February 1876. Nos. 19-21.

37. From A. Mackenzie Esq., C. S. Home-Sanitary. 1884. September Nos. 76-97.

38. Home Sanitary. 1885. January Nos. 87-131.

39. Ibid.

40. Note by J. M. C. 6-8-84. Home-Sanitary. 1884. December. No. 129.

41. J. M. Cunningham's note on CDA, 25-7-84. Home-Sanitary. 1884. No.76.

42. From A. Mackenzie Esq., C. S. Home-Sanitary. 1884. September. Nos. 76-97.

43. From the Government of Bengal. No. 1037. Dated 30 August 1881. Home-Sanitary 1881 A. September. Nos. 38-39.

44. From A. Mackenzie Esq., C. S. Home-Sanitary. 1884.

September. Nos. 76-97.

45. Letter from H. M. Kisch Esq., Officiating Secretary to the Government of Bengal, to the Secretary to the Government of India, Home Department, 30 August 1881. Home-Sanitary 1881 A. September. Nos. 38-39.

46. From the Government of Bengal, dated 30 August 1881. Home-Sanitary 1881 A. No. 1037.

47. Letter from H. M. Kisch Esq. Home-Sanitary 1881 A. September. Nos. 38-39.

48. Ibid.

49. Ibid.

50. Home-Sanitary. 1885. January. Nos. 87-131.

51. Home-Sanitary. 1886. January. Nos. 26-28.

52. Home-Sanitary. 1887. June. Nos. 34-58.

53. Ibid.

54. Reports by the Commissioner of the Patna, Presidency and Rajshahey Divisions on the working of the cantonment lock hospitals in their respective divisions, for the year 1884. Home-Sanitary. December. 1885 A. Nos. 113-133.

55. Letter from Major J. B. Hardy, R. A. Commanding A. Battery, 19th Brigade, to the Station Staff Officer, Jhansie. No. 374. Dated Jhansie, 18 May 1870. Home-Public. December 1870. pp. 947-967.

56. Home-Sanitary. June 1887. Nos. 34-58.

57. Quoted in Benjamin Scott, *A State Iniquity* (London, 1830), p. 245.

58. For a detailed discussion of the anti-CDA campaign in England, see Judith R. Walkowitz, *Prostitution and Victorian Society*.

59. Quoted in Benjamin Scott, *A State Iniquity*, pp. 254-55. See also Antoinette Burton, *Burdens of History*.

60. Memorandum from Babu Peary Mohan Mookerjee to the Secretary to the Government of Bengal. 17 November 1887.

61. Home-Sanitary. 1888 A. June. Nos. 102-129.

62. Ibid.

63. Home-Sanitary. 1888. October. Nos. 61-75

64. Ibid.

65. Home-Sanitary. 1888 A. June. Nos. 102-129.

66. Home-Sanitary. 1888. October. Nos. 61-75.

67. Note signed by G. C. dated 5-6-88. Home-Sanitary. 1888. October. Nos. 61-75.

68. Note dated 11-6-88. Ibid.

69. Note by A. R. S. 1-10-88. Ibid.

70. Home-Sanitary. 1888. October. Nos. 61-75.

71. Home-Sanitary. 1895. May. Nos. 67-71.

72. Letter from General P. J. Maitland, Secretary to the Government of India, Military Dept., to the Quarter-Master General in India, 20 November 1897. Home-Sanitary. 1897. December. Nos. 101-102.

73. Ibid.

74. Re: Kenneth Ballhatchet, *Race, Sex, Class under the Raj*, p. 131.

75. Ibid., p. 132.

76. Home-Judicial. 17 October. 1872. No. 156

77. From the report of John Lambert, Police Commissioner, Calcutta. Dated 9 March 1894, quoted in B. Joardar, *Prostitution in Nineteenth and Early Twentieth Century Calcutta* (Inter-India Publications,1985), pp. 33-34.

78. Home Department Proceedings. 20 February 1869. Home-Public. 20 February 1869. Nos. 112-15.

79. S. M. Edwardes, *Crime in India* (OUP, 1924), pp. 160-61.

80. From an article by H. Anderson, quoted in S. K. Mukherjee, *Prostitution in India* (Das Gupta and Co., 1935), pp. 467-68.

81. From Dr C. Fabre-Tonnerre. Home-Public. 20 February 1869.

82. *Sanjeebani*. Jaistha 20, 1311 (Bengali era; approx. 1904). Excerpted in Kanailal Chattopadhyay (ed.), *Sanjeebani* (Dey's Publishing, 1989), p. 336.

83. Lieut. General Sir George MacMunn, *The Underworld of India* (Jarrold Publishers, 1933), p. 90.

84. Ibid., pp. 90-91.

85. Ibid., p. 92.

86. Ibid.

Epilogue

1. Paragraph 83 of the Report of the Special Commission appointed to inquire into the working of the Cantonment Regulations regarding Infections and Contagious Disorders. The Commission, set up by the Government of India, for on-the-spot inquiries, consisted of three members—Denzil Ibbetson, a Deputy Commissioner, Surgeon Colonel Cleghorn, Inspector General of Civil Hospitals, and Maulvi Samiullah Khan, a 'native gentleman'. It submitted its report in 1893, and it became a part of the Report of

the Committee appointed by the Secretary of State for India to inquire into the Rules, Regulations and Practice in the Indian Cantonments and Elsewhere in India with regard to Prostitution and the Treatment of Venereal Disease. 1893.

2. From Dr C. Fabre-Tonnerre. Home-Public. 20 February 1869.

3. Note by W. J. Moore, C. I. E., Surgeon-General. October 1886. Reproduced in Report by Brigadier-General F. A. Adam, Quarter-Master General, No. 10-154-24. Dated Poona, 3 January 1888. Home-Sanitary. June. 1888.

4. Ibid.

5. Ibid.

6. Bhudeb Mukhopadhyay, *Shekal Aar Ekal*, vol. III (1st edition: 1874; Reprinted in *Dushprapya Sahitya Sangraha*, Reflect Publications, 1992), p. 159.

7. *Indian Mirror*, quoted in *Hindoo Patriot*. 13 October 1873. No copy of Nabinkali's book has yet been traced—at least to my knowledge.

8. This literary tendency reached its culmination in the construction of the crypto-chaste image of the prostitute in the novels of Sarat Chandra Chattopadhyay, and later generations of Bengali pulp-fiction writers have followed in his footsteps.

9. Sukumar Sen, *Bangla Sahityer Itihash*, vol. II. Quoted in Bijit Dutta (ed.), *Sukumari Dutta Ebong Apurba Sati Natak*, p. 9.

10. Harindranath Dutta's introduction to the reprint of Upendranath Vidyabhushan's biographies of three actresses—Tinkari, Binodini and Tarasundari (Rama Prakashani, 1985), pp. 14-15.

11. Cf. (i) Nirmalya Acharya and Soumitra Chattopadhyay (ed.), *Amar Katha o Anyanya Rachana* by Binodini Dasi. (ii) Bijit Dutta (ed.), *Sukumari Dutta Ebong Apurba Sati Natak*. (iii) Rimli Bhattacharya, 'Public Women: Early Actressses of the Bengali Stage—Role and Reality'.

12. A term used in the methodology of research in popular culture. Cf. Michel Vovelle, *Ideologies and Mentalities*.

13. In Bengali folklore research, one of the best examples of this method has been provided by Sudhir Chakravarty in his analysis of the life and songs of the early 19th century Bengali mystic poet and folk-singer Lalan Fakir, in his book *Bratya Lokayata Lalan* (Pustak Bipani, 1992).

Select Bibliography

Books

Ahmed, Wakil. *Unish Shatokey Bangali Musalmaner Chinta ChetanarDhara.* Dhaka: Bangla Academy. 1983.

Ballhatchet, Kenneth. *Race, Sex, Class under the Raj.* New York: St. Martin's Press. 1980. Indian edition. 1979.

Bandyopadhyay, Bhabanicharan. *Rasarachana Samagra.* Calcutta: Nabapatra Prakashan. 1987.

Bandyopadhyay, Brojendranath. *Sangbadpatrey Sekaler Katha* .Vol. I and II. Calcutta: Bangiya Sahitya Parishad. 1377 (Bengali era; approx. 1970).

Banerjee, Sumanta. *The Parlour and the Streets:Elite and Popular Culture in Nineteenth Century Calcutta.* Calcutta: Seagull Books, 1989.

Basak, Baishnabcharan. *Bharatiya Sahasra Sangeet.* Calcutta: Basak & Sons. No date mentioned. Early 20th century.

Basham, A. L. *The Wonder that Was India.* India: Fontana Books. 1971.

Basu, Kanchan (ed.). *Dushprapya Sahitya Sangraha.*Vol. II. Calcutta: Reflect Publication. 1992.

Basu, Manomohan. *Manomohan Geetabali.* Calcutta: 1886.

Baudelaire, Charles. *The Essence of Laughter and Other Essays, Journals and Letters.* New York: Meridian Books. 1956.

Bhattacharya, Ashutosh. *Banglar Loknritya.* Vol. II. Calcutta: A. Mukherjee and Co. Pvt. Ltd. 1982.

Brander, Michael. *The Victorian Gentleman.* London: Gordon Cremonesi. 1975.

Burton, Antoinette. *Burdens of History* . Chapel Hill, USA: The University of North Carolina Press. 1994.

Carre, Abbe. *Travels in India and the Near East.* N. Delhi: Asian Educational Services. 1990.

Chakravarty, Haripada. *Dasharathi o Tanhar Panchali.* Calcutta: A. Mukherjee & Co. Pvt. Ltd. 1960.

Chakravarty, Nilmoni. *Atmajeebansmriti.* Calcutta: Sadharon Brahmo Samaj. 1382 (Bengali era; approx. 1975).

Chakravarty, Somnath. *Baiji Bilash.* Calcutta: Bookland Pvt. Ltd. 1991.

Chakravarty, Sudhir. *Bratya Lokayata Lalan.* Calcutta: Pustak Bipani. 1992.

Chakravarty, Usha. *Condition of Bengali Women around the Second Half of the Nineteenth Century.* Calcutta: 1963.

Chattopadhyay, Kanailal (ed.). *Sanjeebani.* Calcutta: Dey's Publishing. 1989.

Chattopadhyaya, Naliniranjan. *Sri Ramakrishna o Banga Rangamancha.* Calcutta: Mandal Book House. 1978.

Dange, Sadashiv Ambaday (ed.). *Encyclopaedia of Puranic Beliefs and Practices.* Vol. IV. N. Delhi: Navrang. 1989.

Das, Upendra K. *Shastramoolak Bharatiya Shakti-sadhana.* Santiniketan: Vishwabharati. 1988.

Das Gupta, Anil Chandra (ed.). *The Days of John Company*. Calcutta: West Bengal Government Press. 1959.

Dasi, Binodini. *Amar Katha o Anyanya Rachana.* Calcutta: Subarnarekha. 1394 (Bengali era; approx. 1987.)

Deb, Raja Binay Krishna. *The Early History and Growth of Calcutta.* Calcutta: Riddhi India. 1977.

Denver, F.C. *Memorials of Old Haileybury College.* London: 1894.

Dey, Sushil Kumar. *Bangla Prabad.* Calcutta: A. Mukherjee & Co. Pvt. Ltd. 1392 (Bengali era; approx. 1985).

Dutta, Akhil Chandra. *Sonagajir Khun.* Calcutta: 1875/6.

——. *Sonagajir Khunir Phanshir Hukum.* Calcutta: 1875/6.

Dutta, Bijit K. (ed.). *Sukumari Dutta Ebong Apurba Sati Natak.* Calcutta: Paschim Banga Natya Akademi. 1992.

Dutta, Kedar Nath. *Sachitra Guljar-nagar.* Reprint. Calcutta: Pustak Bipani. 1981.

Dutta, Prankrishna. *Kolikatar Itibritta.* Calcutta: Pustak Bipani. 1981.

Edwardes, S. M. *Crime in India.* London: OUP. 1924.

Engels, Frederick, and Marx, Karl. *Selected Works.* Moscow: Progress Publishers. 1970.

Farwell, Byron. *Armies of the Raj: From the Mutiny to Independence, 1858-1947.* London: Viking. 1990.

Gangopadhyay, Ardhendra Kumar. *Bharater Shilpa o Amar Katha.* Calcutta: A. Mukherjee & Co. Pvt. Ltd. 1969.

Ghosh, Aghor Chandra. *Panchali Kamal-koli*. Calcutta: 1873.

Ghosh, Benoy (ed.). *Samayik Patrey Banglar Samajchitra*. Vols. I-V.

Calcutta: Papyrus. 1962-81.

Gupta, Bepin Behari. *Puratan Prasanga.* Calcutta: Vidyabharati Sanskaran. 1966.

Gupta, Meghnad. *Rater Kolkata.* Calcutta: Hemanta K. Ray. 1923.

Henriques, Dr. Fernando. *Stews and Strumpets: A Survey of Prostitution.* Vol. I. London: MacGibbon and Kee. 1961.

Hobbs, Major H. *John Barleycorn Bahadur: Old Time Taverns in India.* Calcutta: 1943.

Joardar, B. *Prostitution in Nineteenth and Early Twentieth Century Calcutta.* New Delhi: Inter-India Publications. 1985.

Kosambi, D. D. *The Culture and Civilization of Ancient India in Historical Outline.* New Delhi: Vikas Publishing House. 1977.

Le Goff, Jacques. *Time, Work and Culture in the Middle Ages.* Chicago: The University of Chicago Press. 1980.

Long, Rev. James. *Selections from Unpublished Records of the Government of India.* Calcutta: Firma K. L. M. 1973.

MacMullen, J. *Camp and Barrack-room, or the British Army As It Is.* London: Chapman and Hall. 1846.

MacMunn, Lieut. Gen. Sir George. *The Underworld of India.* London: Jarrold Publishers. 1933.

Mamun, Muntasir. *Unish Shatokey Bangladesher Sangbad-Samayikpatra* . Vols. I-IV. Dhaka. Bangla Academy. 1985-91.

——. *Smritimoy Dhaka.* Dhaka: Pallav Publishers. 1992.

——. *Unish ShatokeyDhakar Theatre.* Dhaka: Bangladesh Shilpakala Academy. 1979.

Marx, Karl. *Economic and Philosophic Manuscripts of 1844.* Moscow: Progress Publishers. 1977.

Mitra, Arun (ed.). *Amritalal Bosur Jeeboni o Sahitya.* Calcutta: Navana. 1970.

Mitra, Pyarichand. *Alaler Gharer Dulal.* Calcutta: Bani Prakash. 1389. (Bengali era; approx. 1982).

Mitra, Sudhir Chandra. *Hugli Jelar Itihash.* Calcutta: Mitrani Prakashan. 1962.

Mookerji, Amarendranath (ed.). *Glimpses of the Old Times.* Calcutta: Eastlight Book House. 1968.

Mukherjee, Arun. *Crime and Public Disorder in Colonial Bengal.* Calcutta: K. P. Bagchi. 1995.

Mukherjee, Santosh K. *Prostitution in Calcutta.* Calcutta: Das Gupta & Co. 1935.

Mukherjee, S. N. *Calcutta: Myths and History.* Calcutta: Subarnarekha. 1977.

Mukhopadhyaya, Bholanath. *Aponar Mukh Apuni Dekho.* Calcutta: Pragmya Bharati. 1389 (Bengali era; approx. 1982).

Mukhopadhyay, Bhuban Chandra. *Samaj Kuchitra.* (1st edition:

1865) Reprinted in Bandyopadhyay, Brojendranath and Das, Sajanikanta (eds.). *Hutom Penchar Naksha o Anyanya Samaj-chitra.* Calcutta: Bangiya Sahitya Parishad. 1384 (Bengali era; approx. 1977).

Mukhopadhyay, Santosh Kumar. *Amar Smriti.* Calcutta: Institute of National Culture. 1974.

Mullick, Pramathanath. *Sachitra Kolikatar Katha.* Calcutta: Juno Printing Works. 1935.

Nair, P. Thankappan. *Calcutta in the 18th Century*. Calcutta: Firma K. L. M. 1984.

—. *Calcutta in the 19th Century.* Calcutta: Firma K. L. M. 1989.

Oldenburg, Veena Talwar. *The Making of Colonial Lucknow.* New Jersey: Princeton University Press. 1984.

Palme Dutt, R. *India Today.* Bombay: People's Publishing House. 1947.

Pepys, Samuel. *The Diary of Samuel Pepys.* London: Macmillan. 1905.

Ray, Durgacharan. *Debganer Martye Agaman.* Calcutta: Dey's Publishing. 1984.

Ray, Dewan Kartikeya Chandra. *Atmajeeban-charit.* Calcutta: Pragmya Prakashan. 1990.

Ray, Dinendra Kumar. *Palli Baichitra.* Calcutta: Ananda Publishers. 1982.

Ray, Niharranjan. *Bangalir Itihash: Aadi Parba.* Calcutta: Dey's Publishing. 1993.

Sanger, William. *The History of Prostitution.* N. Delhi: Inter-India Publications. 1986.

Scott, Benjamin. *A State Iniquity.* London: 1830.

Sen, Dinesh Chandra. *Gharer Katha o Juga Sahitya.* Calcutta: Jijnasa. 1969.

Sen, Geeti (ed.). *The Calcutta Psyche.* New Delhi: India International Centre. 1991.

Sen, Sukumar. *Women's Dialect in Bengali.* Calcutta: Jijnasa. 1979.

Shastri, Shibnath. *Ramtonu Lahiri o Tatkalin Banga Samaj.* Calcutta: Signet Press. 1955.

—. *Atmacharit.* Calcutta: Signet Press. 1359 (Bengali era; approx. 1952).

Sharif, Ahmad. *Madhyajuger Sahitya Samaj o Sanskritir Roop.* Dhaka: Muktadhara. 1977.

Sinha, Kaliprasanna. *Hutom Penchar Naksha.* Calcutta: Bangiya Sahitya Parishad. 1384 (Bengali era; approx. 1977).

Somerville, Augustus. *Crime and Religious Belief in India.* Calcutta: Thacker Spink & Co. 1966.

Swami Vivekananda. *Bani o Rachana.* Calcutta: Udbodhan Karyalay. 1965.

Walkowitz, Judith R. *Prostitution and Victorian Society.* Cambridge:

Cambridge University Press. 1980.
Vovelle, Michel. *Ideologies and Mentalities.* Oxford, UK: Polity Press. 1990.
Yang, Anand A (ed.). *Crime and Criminality in British India.* The Association for Asian Studies Monograph. No. XLII. Tucson: University of Arizona Press. 1985.

Periodicals

Antahpur, 1889. Calcutta.
Baromash, No. 1. 1986. Calcutta.
Hindoo Patriot, 1873. Calcutta.
Madhyastha, 1873. Calcutta.
Natyamandir, 1319 (Bengali era; approx. 1912). Calcutta.
Pandulipi, Vol. III, 1380 (Bengali era; approx. 1973). Dhaka.
Purasree, 29 December, 1979.
Sadharani, 1874. Chinsura.
Sangbad Bhaskar, 1849. Calcutta.
Sulabh Samachar, 1281 (Bengali era; approx. 1874). Calcutta.
Weekly Reporter, 1869. Calcutta.

Official Documents and Reports

Govt. of India Home-Education files. 1878.
Govt. of India Home-Judicial files. 1872-73.
Govt. of India Home-Public files. 1865-1870.
Govt. of India Home-Sanitary files. 1875-1895.
Report of the Committee Appointed by the Secretary of State for India to inquire into the Rules, Regulation and Practice in the Indian Cantonments and elsewhere in India, with regard to Prostitution and the treatment of Venereal Diseases. London. 1893.
Report on Native Papers. 1864-68.

Index